Women during the English Reformations

Women during the English Reformations

Renegotiating Gender and Religious Identity

Edited by Julie A. Chappell and Kaley A. Kramer

palgrave
macmillan

First published in 2014 by PALGRAVE MACMILLAN® in the United States—a division of St. Martin's Press LLC, 175 Fifth Avenue, New York, NY 10010.

Where this book is distributed in the UK, Europe and the rest of the world, this is by Palgrave Macmillan, a division of Macmillan Publishers Limited, registered in England, company number 785998, of Houndmills, Basingstoke, Hampshire RG21 6XS.

Palgrave Macmillan is the global academic imprint of the above companies and has companies and representatives throughout the world.

Palgrave® and Macmillan® are registered trademarks in the United States, the United Kingdom, Europe and other countries.

ISBN: 978-1-137-47473-5

Library of Congress Cataloging-in-Publication Data

Women during the English Reformations : renegotiating gender and religious identity / edited by Julie A. Chappell and Kaley A. Kramer.
        pages cm
    Includes bibliographical references and index.
    1. English literature—Women authors—History and criticism. 2. Women—Identity. 3. Identification (Religion) 4. Women and religion—England—History. 5. Women in Christianity—England—History. 6. Women and literature—England—History. 7. Women in motion pictures—History. 8. Reformation—England. 9. England—Religion. I. Chappell, Julie, 1950- editor. II. Kramer, Kaley A., 1977- author, editor. III. Title: Renegotiating gender and religious identity.

PR111.W646 2014
820.9'99287—dc23
                                                        2014022067

A catalogue record of the book is available from the British Library.

Design by Amnet.

First edition: November 2014

10 9 8 7 6 5 4 3 2 1

For Evelyn Marie, Saxon Eldred, and Cameron Elizabeth, with love

—JAC

For my parents and for Nasser, for everything

—KAK

Contents

Acknowledgments

The editors wish to express their gratitude to all those involved in the preparation and production of this volume, especially our brilliant contributors, who responded so quickly and cheerfully to all of our comments and requests for information. We would especially like to thank the reviewer of this volume whose perspective on this collection of essays significantly enhanced individual chapters as well as the volume as a whole. We are extremely grateful to our Palgrave editor, Brigitte Shull, for her belief in this project, and to our editorial assistant, Ryan Jenkins, whose professionalism and attention to detail have been invaluable. Their prompt and generous assistance throughout this process has been most appreciated. We would also like to express our sincere love and appreciation for our families who provided support and encouragement throughout this process while enduring our absences of mind and body.

INTRODUCTION

Julie A. Chappell

The seismic cultural shift of the Reformation cannot be fully explained without reference to women.[1]

The reformations in religion in England during the sixteenth century and beyond required individual and collective renegotiation of both gender and religious identities for women. The shifts in political and religious rhetoric, as well as in structure, demanded of women more complex maneuvers for reasserting their identity in both realms. As Henry VIII's dissolution of the monasteries began, along with male religious, the women were dismissed from their religious houses and, at first, able to opt out of the religious life altogether or to allow themselves to be moved to other larger houses. In the end, all religious houses would be dissolved and the religious left to their own devices with small pensions for compensation. As Patricia Crawford has pointed out, "women fared worse than men," with the records for the Lincoln diocese revealing that "those who received pensions of £2 or less lived in penury. Only 6 per cent of men were on this stipend or less, but 60 per cent of the women were."[2] Women's options were shrinking. They could no longer be Brides of Christ, serving God as they had for centuries as women religious in diverse orders throughout England.[3] Nor in the first decade of reform could they be brides of man. Only after 1549 was marriage legalized for former religious.[4] Crawford asserts that "19 percent of the Lincoln ex-nuns married. A few joined together to keep house."[5] Male clerics in independent livings may have fared better overall. Eamon Duffy claims that "the conformity of the overwhelming majority of clergy, despite their conservative opinions" allowed many male clergy to maintain their livings by adapting, adopting, or sometimes even avoiding, for a while, the reforms in religion.[6] The mysticism and affective piety practiced by a number of late medieval women, both religious and lay, enclosed or not, which had provided paths to the divine and relief from traditional social roles for women, were dissolved along with religious houses in England. After the Henrician Reformation, these means for women to inscribe their religious and gender identities were no more. How, then, were women to understand and, consequently, redefine themselves in the face of collapsing religious and social spaces? The new boundaries imposed by the reformations of the next three centuries on women's gender and religious identities would force each woman to renegotiate these for herself.

Catholic or Protestant, recusant or godly rebel, early modern women of singular conscience, powerful or powerless in the main, reinvented or reasserted their spiritual and gendered spaces.[7] Arthur Marotti has contended that the "recusant woman was, like Catholicism itself . . . the target of Protestant misogyny: a masculinized, reform Christianity, which attacked not only the cult of the Virgin, but also devotion to female (as well as male) saints, associat[ing] women's 'carnality' with some of the alleged corruption of Catholicism. . . . Women and Catholics were both feared as intrinsically idolatrous, superstitious and carnal, if not also physically disgusting."[8] After all, the reactions of English Protestants to Mary, Queen of Scots, as a "wicked Popish woman" demonstrates the equivalency of these last two concepts in the reformist mind.[9] This egregious misogyny may have been instrumental in pushing some women to blatant or more surreptitious resistance as reform and counter reform in religion clashed with political power. English Catholic families would marry their sons and daughters to those of other Catholic families to keep the faith secure and in the family. In similar ways, English Protestants formed their own alliances drawn along lines of faith.[10] Women of whatever religious persuasion would sometimes pay dearly to maintain their convictions and alliances.

Henry VIII's reformation bloodied the landscape without consideration for rank or gender. According to Sharon L. Jansen, "many reports of women's words," during the decade when Henry was instituting his religious and marital changes, indicate that "women expressed their opinions . . . about the king's marriage and his political and religious reforms" and "were as much a source of concern to the government as men's views were."[11] Early in 1534, Henry VIII's regime silenced its first woman by hanging her when she would be silenced no other way. Elizabeth Barton, a young nun of low birth, refused to stop prophesying the demise of Henry's kingship if he persisted in the annulment of his marriage from Katherine of Aragon and his efforts to marry Anne Boleyn.[12] Between the more infamous executions of Anne Boleyn and Katherine Howard, two of Henry VIII's wives, the executions of women of varying rank and prestige were carried out as women's bodies became the contested space for religious change.

Margaret Cheyne, a woman of uncertain parentage but possibly an illegitimate daughter of Edward Stafford, Duke of Buckingham, was executed

for her connection to the northern rebels in 1537.[13] Margaret Pole, Countess
of Salisbury, was attainted and suffered a bungled beheading in 1541 for her
alleged connection to the northern risings and her clear support of Katherine
of Aragon and Princess Mary. Neither her brilliant defense of herself, nor her
connections to "the ladies-in-waiting of Katherine Parr," could save Anne
Askew from being burned at the stake for her too reformist views in July
1546.[14] Margaret Giggs Clement, foster daughter of former chancellor and
recent martyr, Sir Thomas More, bribed a jailer so that she could give aid to
the ten Carthusians from the London charterhouse incarcerated in horrific
conditions in Newgate from late May 1537. Although Clement was soon
denied access by the jailer for fear of reprisal by Henry's agents, she escaped
execution for her efforts.[15] After Edward VI's death in 1553, Lady Jane Grey,
once part of Katherine Parr's household, was soon imprisoned and executed
as a threat by faith and by blood to Mary I's regime. The Duchess of Suffolk,
Katherine Willoughby's "friendship with Katherine Parr [and] her appointment to Parr's household . . . placed her for the first time in the inner reform
circle at court." As Willoughby's support of the reform cause grew through
Edward VI's reign, she would also become immediately suspect under Mary
I. Less than two years into Queen Mary's reign, holding firm to her faith,
Katherine Willoughby chose exile.[16] Perhaps her proximity to the tragic ends
of both Askew and Lady Jane allowed Willoughby to see her way clear to a
different strategy.[17] Margaret Clitherow, a butcher's wife from York, would
be pressed to death as the first woman to die for refusing to conform under
the Elizabethan anti-recusancy laws in March 1586. The well-known fate of
Mary, Queen of Scots, under her cousin, Elizabeth I, is another example of
the absence of regard by the Tudors for familial connections, when Mary's
long imprisonment ended with her execution in 1587. Under the Tudors'
Catholic-Protestant struggle for dominance, gender served as a flash point.
As Corthell, et al. have asserted:

> Anti-Catholic discourses relied on gendered invective as an adaptable, resonant
> vocabulary for describing and condemning Catholicism as both the traitors
> within and the exotic, foreign seductress. [In contrast, the Catholics'] associa-
> tion of Catholicism with the feminine might also work positively, positioning
> the "old faith" as a mother, a nurse, or an object of desire.[18]

Erasmus' notion of inward and outward, spirit and flesh was not man's alone
but woman's as well when it came to mapping the strategy for the theology
of the post-medieval world.

The revisionist tack that Christopher Haigh once termed the "English Reformations" has adjusted over time and scholarly debate.[19] But this collection

stems from Haigh's original notion of England's reform in religion as not "an inexorable process" of conversion but more "as the accidents of everyday politics and the consequences of power struggles."[20] "Everyday politics" and "power struggles" were engendered by human agency among the powerless as well as the powerful. Women as well as men participated. This collection intends to enhance our understanding of women's responses to and participation in the originary trauma of reforms in religion occurring in England out of the sixteenth-century edicts of Henry VIII and his successors. Although much groundbreaking work by scholars, such as A. G. Dickens, Christopher Haigh, Eamon Duffy, Diarmaid MacCulloch, Patrick Collinson, and Alexandra Walsham, among others, has examined the extent of the conservative resistance and/or evangelical progress during this long period of English reformations, the arguments have been largely focused on the writings of early modern men of varying cultural significance.[21] While these and other scholars have also been studying the critical roles that women played in the centuries of reform in England, the availability of documentary and other material evidence on women of rank—Anne Boleyn, Katherine of Aragon, Katherine Willoughby, Mary I, Elizabeth I—has made these women the focus of much of this scholarship. The lack of availability of material evidence for women of lesser rank has, naturally enough, produced fewer studies of such women, though we know of some of the more notorious ones, such as Elizabeth Barton, the Holy Maid of Kent, and Margaret Clitherow, the butcher's wife.

This collection intends to contribute to the continually growing discourse on women's renegotiation of their religious and gender identities during the English reforming movements of the sixteenth century and the political and popular responses in the centuries that followed. The essays collected here explore the ways in which some Englishwomen of various backgrounds and notoriety, openly or covertly, engaged the struggle to erase, rewrite, or reimagine their religious and gender identity during a time of much erasure and rewriting of self on paper and parchment, stone, and wood. As Margaret Aston has observed, "In the sixteenth century England acquired a whole suite of ruins. . . . The agonizing sight of wholesale destruction spurred people into activity—even those whose Protestant convictions made them wholly endorse the process at large."[22] The devastation wrought by the sixteenth-century reforms in religion begun by Henry VIII included not only stone ruins, whitewashed church walls, broken altar tables, burned and torn manuscript pages, and other acts of material destruction but also the equivalent in human terms, as we have seen above. Some of these destructive acts were illustrated in woodcut images in books and broadsheets of the period.[23] The devastation in human and material terms testifies to the iconoclasm of religious fervor, conservative and evangelical, occurring in varying degrees of destruction from at least 1534. The late medieval spiritual writing we know as *The Book of Margery Kempe*, survived such destruction when one Carthusian monk spirited the manuscript away to his staunchly Catholic family who then kept the faith over the next centuries of reform.[24] The written word was a powerful transmitter of religious identity, and women, one way or another, participated in the creation and dissemination of writings of various sorts from the beginning.

In her detailed study of an early sixteenth-century devotional manuscript, "a book that belonged to a woman (possibly two women, mother and daughter) . . . with connections to two groups of women religious" and that had been produced at the cusp of "disturbing events, which were to culminate in the destruction of the religious life in England and of the devotional traditions that it represented," Alexandra Barratt revivifies both the woman, "a member of the gentry rather than the aristocracy," whose name appears on the flyleaf, Dame (or Lady) Anne Bulkeley, and her book.[25] Such studies lead us further toward understanding how women positioned themselves in relation to religion and gender during this turbulent period of reformations in religion. In an examination of the lives of four late medieval and early modern women, David Wallace demonstrates how the creation of Somerset House itself in 1549 materially illustrated what Alexandra Walsham has asserted about the Reformation landscape: "It is widely compared with a parchment and palimpsest, a porous surface upon which each generation inscribes its own values and preoccupations without ever being able to erase entirely those of the preceding one."[26]

The Duke of Somerset "had torn down a parish church and the inns of bishops to make room for the building that bears his name." Wallace further noted that more materials for the creation of this initially Protestant project "were freed up by demolishing a chapel in the north cloister of St. Paul's." By 1632, Queen Henrietta Maria had constructed a "Roman Catholic chapel at Somerset House" that caused "a national sensation" in this officially Protestant nation.[27] The material evidence reveals the palimpsestic nature of the power struggle negotiated by men and women during the long period of reformation. Arthur Marotti's study of religious discourse between 1580 and 1688 posits that "real as well as fabricated historical 'evidence' and events were translated [in the polemical literature] into a developing set of rhetorical codes and ideological fantasies."[28] But conversion and palimpsest building occurred internally in the individual as well as externally on both sides of the religious divide. Women were particularly challenged as they had to make a sometimes life-altering choice to follow (as custom and law dictated) or stand in opposition to the men who ruled them at home and at court.

Whether women held firmly to the conservative position, embraced reforms in religion, or converted one way or the other in opposition to their husbands, they often struggled and suffered for their expressions of their faith and their identities as individuals. Ironically, the charges of heresy and treason against conservative or evangelical women stemmed perhaps as much from political expediency as religious intolerance. Elizabeth Barton and Margaret Clement refused the prescribed female passivity and silence. Margaret Cheyne's possible connection to Edward Stafford and liaison with Sir John Bulmer, also charged and executed during the northern risings, made her expendable. Anne Askew had been attempting the unthinkable for a woman, a public estrangement from a husband she had been forced to marry,—one who didn't share her religious views. Lady Jane Grey's so-called crimes were her faith and her bloodlines. The former she would not alter, and the latter she could not. Like Lady Jane, Mary Stuart could not change her bloodlines nor control the intrigue around her, even if she had wanted to do so. Margaret Clitherow would neither reform her views nor obey her monarch's injunctions. Conservative or reformed, women were deemed suspect by the (mis) use of the qualities, the "humours," associated with women, an association that would be firmly entrenched during subsequent centuries of the aggressive masculinity of nation and empire building. Englishwomen would not see even a modicum of equality until they became fully fledged participants in the English legal system in the twentieth century.

The essays in this book reveal that although "Catholic[s were] collecting, preserving, translating, and transcribing . . . medieval spiritual texts [as] a way of safeguarding a religious heritage that the passage of time and the iconoclastic phases of the reformation[s] threatened to erase" and Protestant polemicists reformed texts, rituals, and practices to establish a new religious heritage, Catholic and Protestant women alike were reinscribing their gender and their faith through diverse forms of textual production—letters, spiritual treatises, dramatic texts, novels, translations, memoirs, and more.[29] These women's writings and their lives exploded myths of gender in their own time while altering the course of the construction of gender and faith in the centuries to come.

Valerie Schutte examines the ways in which Tudor queens exploited and were exploited by book dedications for political advantage and personal aggrandizement. Schutte examines dedications made to a number of Tudor queens, confirming the significance of this positioning in textual space, since these "book dedications were the first words in an early modern printed book." These book dedications indicate "the importance of women to the first generations of printed texts in England [as these] illuminate the patronage system, political and religious positions, and demonstrate the power of

Tudor queens at court." This positive aspect of women's roles in the early years of reform contrasts markedly with Janice Liedl's revelation of the tragic consequences of the coupling of women and power close to the Tudor court for another noble woman, Margaret Pole, Countess of Salisbury.

Janice Liedl asserts that the Countess's "gender was no protection against accusations of her involvement in the Exeter Conspiracy or on behalf of conservative religion in the early Reformation." Liedl contends that loyalty to the Crown during the first waves of reform under Henry VIII were the undoing of a woman with too "close ties to Katherine of Aragon and Princess Mary." Adding to the case against her was her son Reginald Pole's appointment as a cardinal and the Countess's own "active role in her home parish of Warblington." For loyalty to Mary and to the religion that had fueled spiritual fires for nearly a thousand years, the Countess of Salisbury would be attainted for treason in May 1539 and executed two years later. Liedl demonstrates how documents of the trial, as well as letters and state papers reveal that Margaret Pole's independence and vast wealth undoubtedly added most to her vulnerability in a time when men in power sought to stifle violently others' power, especially that of women, in the acquisition of more power for themselves.

Letters provide textual evidence for Rebecca A. Giselbrecht's study of the influence of Heinrich Bullinger on the reformed beliefs of Englishwomen during the years of Edward VI's reign and of the Marian Exile. Though she acknowledges the seeming paucity of this correspondence, Giselbrecht demonstrates that Bullinger's extant epistolary exchange with these women indicates that Bullinger supported women's intellectual endeavors in the reform in religion. In opposition to other male reformers, he even supported Elizabeth I's position, not only as a ruling monarch but also as the supreme governor of the Church of England. Ultimately, Giselbrecht offers the first close look at Bullinger's correspondence with women who were not queens or aristocrats but of lesser rank, grappling with the intellectual and psychological changes of reform. Giselbrecht reveals this correspondence's significance not only to the women being influenced by humanist writers but also in influencing those writers in their turn.

In contrast to these Protestant women, Lisa McClain challenges historians and literary critics circumscription of Elizabeth Cary's publicized conversion to Catholicism and her dislocation of the chaste, silent, and obedient yoke of early modern woman in marriage. McClain asserts that Cary stands as "an alternative model of Catholic womanhood that sought to negotiate a new balance between religion and gender." In a careful study of Cary's writings, including her literary output and her correspondence, McClain depicts an early modern woman who stood her ground but suffered her own "conflicts between the demands of gender and faith." Ultimately, McClain sees

Elizabeth Cary's life and writings as "contribut[ing] to larger European-wide re-negotiations of the rules of masculine and feminine behavior in the seventeenth century."

Amanda L. Capern contends that Eleanor Davies' "prophetic ideas" expressed in her writings can "throw light on why [recent] historiographies of reformation and civil war have so elided." Capern asserts that Davies' first treatise, *A Warning to the Dragon* (1625), simultaneously addressed the current crisis of religion in the mid-1620s and the role of the state in acting in both the nation's and Protestantism's best interests. Over nearly thirty years, Davies would express her prophetic ideas and apocalyptic visions in diverse writings. Capern argues that these writings reveal a woman "who literally reconceptualized the English and British reformations, [and] was a theologian" in her own right.

Sharon L. Arnoult demonstrates how religion and gender interconnected in the formation of early modern woman's identity in the case of Lady Elizabeth Delaval, who was born in late 1648 and subsequently abandoned as an infant by Royalist parents who went into exile in 1649. Arnoult examines Delaval's autobiographical meditations, a "diary for spiritual purposes," written in her teens and early twenties between 1662 and 1672. Arnoult asserts that Delaval's narrative suggests an identity struggling and divided, a "post-Restoration Anglican woman," who had absorbed the "religio-gender standards of her day." Delaval's autobiographical narrative might be "flavored with fictional romance," but Arnoult illustrates a genuine identity conflict for a young woman brought up by an emotionally distanced aunt amid the overtly sensual court of Charles II in the 1660s.[30] Ultimately, in Delaval's "failures and frustrations, and her eventual actions," Arnoult sees the emergence of a woman who managed to "remix and reformulate religious and gender identities."

Kaley A. Kramer contends that Sophia Lee's Gothic novel, *The Recess*, "articulates the fascination that Protestant Britain had with Catholicism late into the eighteenth century" as it also reveals strategies of rewriting British history with particular attention to the representation of Catholicism as a site of, what David Punter has described as, "vanished cultural territory."[31] Kramer asserts that Lee's adaptation of British religious history is apparent in some respects and subtle in others. As Kramer demonstrates, Catholicism is explicitly condemned but not expelled from the novel; it enables particular discourses associated with those of haunting and spectrality that the so-called Age of Reason sought to distance. Kramer argues that *The Recess* returns to the site of Protestant Britain's mythological origin and reproduces possible strategies for traversing different modes of narrating history, negotiating the secular and the sacred.

William B. Robison explores at length the popular afterlife of many of the most notable early Tudor women, demonstrating how filmic representations of these women eschew their lived context during sixteenth-century reform by using religion "merely as a subplot." Robison focuses on filmic depictions of Tudor royal women in such productions as *When Knighthood Was in Flower* (1922), *The Shadow of the Tower* (1972), and *The Tudors* (2007), among others. His study reveals that filmmakers persist in portraying Tudor royal women as "secondary, transitory, and 'traditionally female,'" even though historically the same women were "church benefactors" and "intelligent influential Christian humanists." Ultimately, Robison exposes the ahistoricity of such portrayals as not only seriously undermining women's cultural contributions in matters of faith but also negatively influencing modern "popular belief" about the period more broadly. Yet Robison also contends that this ahistoricity allows "Tudor historians to expose their errors while exploiting their appeal" to more general audiences.

This collection of essays examines the effects of reforms in religion on the gender and religious identity of women during the English reformations from Henry VIII's earliest iterations in the 1530s to filmic representations of reforming women in the last two centuries. As a whole, the authors offer a cross section of contributions, influences, and activities by women in matters of faith in early modern England, focusing on women's creative undoings and reimaginings during a long period of reform in religion and the ramifications of these activities well beyond their own time. The essays explore the inspirations for and expressions of women's actions, whether those actions were ultimately intended to serve the conservative or evangelical cause, and they provide a sample of the consequences and contradictions inherent in women's reimagining of religious and gender boundaries, as these manifested internally in the individual woman to effect a renegotiation of her own gender and religious identity.

Notes

1. Amanda Capern, *The Historical Study of Women: England 1500–1700* (Basingstoke, UK: Palgrave Macmillan, 2010), 4.
2. Patricia Crawford, *Women and Religion in England 1500–1720* (New York: Routledge, 1996), 30.
3. Eileen Power, *Medieval English Nunneries, c. 1275 to 1535* (Cambridge: Cambridge University Press, 1922). Power estimated "some 138 nunneries" in England "excluding double houses of the Gilbertine order" in the late medieval period, representing at least ten different religious orders. She further notes more than 110 still remained in 1535 when information began to be gathered for the dissolution (1–2).

4. For clerical marriage, see G. A. J. Hodgett, *The State of the Ex-Religious and Former Chantry Priests of the Diocese of Lincoln, 1547–1574* (Lincoln: Lincoln Record Society, 53, 1959); John K. Yost, "The Reformation Defense of Clerical Marriage in the Reigns of Henry VIII and Edward VI," *Church History*, 50.2 (June 1981): 152–65; Eric Josef Carlson, "Clerical Marriage and the English Reformation," *Journal of British Studies*, 31.1 (January 1992): 1–31; and Helen L. Parish, *Clerical Marriage and the English Reformation: Precedent Policy and Practice* (Aldershot, UK: Ashgate, 2000).

5. Crawford, *Women and Religion*, 30.

6. Eamon Duffy, *The Voices of Morebath: Reformation & Rebellion in an English Village* (New Haven, CT: Yale University Press, 2001), 175.

7. Since this introduction is not intended to debate the nuances of the broader Catholic or Protestant rubrics, I will sometimes use these terms to encompass any and all conservative and evangelical/reformist positions in this period.

8. Arthur F. Marotti, "Alienating Catholics in Early Modern England: Recusant Women, Jesuits and Ideological Fantasies," in *Catholicism and Anti-Catholicism in Early Modern English Texts*, ed. Arthur F. Marotti (New York: St. Martin's Press, 1999), 4 [1–34].

9. Quoted in Marotti, "Alienating Catholics," 4.

10. For the Catholic side, see Julie A. Chappell, *Perilous Passages: The Book of Margery Kempe, 1534–1934* (New York: Palgrave Macmillan, 2013), chapter 4; for the Protestant propensity for the same, see Elaine V. Beilin, ed., "Introduction," *The Examinations of Anne Askew* (Oxford: Oxford University Press, 1996), xvii–xviii.

11. Sharon L. Jansen, *Dangerous Talk and Strange Behavior: Women and Popular Resistance to the Reforms of Henry VIII* (New York: St. Martin's Press, 1996), 83.

12. Henry VIII never technically sought a divorce from Katherine of Aragon. Diarmaid MacCulloch, among others, has pointed out that Henry sought to have his twenty-year marriage to his brother's widow "declared null." (*The Reformation: A History*, [New York: Penguin Books, 2005], 198.) However, contemporary complainants about Henry's attempts to annul his marriage, like William Tyndale, did call this "deuorcement." In his 1530 treatise, *The Practise of Prelates*, Tyndale devotes an entire section of this work to the matter, entitling this section, "Of the deuorcement." (sig. H.vii.r) (Antwerp: Joannes Hoochstraten, 1530), STC 24465, Early English Books Online. Of course, Tyndale's target was actually Wolsey, who, he claimed, "sought all meanes to displease the emperoure [Charles V] and imagined this deuorcement betwene the kynge and the queen" (sig. H.vi.r). Tyndale's treatise begged Henry VIII to "serch the lawes of god / whether it be lawfull or not" to seek another wife (sig. H.vii.r). See also Amanda L. Capern, "Adultery and Impotence as Literary Spectacle in the Divorce Debates and Tracts of the Long Eighteenth Century" in *Spectacle, Sex, and Property in Eighteenth-Century Literature and Culture*, ed. Julie A. Chappell and Kamille Stone Stanton (New York: AMS Press, Inc., forthcoming 2014), 197–225; and Tim Stretton, "Marriage, Separation and the Common Law in England, 1540–1660 in *The*

Family in Early Modern England, ed. Helen Berry and Elizabeth Foyster (Cambridge: Cambridge University Press, 2007), 18–39.

13. See Jansen, chapter 1, "A Woman's Treason: The Case of Margaret Cheyne," 5–39.

14. Paul F. Zahl, *Five Women of the English Reformation* (New York: W. B. Erdsman Publishing Co., 2001), 28; Zahl also points out that Askew "refused to give away the names of any of that group [of women like Willoughby and Parr accused of treason and heresy] . . . and thus stood fully firm in her confession" (28); see also Beilin for the first edition of Askew's *Examinations* with John Bales' *Elucidation* and John Foxe's version in his *Acts and Monuments*. In her introduction to this edition of these documents, Beilin claims that Askew "sought a divorce from her Catholic husband and went to London" (xv). Others have asserted that Askew "unsuccessfully petitioned for divorce": Theresa D. Kemp, "Translating (Anne) Askew: The Textual Remains of a Sixteenth-Century Heretic and Saint," *Renaissance Quarterly*, 52.4 (1999): 1021–22 n3 [1021–1045]; Patricia Pender, "Reading Bale Reading Anne Askew: Contested Collaboration in *The Examinations*," *Huntington Library Quarterly*, 73.3 (2010): 507 [507–22]; and Tarez Samra Graban, "Feminine Irony and the Art of Linguistic Cooperation in Anne Askew's Sixteenth-Century *Examinacyons*," *Rhetorica: A Journal of the History of Rhetoric*, 25.4 (2007): 387 n8 [385–411]; among others. Whether Askew intended her estrangement from her husband to lead to divorce or legal separation, either would have made her more vulnerable to the authorities along with her "gospelling" activities.

15. See David Knowles, *The Religious Orders in England, Vol. III The Tudor Age* (Cambridge: Cambridge University Press, 1959), 235–36.

16. Melissa Franklin Harkrider, *Women, Reform and Community in Early Modern England: Katherine Willoughby, Duchess of Suffolk, and Lincolnshire's Godly Aristocracy, 1519–1580* (Woodbridge, Suffolk: The Boydell Press, 2008), 48.

17. Harkrider, *Women, Reform and Community*, claims that "Parr included Willoughby among a select group who witnessed her wedding to Henry VIII and appointed her as one of her ladies-in-waiting" (48). Her proximity to court circles would have potentially necessitated some careful negotiation by Willoughby when Parr was under suspicion, as well as when others of that circle, Anne Askew and Lady Jane, were brought to trial and suffered.

18. Ronald Corthell F. Dolan, C. Highley, and A. F. Marotti. "Introduction," *Catholic Culture in Early Modern England* (Notre Dame, IN: University of Notre Dame Press, 2009), 5 [1–18].

19. See Christopher Haigh, *English Reformations: Religion, Politics, and Society under the Tudors* (Oxford: Clarendon Press, 1993); Haigh, "Success and Failure in the English Reformation," *Past and Present*, 173 (2001): 28–49; Nicholas Tyacke, *England's Long Reformation, 1500–1800* (London: UCL Press, 1998); Peter G. Wallace, *The Long European Reformation: Religion, Political Conflict and the Search for Conformity, 1350–1750* (Basingstoke, UK: Palgrave Macmillan, 2004); among others.

20. Haigh, *English Reformations*, 13.
21. For examples of the relative positions of these scholars, see A. G. Dickens, *The English Reformation* (University Park, PA: Penn State University Press, 1964, repr. 1989); Dickens, *Reformation Studies* (London: Hambledon Press, 1982); Christopher Haigh, *The English Reformation Revised* (Cambridge: Cambridge University Press, 1987); Haigh, *English Reformations*; Eamon Duffy, *The Stripping of the Altar: Traditional Religion in England 1400–1580* (New Haven, CT: Yale University Press, 1992); Duffy, *The Voices of Morebath;* Diarmaid MacCulloch, *The Reign of Henry VIII: Politics, Policy, and Piety* (New York: St. Martin's Press, 1995); MacCulloch, *The Reformation*; Patrick Collinson, *The Religion of Protestants: The Church in English Society 1559–1625* (Oxford: Clarendon Press, 1982); Collinson, *The Birthpangs of Protestant England: Religious and Cultural Change in the Sixteenth and Seventeenth Centuries* (Basingstoke, UK: Palgrave Macmillan, 1988); Alexandra Walsham, *Church Papists: Catholicism, Conformity and Confessional Polemic in Early Modern England* (Woodbridge, Suffolk: Boydell and Brewer, 1993); Walsham, "The Reformation and 'The Disenchantment of the World' Reassessed," *The Historical Journal*, 51.2 (2008): 497–528; Walsham, *The Reformation of the Landscape: Religion, Identity, and Memory in Early Modern Britain and Ireland* (Oxford: Oxford University Press, 2011); among others.
22. Margaret Aston, "English Ruins and English History: The Dissolution and the Sense of the Past," *Journal of the Warburg and Courtauld Institutes*, 36, (1973): 231–32 [231–55]. See also her *England's Iconoclasts, Volume 1: Laws against Images* (Oxford: Oxford University Press, 1988); and see Eamon Duffy, *The Stripping of the Altars*.
23. Testaments in stone to the Henrician destruction remain throughout England, but two of the most remarkable are the ruins of St. Mary's Abbey in York and the most well preserved of the ruins of Henrician dissolution, the Carthusian charterhouse, Mount Grace Priory, near Northallerton in Yorkshire. See Anne Dillon's *Michelangelo and the English Martyrs* (Aldershot, UK: Ashgate, 2012) for a detailed account of the broadsheet produced in Rome in 1555 depicting the martyrdom of the Carthusians in London between 1534 and 1537. For the evangelical side see, of course, John Foxe's *Acts and Monuments*. John N. King's *Foxe's Book of Martyrs: Select Narratives* (Oxford: Oxford University Press, 2009) reproduces twenty-one of the original woodcuts. The essential *Unabridged Acts and Monuments Online* or TAMO (Sheffield: HRI Online Publications, 2011) offers online, with commentary and woodcuts, the four editions of Foxe's martyrology at http://www.johnfoxe.org/.
24. See Chappell, *Perilous Passages*, chapters 3 and 4.
25. Alexandra Barratt, *Anne Bulkeley and her Book: Fashioning Female Piety in Early Tudor England* (Turnhout, Belgium: Brepols, 2009), 2, 6, 43.
26. Walsham, *The Reformation of the Landscape*, 6.
27. David Wallace, *Strong Women: Life, Text, and Territory 1347–1645* (Oxford: Oxford University Press, 2011), 201, 203.
28. Arthur Marotti, *Religious Ideology and Cultural Fantasy* (Notre Dame, IN: University of Notre Dame Press, 2005), 2.

29. Corthell et al., *Catholic Culture*, 13; see also Chappell, *Perilous Passages*, for a full-length study of the complicated path of preservation of one late medieval spiritual text.
30. Susan Brown, Patricia Clements, and Isobel Grundy, eds., "Elizabeth Delaval" in *Orlando: Women's Writing in the British Isles from the Beginnings to the Present* (Cambridge: Cambridge University Press Online, 2006), http://orlando.cambridge.org/.
31. David Punter, *Gothic Pathologies: The Text, the Body, and the Law* (Basingstoke, UK: Palgrave Macmillan, 1998), 1.

CHAPTER 1

"To the Illustrious Queen": Katherine of Aragon and Early Modern Book Dedications

Valerie Schutte

In 1979, Elizabeth Eisenstein challenged early modern historians to reassess the period immediately after the invention of the printing press as a time of communication revolution—one that stimulated renaissance and reformation and instituted a break with the past.[1] It was no longer enough to simply understand the importance of early texts in terms of content or the processes of production; it was now time to consider the roles of those texts in cultural and ideological formations. Since then, the printing press and the revolutions of which it was a part have been scrutinized from many angles, including the process of printing, book readers and literacy rates, and the ways in which books were used. The history of the book has become a recognized field of study. Yet this field has overlooked a crucial part of early modern texts: book dedications. Following the title, book dedications were the first words in an early modern printed book, but only a few modern studies exist that are devoted entirely to dedications. When modern scholarship does address dedications, authors still favor the body of the text as having more literary importance. These underutilized sources illuminate patronage relationships and, particularly, the importance of women to the first generations of printed texts in England.

The study of book dedications has been primarily left to amateur historians as compilers of anthologies, but these resources present little or no explanation of the dedications. Clara Gebert, Mary Elizabeth Brown, and Henry Benjamin Wheatley have all offered anthologies; although these have enabled greater access, they lack the critical analysis necessary to fully recognize the importance and place of dedications in early modern texts.[2] Franklin B. Williams, Jr.'s anthology is the most important work that has been done on English book dedications.[3] Meant to be a research aid to the English Short Title Catalogue, Williams's book created a key by which to search the intended recipient or recipients of nearly every book printed in England prior to 1641. He organized his study as a personal index, alphabetically listing every book dedicatee followed by the English Short Title Catalogue numbers of each book dedicated to that person.

Modern scholarship has seen some interest from doctoral candidates in their dissertations, as well as a few articles and mentions in book chapters. John Buchtel's 2004 dissertation at the University of Virginia examines dedications associated with Henry Stuart, Prince of Wales, and two articles have been published out of his research.[4] Tara Wood's unpublished dissertation at Arizona State University in 2008 examines the 183 books dedicated to Elizabeth I, situating them within the Tudor patronage system.[5] As both dissertations are necessarily limited in scope, they leave much to be done with the study of book dedications. William Wizeman's revisionist study on Marian Catholicism offers a chapter on Marian texts, authors, and dedicatees, concluding that dedicators to Queen Mary I saw themselves as contributing to the Catholic restoration of England.[6] Jaime Goodrich has offered a case study of Mary Roper Clarke Basset's manuscript dedication to Queen Mary I to show that Basset's dedication and translation was an example of a Catholic woman writer challenging Edward VI's religious settlement.[7] Helen Smith has recently used book dedications as "new" evidence of women's participation in the processes of book composition.[8]

Nieves Baranda Leturio's work on book dedications focuses on dedications directed to women in early modern Spain from 1500 to 1700.[9] She posits that dedications are useful sources that provide information on women's reading habits, rather than simply recording patronage and social relationships. They also illuminate correlations between subject matter and readership, with the majority of books covering topics of religion, while the rest consisted mainly of literature, etiquette, and education. Admittedly, she does not include books dedicated to women of the royal family, as they had different duties and demands than did the rest of Spanish women; nonetheless, her argument is also relevant to royal dedications. Dedications to Tudor queens provide similar evidence in the English royal court of the complexity of relationships between the queen, her household, and the broader social and political world.

Book dedications, particularly those printed during the early phase of the English reformations, have many uses for historians. Firstly, they provide insight into the patronage system of the early Tudor period: dedicating a book to an important person could result in monetary or political favor. Secondly, book dedications reflect some of the most important religious and political matters of the period. As prefaces to important works on marriage, education, and Christianity, book dedications allow the authors a chance to explain why they chose to write the works that they wrote and why they wrote them in the way that they did. Thirdly, book dedications to the wives of Henry VIII, particularly those only dedicated to the queens, not the king and queen together, demonstrate the extent of the queen's patronage power at the Tudor court. In appealing to queens, the authors demonstrate a canny understanding of the queens' influence over the king's policies, particularly relevant during a time of religious change and upheaval. Book dedications offer a glimpse of an author's choice of patron and show interconnectedness of nobles and humanists across Europe. The tradition, as well as the standards and protocols, of dedicating printed books to English queens began with Lady Margaret Beaufort.

Lady Margaret, mother of Henry VII, had approximately ten books dedicated to her. She was a patroness of William Caxton, and the two enjoyed a close relationship; Caxton dedicated *Blanchardyn and Eglantine,* a thirteenth-century romance, to Lady Margaret.[10] Lady Margaret ran her own household, established colleges, and was even declared a *feme sole* by Parliament in 1485. Because of this odd position, she functioned as an important model that later writers followed in their dedications to actual queens. Dedications to Lady Margaret tended to be brief remarks made for commercial purposes, connecting Lady Margaret to a book so that it would sell better and help establish the new market of printed books. Dedications to the six wives of Henry VIII took the format of more traditional dedications, lavishly praising the queens and pleading for patronage. The authors were much more concerned with the queens appealing to Henry on their behalf than increasing the sale potential of a book. Of course, a handful of manuscripts had been dedicated to previous English queens,[11] but Katherine of Aragon was the first queen to have a printed book dedicated to her.[12]

As Henry VIII's first wife and queen of England for the first twenty-four years of Henry's reign, Katherine of Aragon was known for her passion for learning, her religious devotion, and her desire to pass as much knowledge to her daughter, Mary, as possible. Katherine was the recipient of at least seven book dedications, all of which show that she was a respected and educated queen on whom authors and printers relied. Moreover, she was a source of patronage and wielded considerable power at court. The books dedicated to her came from well-known humanists, such as Erasmus and Juan Luis Vives; religious men, such as Alphonsus de Villa Sancta; and courtiers, such as Thomas Wyatt. Henry's remaining five wives collectively received approximately ten book dedications, coming from similarly stationed men. For these later queens, the patronage system of book dedications did not really change. As before, men dedicated books to these queens in hopes of a reward. Yet one aspect of these book dedications that did change was the nature of their received devotional literature. As expected, when Katherine of Aragon was queen, the devotional works were orthodox and spoke directly against Martin Luther and Philip Melanchthon. But the devotional works dedicated to the five wives after Katherine of Aragon took on a much more evangelical flair. Both Anne Boleyn and Katherine Parr received dedications to English translations of scripture. As with subject matter, dedications could also change to reflect different religious tones. Erasmus's dedication to Katherine was rarely reprinted and the extant copies are exactly the same. This is not necessarily typical: Juan Luis Vives's dedication to Katherine of Aragon of *The Instruction of a Christen Woman* (1526) underwent many changes in its nine editions.[13] Its translation into English by Richard Hyrde in 1529 included both Vives's original dedication and a new dedication by Hyrde. Vives's and Hyrde's names appear on all editions, but Hyrde's preface, which was extremely laudatory of Katherine, is omitted from all editions after 1531, and all mentions of Katherine as queen were changed to princess, to reflect her demoted status after the annulment of her marriage to Henry. Only the 1585 and 1592 editions returned to calling Katherine queen, when the annulment no longer faced as much open hostility. Yet Erasmus's dedication of *Institution of Christian Matrimony* to Katherine of Aragon has received very little scholarly attention and provides a key example of the historical and literary richness of book dedications.

Erasmus's *Institution of Christian Matrimony* was initially printed in Latin in Basel in 1526 by Johannes Froben in both folio and octavo editions, as *Christiani matrimonii institutio*.[14] Another Latin edition was published in Antwerp in 1526, followed by two undated sixteenth-century editions, one published in Cologne and the other with no place of publication given. Translations were offered in German in 1542, Italian in 1550, French in 1714, and, allegedly, English in 1568, with one undated edition. The first reprinting in its entirety since the eighteenth century appeared as an English translation by Michael Heath as part of the *Collected Works of Erasmus* project.[15] But Heath's identification of these last two (at least) seems problematic. Firstly, he takes his information from two other sources, Émile Telle's *Erasme de Rotterdam et le septième sacrament* and Ferdinand van der Haeghen's *Bibliotheca Erasmiana*, which he corroborates with an examination of a first octavo in the *Opera Omnia* of 1540 and the 1703 to 1706 edition.[16] Although his sources may be reliable studies of Erasmus, they are simply outdated. Secondly, the two English translations listed are misidentified. A quick search of the electronic English Short Title Catalogue reveals that the treatise on marriage printed in 1568 and credited to Erasmus really contains excerpts from Erasmus's *Colloquia*, not *Institution of Christian Matrimony*, and that the undated edition has a putative date of 1536 and is really a translation of Erasmus's *Matrimonii encomium*.[17] The former is dedicated to Francis Rogers and the latter to Thomas Cromwell. Therefore, it appears that no English translations of *Institution of Christian Matrimony* were made.

Institution of Christian Matrimony is regarded as one of the most important texts on concepts of marriage in the sixteenth century, yet it is also one of the most understudied, probably because it was not available in modern English translation until 1999. It has only recently been made widely available, digitized through the Universal Short Title Catalogue Project.[18] As a humanist, Erasmus valued female education and departed from traditional thought on marriage, but he assigned women conventional roles within marriage and the home. Examining marriage from the choice of partner to mutual respect to child rearing, of particular importance is that it was written by a priest and explicated the value of marriage, not preferring virginity or celibacy, which was traditionally the favored opinion of the Church. Most other contemporary texts on matrimony, even if not written by churchmen, also included virtues and chastity, such as Juan Luis Vives's *Instruction of a Christian Woman*, which was also dedicated to Katherine of Aragon. Heath situates *Matrimony* within Erasmus's other works on marriage, such as *Colloquia* (1523) and *Matrimonii encomium* (1518), to show how the conclusions in *Matrimony* were more controversial than those of Erasmus's previous writings on marriage. With the debate over the sacramental status of marriage taking place all over Europe, this work fit into a larger dialogue. It somewhat predated the most heated debates, but it presaged many of the changes that were made at the Council of Trent, though its contents, particularly its preference of marriage over celibacy, led to its inclusion in the *Index of Forbidden Books* in 1559. If the text of *Matrimony* has been understudied, then the dedication has barely been acknowledged.

The opening, which praises Katherine as an "illustrious queen" who was the "glory of matrons," establishing his deference to her, was a typical way to begin such a dedication. Vives began his dedication to Katherine of Aragon similarly: "unto the most gratious princes Katharine quene of Englande . . . I have ben moved partly by the holynes and goodnes of your lyvyng," as did his English translator, Richard Hyrde, who dedicated his translation "unto the moste excellent prynces quene Catharine."[19] Immediate praise for a patron or patroness placed the dedicator lower than the person addressed, a position calculated to acquire favor and patronage. Typically, beginning praise was aimed at individual virtue or social position, two of the most important things that patrons held, apart from wealth. Like many other humanists, Erasmus, though a well-known theologian, relied on financial patronage for his survival. Virtue and status counted for much, but wealth remained the most desirable aspect in a patron.

Erasmus and Katherine of Aragon had established a relationship through Lord William Mountjoy, Katherine's chamberlain. In his dedication, Erasmus credits Mountjoy for arranging for the writing of *Matrimony*. The connection between the two men was long-standing: Erasmus was Mountjoy's tutor in Paris in 1499, and it was Mountjoy who first invited Erasmus to England. [20] They remained lifelong friends, with Erasmus dedicating at least two other works to his former student. When Erasmus came to England upon Mountjoy's request, he served as a lecturer at Cambridge for a few years at the invitation of John Fisher, Bishop of Rochester. Erasmus also wrote the epitaph for Lady Margaret Beaufort's tomb, and Fisher wrote her remembrance sermon. Lady Margaret was one of the main supporters of Cambridge, as she established St. John's College with the assistance of Fisher. Through Mountjoy and Fisher, Erasmus was connected to the two most powerful women in England at that time. By the time of Katherine's death, she and Erasmus were close correspondents. The first letter Erasmus addressed to her was the dedicatory letter in *Institution of Christian Matrimony*.[21]

Lord Mountjoy is also associated with Katherine in another book dedicated to her, *De Ratione Studii Puerilis*, a two-part study written by Juan Luis Vives on education for boys and girls. The first part, dedicated to Katherine, was written for her daughter Mary's education; the second part, dedicated to Lord Mountjoy, was written for his son's education. Mountjoy's connection with two books written for Katherine shows the intricacies of patronage, as dedicatees often had to go through circles of patrons even to be able to become clients of kings and queens. Often clients of the queens were clients of others at court, so as to have many possible opportunities for monetary gain or power.[22] Erasmus's careful inclusion of Mountjoy, conscious as he must have been that Katherine was aware of his involvement in the book on marriage, indicates his awareness of Mountjoy's usefulness as a patron and the need to balance praise for both Katherine, as the queen and intended recipient, and Mountjoy, as an important avenue to further patronage. Clearly, there were benefits for both men from working with queens. As a result of their connection with Katherine, both were recipients of money, prestige, and well-placed positions in England. This lucrative patronage engendered followers and imitators. Altogether, the six wives of Henry VIII received nearly twenty book dedications. Given the dynamic and often sudden changes in political and social landscapes, as well as the frequent changes at court during Henry's reign, the number of dedications is significant. Henry VIII received approximately sixty dedications during his reign. While this is two-thirds more dedications than his wives received, it nonetheless demonstrates the power of queens as patrons, even in troubled and unstable courts.

In his dedication, Erasmus was careful to praise Katherine a few times, particularly for her patience, forestalling the queen's anticipated frustration at his dallying on a promised work on matrimony two years previously. A few sentences later, he claimed that part of the reason that this treatise took him so long to complete was that it did not inspire him, so it might not even have been what she was initially hoping to receive. Yet for being uninterested in the subject of marriage, Erasmus still managed to complete a very long, detailed discourse, totaling close to three hundred pages. As a client of Katherine's, Erasmus expected monetary benefit as long as he did something that his patroness asked for, even if it did not suit her needs. Altogether, Erasmus did not seem to be helping his case by highlighting his tardiness. But, Erasmus tried to cover his lateness and indifference by telling Katherine that if she was displeased with his work, she could look to her own marriage as an ideal example.

Katherine, in her turn, was late responding to Erasmus about the treatise even though she was aware of it. Concerned by lack of response from Katherine, in a 1526 letter from Thomas More to Erasmus, More referred to "your *Institutio christiani matrimonii*, for example, which her serene Majesty rightly values most highly, as, I hope, you will discover in some tangible way."[23] It was not until 1527, after Erasmus asked about its reception in a letter to Sir Thomas More, that Lord Mountjoy wrote to Erasmus to let him know that Katherine enjoyed *Matrimony*.[24] But, it was not until 1528, two years after publication, that Erasmus sent a reminder to Katherine of his commissioned work, and she sent a gift in return.[25] Through their correspondence, we see Tudor patronage at work. Queen Katherine commissioned work from a well-known humanist, who was obligated to oblige her request in some way and who also expected some form of favor in return.

Katherine's delayed response was most likely due to a preoccupation with her matrimonial trials that had begun around the time that she would have received this book. For the next seven years, Katherine was more intimately involved with questions of matrimony than she ever could have expected. Although this dedication praised Katherine's current state of matrimony in 1526, it was probably one of the last tracts to do so. For, between the end of 1526 and the beginning of 1527, King Henry VIII became infatuated with Anne Boleyn and started on his seven-year-long quest for annulment. Erasmus had concluded his dedication with a prayer for God to preserve Katherine's happy marriage as a model for all of Europe. But Erasmus's prayer must not have been heard, for Katherine and Henry's marriage was annulled in 1533. The annulment of their marriage reverberated throughout Europe, undermining Erasmus' assertion of it as modeling the ideal state of matrimony. Yet at the time Erasmus's book was written and presented to Katherine, she certainly would not have seen irony in its dedication. In the process of dissolving his marriage to Katherine and marrying Anne, Henry split from the Catholic Church, bringing England into the national politics of Italy, Spain, and the Holy Roman Empire. The pope was under house arrest in Italy, and Katherine's nephew was both king of Spain and Holy Roman Emperor.

Katherine's lack of immediate response could also be partly responsible for the book never being printed in England. If Katherine did not approve, Erasmus would not bring it to England for publication, or Katherine or Henry may not have allowed it to be printed in England. As mentioned earlier, there is no known printing of *Matrimony* in England during Katherine's lifetime and may never have been one. Certainly by the time an English translation could have been undertaken, within a few years of its original Latin printing, an English translation would have been very controversial, connected as it was to the then deposed princess and an annulled marriage. There are several reasons for sensitivity surrounding this text: Firstly, its dedication praised Katherine and her marriage to Henry—a marriage that Henry was actively seeking to end. His cause did not need further public support for Katherine's side. There was already great concern that there would be a popular uprising on Katherine's behalf. Secondly, with the Henrician Reformation underway, the status of marriage was not secure. Marriage was hotly debated during the reformations across Europe, even in England, and the subject itself may have been deemed too controversial for an English press. Thirdly, the work may have been forbidden in England because it was connected to Katherine, and with English print mainly consolidated in London, it would have been very difficult to print something forbidden but very easy to get into trouble for doing so.[26] In 1534, Parliament passed the Act for Printers and Binders of Books, restricting the importation of foreign print,[27] which mandated that the bishop of London approve the importation of foreign books and the domestic printing of religious texts. The act constituted an effort to gain control over the print surrounding Henry's marital and religious choices, especially as more and more printers were setting up shops in London, and could have prohibited *Matrimony* from coming into England, even without the dedication to Katherine. Therefore, this text may have been too controversial to receive the bishop's approval.

In addition to restricting the importation and sale of foreign-printed books, the act allowed the chancellor to set the prices of books printed in England. Passed alongside acts such as the King's Succession and Submission of the Clergy, the Act for Printers was clearly a reaction to Henry's recent marriage to Anne Boleyn and was meant to deliberately exclude European literature that spoke for Katherine and against Anne. For E. Gordon Duff, this act sank English printing into a "badness which has lasted, with the exception of a few brilliant experiments, almost down to our own day."[28] For Duff, the removal of foreign print meant the removal of healthy competition among printers to improve so as to compete in a world market. Erasmus's *Matrimony* could have been the victim of this print restriction.

Although this text was connected to Katherine, it was only through the dedication. The text easily could have been printed in England with the dedication left out, and only those who read the Latin edition would have known that this text supported Katherine's marriage to Henry. This text even could have been used to support Henry's annulment, as Erasmus points to many cracks in marriage contracts, such as language and oaths.[29] Erasmus's eighteen impediments to marriage also seem to have included ideas Henry could have used to dissolve his marriage or prove that it was never valid in the first place. Impediment number four regards "misrepresentation of status or fortune."[30] Erasmus explains that a marriage cannot stand if it has an error of misrepresentation. Henry argued that his marriage to Katherine was not legal because she misrepresented herself as a virgin after the death of her first husband, Henry's brother, Arthur. In this passage alone, Henry could have supported his claim. Erasmus's tenth impediment is affinity, in which Erasmus cites Leviticus 18, prohibiting a man from marrying his brother's wife, which is the exact biblical justification that Henry used for his annulment from Katherine.[31] Erasmus does display some hesitancy over the Leviticus verse: "perhaps only during his lifetime [that of the brother], since, if he dies without issue, his surviving brother is ordered to provide offspring for his dead brother."[32] Even so, if Erasmus was unsure of the meaning of the verse, Henry certainly could have used that to his advantage to secure an annulment. However, if Katherine did engage in sexual intercourse with Henry's brother, the impediment of affinity would have applied, because according to papal law, affinity could arise from sexual intercourse, even if legal. The fact that, *Matrimony* was never printed in England, despite the ammunition it offered for Henry's annulment campaign strongly suggests that because it had a dedication to Katherine of Aragon, it was too political to print.

The first two-thirds of Erasmus's dedication show the Tudor patronage system at work and how dedications were part of a larger discourse of politics and religion. The last third of Erasmus's dedication to Katherine of Aragon shifts focus and demonstrates her power at court. The final lines of the dedication tie Katherine's qualities and virtues to those of her mother, the famous and powerful Queen Isabella of Castile. Isabella was queen outright of her own kingdom in Spain and was known for finishing the Reconquista with her husband, King Ferdinand of Aragon, as well as her patronage of Christopher Columbus and numerous artists. She survived plots on her life immediately after her ascendancy, squashed rebellions, and implemented criminal and financial reforms, creating stability for Castile. Isabella also understood the value of education, teaching herself Latin as an adult and providing both her sons and daughters with a humanist education. This education was very important for all of her children, not just her son, John. John predeceased her, allowing her daughter, Juana, to take the throne, and Ferdinand and Isabella made sure to make beneficial political matches for their other children. She was also deeply pious, believing herself an instrument of God. As such, Isabella gained a reputation for her energy, perseverance, prayer, and success in battle and politics. Altogether, Isabella was a powerful queen.

In calling upon the memory of Katherine's powerful mother, and referring to Katherine as an image of her mother, Erasmus acknowledges that Katherine is also a powerful queen for all of those same reasons. Katherine did act as regent of England in 1513, overseeing forces that defeated the Scots at Flodden Field, which included the death of King James IV of Scotland. Obviously, Katherine was a generous patron to authors, as well as artists and musicians. She also ensured that her daughter, Mary, had a humanist education, under the instruction of Juan Luis Vives, Giles Du Wes, and others, who tutored her in Latin, French, science, other foreign languages, and religion. Importantly, Katherine was also known for her strong religious convictions, frequently going on pilgrimages, giving alms regularly, standing up to Henry about the religious validity of their marriage, and consistently supporting papal authority and decisions. Accordingly, Katherine was also a very powerful queen.

Mary is also mentioned in the final lines of this dedication as a girl who will follow in Katherine's footsteps of virtue and valiance. By mentioning Mary as sure to be like her mother, who was a reflection of *her* mother, Erasmus placed Mary in a line of powerful, educated, respected queens. Erasmus sets the stage, implicitly for Mary's ascension to the throne as Queen of England. In 1526, Mary was the only living heir of Henry and Katherine, and Katherine was beyond her childbearing years, so there was good reason to believe that Mary would become queen regnant of England someday. Therefore, in expecting "a work no less perfect" in Mary, Erasmus alluded to the possibility that Mary would be queen and therefore stressed the necessity of Mary becoming an educated and powerful woman so as to be a good queen like her mother and grandmother.

Erasmus concluded his dedication with a prayer for England to remain in its "happy" state. Erasmus was a priest, and most of his correspondence concludes in this fashion. But, it was also part of a standard topos to bookend a dedication with praise and prayer. For Erasmus, the prayer is straightforward and traditional in tone. Depending on the recipient and nature of the work, the tone of prayers could change. Traditional prayers accompanied traditional theology and patrons, while evangelical prayers accompanied evangelical books and patrons, such as Katherine Parr, whose dedications often mentioned the necessity of grace. Katherine Parr received a dedication from Nicholas Udall, the English translator of *The First Tome or Volume of the Paraphrases of Erasmus upon the Newe Testament* (1548), in which Udall hoped that its readers would be joyous to receive religion, in their mother tongue, that was deciphered by those trained in doctrine.

Although book dedications to Henry's queens remain a relatively new area of interest, they have taken up an odd position in retellings of Tudor history. In an episode in the final series of *The Tudors*, a popular Showtime series depicting the rise and fall of Henry VIII, Katherine Howard is presented with a copy of Richard Jonas's translation of *Byrth of Mankynde*, a book on midwifery dedicated to her.[33] Most of the details are wrong. Among other things, the episode's book is much larger and contains cruder images than the actual edition. Another episode in the final season depicts Katherine Parr telling Henry VIII that she has completed another book, *Lamentation of a Sinner*, and that she has chosen to dedicate it to him, treating him as a Moses within England.[34] This depiction is actually almost entirely wrong. *Lamentation* was not published until November 1547, nearly nine months after Henry's death, although it is surmised that it was composed in late 1546.[35] Moreover there is no actual dedication in *Lamentation*, but a preface by William Cecil is directed at general readers. If the creators of a loosely based historical miniseries recognize the importance of queenly literary patronage and book dedication, even if haphazardly, it is time that scholars do the same and better. As this essay has demonstrated, book dedications have historical value in illuminating the patronage system, as well as political and religious positions, and in demonstrating the power of Tudor queens at court. The dedication by Erasmus in *Institution of Christian Matrimony* to Katherine of Aragon is no exception, as it brings all three of these elements together while prefacing one of the most important books written on matrimony during the early Tudor Reformation.

Notes

1. Elizabeth Eisenstein, *The Printing Press as an Agent of Change* (Cambridge: Cambridge University Press, 1979).
2. Clara Gebert, *An Anthology of Elizabethan Dedications and Prefaces* (Philadelphia: University of Pennsylvania Press, 1933); Mary Elizabeth Brown, *Dedications: An*

Anthology of the Forms Used from the Earliest Days of Book-Making to the Present Time (New York: Burt Franklin, 1913); and Henry Benjamin Wheatley, *The Dedication of a Book to Patron and Friend* (New York: A. C. Armstrong, 1887).

3. Franklin B. Williams, Jr. *Index of Dedications and Commendatory Verses in English Books before 1641* (London: The Bibliographical Society, 1962).

4. John Buchtel, *Book Dedications in Early Modern England: Francis Bacon, George Chapman, and the Literary Patronage of Henry, Prince of Wales* (PhD diss., University of Virginia, 2004); "'To the Most High and Excellent Prince': Dedicating Books to Henry, Prince of Wales," in *Prince Henry Revived: Image and Exemplarity in Early Modern England*, ed. Timothy V. Wilks (London: Holberton, 2008); and "Book Dedications and the Death of a Patron: The Memorial Engraving in Chapman's Homer," *Book History* 7 (2004): 1–29.

5. Tara Wood, "*To the most Godlye, virtuous, and myghtye Princes Elizabeth*": Identity and Gender in the Dedications to Elizabeth I (PhD diss., Arizona State University, 2008).

6. William Wizeman, SJ, *The Theology and Spirituality of Mary Tudor's Church* (Aldershot, UK: Ashgate, 2006).

7. Jaime Goodrich, "The Dedicatory Preface to Mary Roper Clark Basset's Translation of Eusebius' Ecclesiastical History." *English Literary Renaissance* 40 (2010): 301–28.

8. Helen Smith, *"Grossly Material Things": Women and Book Production in Early Modern England* (Oxford: Oxford University Press, 2012).

9. Nieves Baranda Leturio, "Women's Reading Habits: Book Dedications to Female Patrons in Early Modern Spain," in *Women's Literacy in Early Modern Spain and the New World*, ed. Anne J. Cruz and Rosilie Hernández (Aldershot, UK: Ashgate, 2011), 19–39.

10. Elizabeth Woodville received a dedication in Liverpool Cathedral MS Radcliffe 6. See Anne F. Sutton and Livia Visser-Fuchs, "The Cult of Angels in Late Fifteenth-Century England: An Hours of the Guardian Angel Presented to Queen Elizabeth Woodville," in *Women and the Book: Assessing the Visual Evidence*, ed. Lesley Smith and Jane H. M. Taylor (London: The British Library, 1996), 230–65. For Elizabeth of York, British Library Royal MS 17 D xv includes "The Balet off the Kynge," a political poem on the return of Edward IV into London, reprinted in Thomas Wright, ed., *Political Poems and Songs Relating to English History*, II (London: Longman, Green, Longman and Roberts, 1861), 271–82. The final three paragraphs begin "O quene Elizabeth, o blessid creature . . . good ladye, in youre felicite, remembere olde trowblis and thynges paste."

11. Juan Luis Vives, *A Very Frutefull and Pleasant Boke Called the Instruction of a Christen Woman,* trans. Richard Hyrde (London: Thomas Berthelet, ca. 1529). STC 24856.

12. Margaret Beaufort received the dedication of William Caxton's *Blanchardyn and Eglantine* (1489).

13. Anne Clark Bartlett, "Translation, Self-Representation, and Statecraft: Lady Margaret Beaufort and Caxton's *Blanchardyn and Eglantine* (1489)," *Essays in Medieval Studies* 22 (2005): 53–66.

14. The modern translator, Michael Heath, lists the known printings of *Matrimony* that occurred in the sixteenth and seventeenth centuries in his introduction. *Institution of Christian Marriage*, trans. Michael Heath, in *Collected Works of Erasmus: Spiritualia and Pastoralia*, ed. Josh O'Malley and Louis Perraud (Toronto: University of Toronto Press, 1999), 203–438. It is difficult to trace the transmission as very few copies of the text still exist. The British Library has one copy of the 1526 Basel edition, as well as a 1650 Leiden edition. This 1650 edition is not mentioned in this chapter because I believe it is a part of the *Opera Omnia* published that year by J. Maire in Paris. The *Opera Omnia* of 1540 also includes *Institutio*, as does that of 1703, according to Michael Heath. I did not have access to any of the editions beyond copies of the original 1526 edition. I suspect that the dedication to Katherine was included only in the first edition, as the collection of Erasmus's correspondence does not mention the dedication letter as published any other time, yet it does note all other correspondence relating to this dedication.

15. Excerpts of Heath's translation also appear in Ericka Rummel, *Erasmus on Women* (Toronto: Toronto University Press, 1996). Rummel concludes that *Matrimony* (or *Institution of Marriage*, as she calls it) is not so much innovative as it is an elegant summary of traditional thought and authoritative voices, traced to biblical, classical, and patristic sources.

16. Émile Telle in *Erasme de Rotterdam et le septième sacrament* (Geneva: Droz, 1954); Ferdinand van der Haeghen, *Bibliotheca Erasmiana: repertoire des oeuves d'Erasme* (Ghent: Bibliothèque de l'Université de l'État 1893).

17. English Short Title Catalogue (ESTC) 10499 and 10492. If there is a sixteenth-century English translation of *Matrimony*, it has not been identified by the ESTC or by Early English Books Online.

18. *Matrimony* has received some attention from French scholar Émile Telle in *Erasme de Rotterdam et le septième sacrament*. Like other works on Erasmus's view of marriage, it gives more focus to Erasmus's other treatises on marriage and hardly offers any analysis on *Matrimony*. *Matrimony* also received less than three full pages of attention in Reinier Leushius, "The Mimesis of Marriage: Dialogue and Intimacy in Erasmus's Matrimonial Writings," *Renaissance Quarterly*, vol. 57 no. 4 (Winter 2004): 1278–1307, even though *Matrimony* is Erasmus's largest and latest text on marriage.

19. Vives, *Instruction*, Br and Aiiv.

20. Maria Dowling, *Humanism in the Age of Henry VIII* (Kent, UK: Croom Helm, Ltd., 1986), 13.

21. *The Correspondence of Erasmus: Letters 1658 to 1801, January 1526–March 1527*, trans. Alexander Dalzell (Toronto: University of Toronto Press, 2003), letter 1727.

22. Wood makes a similar point in *Identity and Gender*, 52.

23. *Correspondence*, letter 1770.

24. *Correspondence*, letter 1727. See introduction to letter.

25. *Correspondence*, letter 1727. See introduction to letter.

26. See Andrew Pettegree, *The Book in the Renaissance* (New Haven: Yale University Press, 2010). In this, Pettegree explicates the central control of English print.

27. Parliament 25 Henry VIII, c. 15. January 15, 1534.

28. E. Gordon Duff, *The Printers, Stationers and Bookbinders of Westminster and London from 1476 to 1535* (New York: Arno Press, 1977), 240.

29. O'Malley and Perraud, *Collected Works of Erasmus*, 250–54.

30. O'Malley and Perraud, *Collected Works of Erasmus*, 257.

31. O'Malley and Perraud, *Collected Works of Erasmus*, 270.

32. O'Malley and Perraud, *Collected Works of Erasmus*, 270–71.

33. *The Tudors*, "Something for You," SE04EP03. DVD: Sony Pictures Home Entertainment, 2011.

34. *The Tudors*, "Sixth and Final Wife," SE04EP07. DVD: Sony Pictures Home Entertainment, 2011.

35. Janel Mueller, ed., *Katherine Parr: Complete Works and Correspondence* (Chicago: The University Chicago Press, 2011), 425.

CHAPTER 2

"Rather a Strong and Constant Man": Margaret Pole and the Problem of Women's Independence

Janice Liedl

Margaret Pole was an unusual woman, as her weary examiners explained in a letter to Thomas Cromwell: "We have dealid with such a one as men have not dealid with to fore us, Wee may call hyr rather a strong and custaunt man than a woman."[1] Their chagrin at her steadfast protestations of loyalty seems understandable when juxtaposed against the quick confessions offered by her sons in what has come to be known as the Exeter Conspiracy of 1538.[2] As Countess of Salisbury, Margaret Pole enjoyed a remarkable degree of independence, administering her considerable properties, promoting the interests of her family, and participating in the early Tudor court. This same independence, however, ensured she could not be overlooked when her sons and their circle were implicated in treason. With the coming of the Henrician Reformation, noble power came under new scrutiny. Margaret Pole's close ties to Katherine of Aragon and Princess Mary pushed her family to the outskirts of the royal court. However, the Countess's retired life was no protection in an age of religious and political turmoil. Her active role in her home parish of Warblington sparked an investigation that led to the arrest of many in her affinity and her own eventual attainder for treason.

The Countess of Salisbury found herself in a difficult situation in the autumn of 1538. Her protestations of a suitably feminine distance from political and religious power failed to convince her accusers during the Exeter Conspiracy: Margaret Pole was too prominent and independent a noblewoman for those characterizations to apply. Her reputation for intense involvement on the part of her family, her friends, and her faith was too well known for her to convince others that she was an uninformed and uninvolved woman. In the end, Margaret Pole found that her gender was no protection against accusations of her involvement in the Exeter Conspiracy or on behalf of conservative religion in the early period of Henry's reformation.

Early modern Englishwomen enjoyed an invidious relationship with power, political and otherwise. Law and custom barred most women from the exercise of autonomy and authority outside the confines of their own families, yet 20 percent of householders in the early modern period were females who exercised considerable economic independence.[3] Women also exercised power in their religious activities, from nuns and abbesses who populated some of the great and powerful religious houses to laywomen whose bequests could make provision for charitable chantries and other forms of spiritual comfort. In 1547, for example, Anne Whithers of St. Botolph's Aldersgate established five tenements for poor women to pray for the souls of the departed in her family.[4] However, even at the highest ranks, women were subordinate to male relatives, and their power could be ruthlessly circumscribed or leniently indulged, as suited masculine agendas.

It would be difficult to stand much higher in the social order than to be a Plantagenet in late fifteenth-century England. Margaret Pole was born to be a key figure in high-level English politics and society, even if her gender potentially limited her actions and independence. Born Margaret Plantagenet in 1473 to George, Duke of Clarence, and his wife, Isabella Neville, daughter and coheiress of Warwick the Kingmaker, Margaret represented powerful lineages. The Duke of Clarence was a younger brother of Edward IV who had briefly supported the readeption of Henry VI in 1469 but reconciled with his brother for the Yorkist restoration in 1471. Their mother was heiress to the Warwick lands and privilege, and this connection increased her children's standing in Yorkist noble society.[5] Margaret's younger brother, Edward, was the heir to vast estates and titles from both sides of their family tree, and Margaret could expect a dowry befitting a Plantagenet princess.

While they lived, the Duke and Duchess of Clarence maintained households of grandeur and godliness.[6] But both died when Margaret and Edward were very young: their mother due to childbed complications and their father due to political intrigue. George was accused of a second rebellion against his brother, Edward IV, tried by a commission of oyer and terminer in 1477 and executed as a traitor at the Tower in 1478.[7] His attainder left his children as royal wards: Margaret was now of doubtful worth, with most of her inheritance forfeit due to her father's treason, while Edward remained a prize due to his claims on the Warwick lands and title. During these years from 1478 to 1483, Margaret appears rarely in the historical record, although there was no indication of ill treatment; repeatedly Edward IV made provision to pay for her clothing and her servants' wages.[8] Her brother, Edward, was further granted the title of Earl of Salisbury, and his custody and marriage were handed over to Thomas Grey, Marquis of Dorset and the queen's son by her first marriage.[9] The death of their royal uncle, Edward IV, in 1483 and the succession of their younger uncle, Richard III, put the young Plantagenets in an even more precarious position.

Margaret's brother, Edward (Warwick), as Clarence's heir, arguably had the better claim to the succession than his uncle, putting aside the questions of the legitimacy of Edward IV's marriage to Elizabeth Woodville that Richard III gave as reason to disinherit his other nephews.[10] Because of this, both Richard III and Henry VII held Warwick and Margaret under close control. Eventually, Warwick was confined to the Tower in 1486 before being accused of plotting an escape, attainted, and executed in his turn for treason in 1499.[11] His death brought an end to the Plantagenet threat against Henry VII's throne, and his confiscated estates constituted a notable addition to the royal holdings.

Margaret Plantagenet may not have inherited the property or title that her brother claimed, but she did not sink into obscurity. After Henry Tudor secured his throne, he secured Margaret through an arranged marriage with Sir Richard Pole, an undistinguished and loyal Tudor cousin, who guaranteed her safety and position even during the dangerous time of her brother's escape attempt. Richard Pole was appointed chamberlain of North Wales; as such, he was closely associated with Prince Arthur's household and remained a fixture in Welsh administration even after the prince's death.[12] Through this connection, Margaret met and befriended Katherine of Aragon, forming an important connection, although childbearing seems to have kept her from a more active role in the court. Richard Pole's untimely death in 1504 left the family financially as well as emotionally adrift. Margaret took refuge for a time with the nuns of the well-connected Syon Abbey, while the Carthusians educated her young son, Reginald.[13] The family fortunes languished until after Henry VIII's accession when Margaret's petition for restoration to her brother's lands and the earldom of Salisbury was granted in 1512.[14]

As Countess of Salisbury, Margaret Pole was definitively elevated to the highest ranks in the land. Without that restoration, Margaret Pole's family may have had symbolic significance in early Tudor dynastic politics, but her new title and estates catapulted her into political, social, and courtly prominence. Her lineage as an indisputably legitimate Plantagenet made her, as much as her brother had been, a viable claimant to the throne and a perennial thorn in the side of the reigning monarch. Her marriage to Richard Pole, a loyal Tudor adherent, muted that threat but did nothing to reduce the potential of the family's claim on the throne. Margaret's lineage was continued through her five children, Henry, Ursula, Arthur, Reginald, and Geoffrey, ensuring that her claims would carry on to the next generation. Reginald Pole became a cardinal and was the last Roman Catholic Archbishop of Canterbury; Henry, Ursula, Geoffrey, and Arthur all made good marriages. The success enjoyed by Margaret after Richard's death, along with the future promise indicated by her children's marriages and Reginald's placement in the Church, increased the threat that the family posed to the shaky succession of Henry VIII.

Though Margaret Pole's bloodlines ensured that she was a political force to be reckoned with, whatever her station, her restoration to the nobility dramatically altered her place in Tudor court culture. The newly recognized Countess of Salisbury, as a peeress in her own right and with the restoration of estates to support her status, ranked among the most powerful tenants-in-chief during Henry's reign. Her appointment as governess to Mary Tudor signaled an equally significant personal standing in the court.[15] Margaret exercised great power through both her courtly and her titled position, different from her female contemporaries more in scale of her political activities (by virtue of her anomalous legal stance as a woman holding title in her own right) than in style.[16] Obviously, she exercised greater liberty than most early Tudor landholding women in that her property rights came not through a life-interest in widowhood, but they were unburdened by obligations relating to her deceased husband or his kin. This circumstance left Margaret Pole free to control her considerable property across southwest England, negotiate with her peers over the advantageous marriages and advancements of her children, and maintain a powerful presence in the Tudor court. In this respect, her closest parallels were the king's late grandmother, Lady Margaret Beaufort, who, after Henry VII's accession, enjoyed the legal status of *feme sole*, despite her marriage to Lord Stanley, and Katherine Courtenay, Henry VIII's aunt and Countess of Devon, who received a lifetime grant to all the estates of the earldom of Devon in the same year that Margaret was elevated to the peerage.[17] Both of these other royal women exercised a great deal of power through their lineage and landowning, but their efforts were focused on male relatives: Margaret Beaufort concentrated all of her political acumen on supporting her son's royal dynasty, and Katherine Courtenay seemed to defer to her son, Henry Courtenay, who featured prominently at the early Henrician court, was restored to his father's title in 1512, and eventually created as Marquis of Exeter in 1525.[18]

As a courtier, the Countess of Salisbury enjoyed significant royal favor thanks to her close ties to Katherine of Aragon. Their friendship, dating back to Katherine's earlier marriage to Prince Arthur, was considered instrumental in the Poles' restoration after Katherine's marriage to Henry VIII.[19] In 1516, she was one of several high-ranking women who served as godmother to Princess Mary. The Countess continued on in the royal household as the most distinguished of the queen's ladies, as demonstrated by her receipt of a New Year's gift, valued at forty shillings, equal to that received by the Dukes of Buckingham and Norfolk.[20] But in 1520, Margaret achieved the pinnacle of courtly success with her appointment as governess to Princess Mary. She would hold this position, one of great prestige and influence, on and off, until 1533. As governess, Margaret was not only expected to oversee the rearing and education of the princess in the new learning but also to act on behalf of others seeking a position at court.[21] This role consolidated the Countess of Salisbury as a powerful force for patronage, through her position in Princess Mary's household as well as in her own right.

With this influence, Margaret also sought and secured highly advantageous marriages for her own children. Her eldest son and heir, Henry, was twenty-one at the time of her own restoration in 1513 and enjoyed a noble lifestyle. His mother's recovered wealth supported him far more generously than he could have expected from the modest inheritance he had received from his father. Henry also rose in rank thanks to his mother: he was knighted in 1513 and henceforth was referred to as Lord Montague.[22] Henry's marriage to Jane Neville, coheiress of Lord Bergavenny, brought benefits for both parties, and the plans for this union were marked by careful negotiations carried out between the Countess and Lord Bergavenny on behalf of their children.[23] Margaret's influence aided her other children as well: more marriages were arranged, and one of her younger sons, Reginald, enjoyed Henry VIII's direct and rewarding patronage as a royal scholar.[24] His studies in Padua during the early 1530s brought Reginald closer to the papacy, just as his patron was drawing away. The young scholar directly repudiated the nascent royal supremacy in his 1536 composition, *Pro ecclesiasticae unitatis defensione*, more commonly known as *De unitate*. The manuscript called for England's nobility and the emperor to restore the singular, true church in England. The king was angered at this disobedience, which amounted to a public attack for all that Reginald Pole insisted the manuscript was a private communication with his royal cousin. Instead of returning to England as Henry and Cromwell demanded, Reginald accepted a summons to Rome in July of 1536. Although Continental hopes for the success of the Pilgrimage of Grace remained strong in December of that same year, Reginald Pole was elevated to the cardinalate and put in charge of a mission to restore England to the Roman church.[25] With this turn of events, the Poles were inextricably linked with foreign and domestic threats to Henry VIII's reign, a suspicion that extended to Margaret, matriarch of the family and mother of the new cardinal. Deprived of her royal offices, Margaret and her family were banished from Henry's court.

Even retired to family holdings, the Poles posed a problem for Henry and his ministers. As one of the major landowners in England, the Countess played a significant role in several regions—from the southwest across the south and into the east—just as other Tudor magnates exercised authority in the outlying regions.[26] Her holdings included lands of great strategic importance for coastal defense, with a third of her properties clustered near the coastline in Devon, Dorset, Essex, Hampshire, and the Isle of Wight.[27] With these, the Countess of Salisbury was the chief military power in the southwest, a situation that helped contribute to an eventual call for improved Crown control of the region and its defense.[28] As a landowner, she also had numerous religious livings under her control. It was one of these parishes, Warblington, associated with her chief residence in Hampshire, which brought greater scrutiny on the Countess, her family, and her household during the convalescence of a supporter of the "new learning": Gervase Tyndale.

It might have seemed that the downfall of the Countess and the prosecution of the Exeter Conspiracy was an accident. In 1538, Dr. Richard Ayer treated Gervase Tyndale at a hospital that Ayer maintained in his home on the Countess's lands. Tyndale was a fervent supporter of the evangelical shift in English religion. Ayer was an Observant Friar but also sympathetic to the religious changes that the king's reform had brought. Ayer complained to his patient of the interference of his patroness, Margaret Pole, who he characterized as an opponent to the new learning. Ayer suggested that she was suspiciously well-informed about what went on among the people of her estates:

> ther colde be nothynge be done, nether s . . . yn all [the country] wer he dwellyd bout my Lady dyd knoe yt, all thow [yt wer] never so secret yn mens hartes for the curat dyd reuell . . . *sub sigillo secreto* as the papystes sae the may doe to my Lady, and the acordynge to ther owthe wysp[erd] yn my Ladys eer.[29]

In Ayer's view, the Countess could never be characterized as uninformed or uninvolved. With priests breaking the seal of confession to share what they learned with their patroness, Margaret Pole had access to a frightening amount of information regarding her tenants and visitors on her property.

She was not only collecting information. In her capacity as noble landowner, Margaret Pole governed in the king's name. According to Tyndale's informant, however, Margaret's "government" subverted the king's wishes. Tyndale reported that the Countess's council had commanded, in the king's name, that no one was allowed to possess a copy of the New Testament in English or "other new [books] which the Kynges Hynes hathe pryvelyged; which he affermyd [he had] good wyttnes off."[30] From all of these reports, it appears that the Countess was both extremely well-informed about what went on in her community and complicit in action against the royal changes in religion. Tyndale complained about the interrogation he endured at the hands of the Countess's men, including her son, Geoffrey Pole. It was Geoffrey that summoned Tyndale's informant, Ayers, to speak with Thomas Cromwell, the Lord Privy Seal, and supposedly to clear his name.[31]

Tyndale was no idle or disinterested witness to the Countess's transgressions. He was a one-time schoolmaster in Grantham and, while a student at Oxford, had fallen in with men who would later figure prominently in the royal reform, including Richard Morison, a propagandist who wrote against the Pilgrimage of Grace and would also take up the royal case against the Exeter Conspiracy. Equally interesting, as G. W. Bernard has noted, sizeable sums were paid in September of 1538 to transport Tyndale to Lewes to meet with Cromwell: forty shillings to two servants of the Bishop of Thetford to arrange for his travel and twenty-two shillings, six pence, for Tyndale's own costs. The reasons for this arranged and funded meeting remain unclear, but Bernard has queried whether Tyndale "present[ed] so convincing a case this time that something had to be done?"[32] Although suggestions that Tyndale was sent to ferret out resistance to the Henrician Reformation are still unsubstantiated, it is clear that his information and his assessment of the Countess as an informed and dedicated opponent of religious change helped to build the case against the conspirators, particularly the Countess.

Women of all ranks came under scrutiny during the Henrician Reformation for their religious behaviors as legislation criminalized many traditional practices. As Sharon L. Jansen noted, Tudor women charged with the crime of treason "posed no direct, physical threat to Henry . . . [n]evertheless, to Henry's government they also represented a danger to the stability of the realm."[33] The case of Margaret Cheyne, who was arraigned, indicted, and found guilty of treason in regards to the Pilgrimage of Grace in 1537, shows that women were held responsible for their public actions regarding their convictions.[34] Changes to the law in 1534 had widened the range of what was considered treason: words, as well as deeds, could raise suspicions and invite scrutiny. This innovation disquieted many at the court, including Margaret Pole's eldest son, Lord Montague.[35]

The expanded range of the new treason laws brought more women's behavior under scrutiny by church officials and the king's men. Even so, proving treason against a woman was rarely clear-cut as most early Tudor women did not take part in military uprisings, preaching, or political actions that were the primary charges made against traitors. The new law made treasonable speech a crime, but establishing this to the satisfaction of the courts was not always easy. As some prosecutions languished before the courts, Henry's ministers employed the alternative method of attainder to deal with anomalous cases. Elizabeth Barton, the "Holy Maid of Kent," was attainted of treason only after a panel of common law judges failed to return a conviction in November 1534.[36] Barton's prophecies against Henry VIII's divorce and remarriage were eagerly followed by an English and foreign audience in 1533 and 1534.[37] The king and Cromwell resorted to parliamentary attainder to deal with this troublesome woman. While the official business was dealt with in the parliamentary act, Elizabeth Barton's reputation was also savaged in print and from the pulpit. Both were conventional strategies to discredit women. Publicly, the church leaders attacked her as an unnatural woman who stepped outside the natural realm of hearth and home. Her virtue was questioned in the public sermon preached at St. Paul's Cross. In the public confession elicited from Barton before her hanging, she acknowledged her transgressions of the ideals of femininity in an attempt to downplay her role. She demeaned the importance and validity of her earlier acts, reminding listeners that she was only "a poor wench without learning" and, as a woman, she was unfit to speak on matters regarding rule and faith.[38]

Such conventional apologies were often offered after the fact by early modern women to excuse or demean their political actions. Further justifications for women's intervention in public matters could be made, as in the case of the Countess of Westmorland, who apologized for having intervened in the Scots war in 1639, arguing "that her interest in 'the children unborne, inforceth me to utter my minde.'"[39] Gertrude Courtenay, Marchioness of Exeter and Margaret Pole's co-accused in the 1539 act of attainder, employed another such tactic when she sought the king's pardon in 1535 for having heeded the Holy Maid of Kent, describing herself as a woman "most facile, easily, and lightly . . . seduced."[40]

Margaret Pole epitomized a loyal subject and a good mother in her answers to her accusers: her duty to her king came first. As a mother, she also expressed a rightful interest in her son's welfare but only insofar as he obeyed his sovereign lord. In the interrogations, the Countess would have her audience believe that she not only wanted their obedience to Henry, but that she was also ignorant of any political actions of her sons and their circle. When asked about others already implicated in the plot, she averred that each man in question "never opened his mynd" to her, be it son, cousin, or vicar.[41] When confronted with a suggestion that Geoffrey, increasingly implicated in treasonous actions, might cause the family difficulties, her only response recorded was "Nay, Nay, sayd she, he will not bee so unhappe."[42] In many instances, Margaret Pole's defense combined themes of blind maternal affection with feminine disinclination for politics: a somewhat improbable stance for a powerful magnate and longtime courtier.

Those around her, particularly her comptroller, defended the Countess of Salisbury as a true subject of the Tudor monarchy and uninvolved in the treason for which her sons had already been condemned. Interrogations and the reports collected by those who knew her and members of her household emphasized her abiding loyalty to the king. Oliver Frankelyn, her comptroller, reported that the Countess responded to his warnings that Geoffrey would cause her displeasure with his wild actions: "I trowe he is not so unhappye that he wyll hurte his mother, and yet I care neyther for hym, nor for any other, for I am true to my prynce."[43] Frankelyn's account emphasized Margaret Pole's maternal hopes with an additional disavowal of any traitorous relative in favor of loyalty to the king.

Her protestations of loyalty, however, were insufficient to sway her case. That the family had met with Reginald after he had incurred the king's displeasure was bad enough; that others saw the family as a rallying point for resistance against the recent changes in state and religion was even more troubling. From the early evidence gathering in September, the Earl of Southampton reported to Cromwell the opinion of one Johane Sylkden of Waldreton, Sussex:

> that if Sr. Geoff. Poole had prospered till March next he would have sent a band of men over sea to his brother Cardinal Poole; also that if my Lady of Salisbury had been a young woman, the King and his Council would have burnt her at their late being in the country.[44]

This testimony demonstrated that the entire family posed a threat to the ongoing reform efforts and the security of the realm. Indeed, the case made against Geoffrey Pole at the end of 1538 hinged, in part, upon his potential to provide material support to his brother. Sylkden's assertion about Margaret Pole was even more interesting, though, as it posited a view of the Countess as both martyr and rebel.[45]

Margaret's powerful reputation, as well as her refusal to bend, break, or admit any treasonous talk, inspired the Earl of Southampton, one of her interrogators who had the unenviable task of hosting the Countess in genteel imprisonment before she was removed to the Tower, to deem her "rather a strong and custaunt man than a woman," highlighting the ways in which her behavior ran counter to gendered expectations.[46] Yet Margaret's behavior during interrogation and throughout the crisis was, in some ways, hardly transgressive. In the interrogations, Margaret repeatedly invoked her maternal role and bodily weakness as she avoided any implications of treason. For instance, she expressed a mother's desire to be close to her children when she said that she desired "her sonne no more go over the seas." When further questioned about Reginald's absence from England, she responded that "she hathe wished of tym . . . for him over agayne in England with the king's favour, though he were but a poore parishe priest."[47] Margaret's professions were perfectly couched to evoke both maternal care and dutiful loyalty. The Countess was concerned for her son, but more that he should enjoy royal favor than that he prosper outside of the royal circle.

Her evasiveness and refusal to respond directly to questioning cannot be decisively considered as "feminine" behavior either. Southampton suggested that it was a masculine tactic, but other observers and scholars would categorize demurrals as feminine. One comparison comes from the near-contemporary experience of Anne Askew, whose interrogation in 1546 helped establish her as an early Protestant martyr. Askew's answers to interrogations were often evasive, and some of Askew's readers have argued that the Protestant martyr's refusal to assert doctrine reflects less a religious conviction than a gendered interiority. They characterize her resorting to silence or scriptural tags as a gendered response. Megan L. Hickerson has countered that "the discretion exercised by Askew when faced with persecution was far from unique to her, nor was it a symptom of her gender."[48] A refusal to self-incriminate was not particularly masculine or feminine: it was evident in both men and women under interrogation throughout the period.

Even if not uniquely feminine, the plausibility of Margaret Pole's professions of unswerving loyalty and ignorance are questionable. At least some contemporaries were willing to accept that she might appear an innocent bystander in her sons' treason. With fears of Pole's rallying a Franco-Imperial invasion force at their height, a 1539 propaganda pamphlet outlined both the case against the conspirators and the reasons for English subjects to rally around the king. This publication, *An invective ayenste the great and detestable vice, treason, wherein the secrete practices, and traitorous workinges of theym, that suffid of late are disclosed*, by Richard Morison, the old Oxford friend of Gervase Tyndale, justified the quick action taken against what was now being seen as a widespread Anglo-Catholic conspiracy: the Exeter Conspiracy.[49] In Morison's pamphlet, Margaret Pole was less a threat than an object of pity.

In *An invective*, Morison focused on Exeter and Pole kinships as premier examples of ungrateful nobles resorting to treachery against the king. Reginald Pole was his chief target, and Margaret appeared only in reference to this arch-traitor: "all men muste hate the, yea, thy mother her selfe shall thynke her self worthy deth, if she hate not the above all creatures."[50] Margaret's debt to Henry for his generous grant of title and land came into play when discussing Montague's treasonous actions: "was not also his mothers landes lost, she a poore gentyll woman, dwellynge amonge the systers of the Syon, he a poore gentyll manne, not havynge a fote of lande towarde his lyvynge? Was it not a thing worthy thankes, to comme from nothynge to .iii. or. iiii. thousande marke lande, his mother to have this for her lyfe, and he to enherite it after her decease?"[51]

In his interrogation, Oliver Frankleyn had characterized Margaret as more loyal to the king than to her family, an admirable stand for any subject. In *An invective*, Reginald's disloyalty to his king was conflated with disdain of his family, his mother in particular: "[Reginald] sent his mother word, that if he knewe her to be of the same opinion, that ye king is of, he wold treade her under his fete, mother his, as she was. What beast could use such language to his mother, excepte he had utterlye forgotten the reverence, that nature techeth all creatures to ward their parentes?"[52] Ironically, the royal propagandist seemed to place a higher premium on family loyalty than the Countess or her supporters.

Through her tenure as Countess of Salisbury, Margaret Pole was active within her family, on her estates, and within the political realm of the court. Gervase Tyndale painted a picture of a noblewoman who was closely involved in the religious life of her community: so much so that her priests brought her secrets from the confessional and royally sanctioned reform texts were suppressed on her estates. This, combined with her sons' close involvement in her properties and residences, further strained suggestions that the Countess was ignorant of their activities or those of others in her household. Three decades of independent action stood in opposition to the Countess's protestations that none of these men around her had ever opened their mind to her, but in the end, no confession was needed. Margaret Pole was attainted of treason in May of 1539 on the basis of an embroidered surcoat reportedly found in her possession that Thomas Cromwell heraldically interpreted as promoting the marriage of Mary Tudor to Reginald Pole.

On May 18, 1539, John Worth reported to Lord Lisle the latest news from Parliament:

> There was a coat-armor found in the Duchess of Salisbury's coffer, and by the one side of the coat there was the King's Grace his arms of England, that is, the lions without the flower de luce, and about the whole arms was made pansies for Pole, and marigolds for my Lady Mary. This was about the coat-armor. And betwixt the marigold and pansy was made a tree to rise in the midst; and on the tree a coat of purple hanging on a bough, in tokening of the coat of Christ; and on the other side of the coat all the Passion of Christ. Pole intended to have married my Lady Mary, and betwixt them both should again arise the old doctrine of Christ. This was the intent that the coat was made, as it is openly known in the Parliament house.[53]

The Lords Journal for May 12, 1539, noted that immediately after the bill of attainder was read there, Cromwell displayed the same garment. Interestingly enough, however, this earlier account differed significantly in describing the reverse of the garment. In this second account, the coat-armor's reverse was identified as that recently used by the rebels in the north:

> Immediately after the bill was read, Lord Cromwell, Vicegerent for the king in spirituals, proffered a tunic made of white silk, discovered by the Lord Admiral [Southampton] among the possessions of the Countess of Salisbury, on the front of which was the Arms of England, to wit, three lions surrounded by two flowers, in English called pansies and marigolds. On the back was that insignia that was used by the rebels in the north of England in their recent commotion.[54]

The attainder passed Parliament and the Countess, along with the Marchioness of Exeter and her young son, Edward Courtenay, were committed to the Tower. Occasional memoranda regarding their provision and care appeared in Cromwell's papers until his execution in 1540. Margaret Pole survived her parliamentary accuser by a year and was executed in May of 1541. Her chief estate went to the Earl of Southampton who, along with Sir Thomas Wriothesley, the king's secretary, held Warblington until 1551.[55]

Margaret Pole, Countess of Salisbury, had been a prominent part of the Henrician court until the break with Rome. With one son a Roman cardinal and others implicated in treasonous talk, her protestations of loyalty and innocence were insufficient to secure her safety. Southampton may have characterized her as manly, rather than womanly, but her tactics of evasion were not uniquely gendered. What worked against her was her extremely high status and landed power, which amplified her beliefs and policies. Her sons' convictions could not secure Henry against the Pole and Courtenay affinities as long as the Countess of Salisbury held her land and authority. Despite her careful words and the frustration they inspired in her interrogators, Margaret Pole could not be allowed to remain free in Henry VIII's troubled realm.

Notes

1. "William Fitzwilliam, Earl of Southampton and Thomas, Bishop of Ely to Cromwell," November 16, 1538, *Letters and Papers* XIII (2), no. 855.
2. The standard treatment of these events remains Madeleine Hope Dodds and Ruth Dodds, *The Pilgrimage of Grace, 1536–1537, and The Exeter Conspiracy, 1538.* 2 vols. (Cambridge: Cambridge University Press, 1915).
3. Bernard Capp, "Separate Domains? Women and Authority in Early Modern England," in *The Experience of Authority in Early Modern England*, ed. Paul Griffiths, Adam Fox, and Steve Hindle (New York: St. Martin's, 1996), 117–34.
4. "Anne Whithers," *Abstracts of Inquisitiones Post Mortem Relating to the City of London*. Volume 1: 1 Henry VII to 3 Elizabeth (1485–1561), ed. G. S. Fry (London:

British Record Society, 1896), 100–101. For the broader context of women's agency in Tudor religious life, see Patricia Crawford, *Women and Religion in England, 1500–1720* (London: Routledge, 1996), 88–93.

5. Hazel Pierce, *Countess of Salisbury, 1473–1541: Loyalty, Lineage and Leadership* (Cardiff: University of Wales Press, 2003), 1–4.

6. For the spiritual side of the ducal household, see Kate Mertes, *The English Noble Household, 1250–1600* (Oxford: Blackwell, 1988), 148, 151, and 159.

7. Charles Ross, *Edward IV* (Berkeley: University of California Press, 1974), 240–44.

8. Pierce, *Countess of Salisbury*, 5–7.

9. Ross, *Edward IV*, 336.

10. Mortimer Levine, "Richard III: Usurper or Lawful King?" *Speculum* 34.3 (July 1959): 391–92.

11. Pierce, *Countess of Salisbury*, 8–14.

12. Pierce, *Countess of Salisbury*, 20–27.

13. Sue Powell, "Margaret Pole and Syon Abbey," *Historical Research* 78, no. 202 (November, 2005): 563–67.

14. Pierce, *Countess of Salisbury*, 31–37. For the context of restorations at the start of Henry VIII's reign, see Helen Miller, *Henry VIII and the English Nobility* (Oxford: Blackwell, 1986), 6–9.

15. We can date this appointment to sometime between 1519 and 1520, the Countess having already been named one of the princess's godmothers at her christening in February 1516. Pierce, *Countess of Salisbury*, 42–43.

16. See Barbara J. Harris, "Women in Politics in Early Tudor England," *Historical Journal*, 33:2 (1990): 268–70; Patricia Crawford, "Public Duty, Conscience and Women in Early Modern England," in *Public Duty and Private Conscience in Seventeenth-Century England: Essays Presented to G. E. Aylmer*, ed. John Morrill, Paul Slack, and Daniel Woolf (Oxford: Clarendon Press, 1993), 65–67 [57–76], concurs, though she notes that women's opportunity to exercise direct political power decreased over the era.

17. Michael K. Jones and Malcolm G. Underwood, *The King's Mother: Lady Margaret Beaufort, Countess of Richmond and Derby* (Cambridge: Cambridge University Press, 1992); Margaret Westcott, "Katherine Courtenay, Countess of Devon, 1479–1527," in *Tudor and Stuart Devon: The Common Estate and Government*, ed. Todd Gray, Margery Rowe, and Audrey Erskine (Exeter: University of Exeter Press, 1992), 22–23 [13–38].

18. Westcott, "Katherine Courtenay," 24–31.

19. David Loades, *Henry VIII and his Queens* (Stroud: Sutton, 1994), 19. Helen Miller deemphasizes the Aragonese influence, preferring to characterize the Pole restoration as part and parcel of an early Henrician program to rehabilitate important subjects fallen out of favor during his father's reign. Miller, *Henry VIII and the English Nobility*, 7–9.

20. Pierce, *Countess of Salisbury*, 43–45, 58–59.

21. For the growing significance of Mary's household after 1520, see Jeri L. McIntosh, *Sovereign Princesses: Mary and Elizabeth Tudor as Heads of Princely Households and*

the Accomplishment of the Female Succession in Tudor England, 1516–1558 (PhD Diss: Johns Hopkins University, 2003), 73–75.

22. Debate continues over whether this was a courtesy title or a separate creation. Henry Pole was summoned as Lord Montague to the House of Lords in 1529, making the latter seem more likely. Stanford Lehmberg, *The Reformation Parliament, 1529–1536* (Cambridge: Cambridge University Press, 1970), 46.

23. Pierce, *Countess of Salisbury*, 50–51. The marriage agreement is preserved in the state papers, *L&P* XIII (2), no. 1016(1). Bergavenny later fathered another child, considerably reducing the value of the union.

24. For Reginald Pole's early career, see Thomas F. Mayer, *Reginald Pole: Prince and Prophet* (Cambridge: Cambridge University Press, 2000), 47–49.

25. Mayer, *Reginald Pole*, 61–65.

26. See Steven G. Ellis, *Tudor Frontiers and Noble Power: the Making of the British State* (Oxford: Clarendon Press, 1995) for a discussion of the estate management policies of the Percy earls of Northumberland in the early Tudor period (41–42).

27. Taken from Appendices II ("Map of the Lands of the Countess of Salisbury in 1538") and III ("The Lands of the Countess of Salisbury in 1538 and their Descent") in Pierce, *Countess of Salisbury*, 186–89.

28. Ellis, *Tudor Frontiers*, 173–75.

29. "Information against the Countess of Salisbury," n.d. 1538, *Letters and Papers*, XIII (2), no. 817.

30. "Information against the Countess of Salisbury," n.d. 1538, *Letters and Papers*, XIII (2), no. 817.

31. This was the recollection of the Countess's comptroller: Oliver Frankelyn's examination, November 20, 1538. The National Archives (UK), TNA SP1/139, f. 154.

32. G. W. Bernard, *The King's Reformation: Henry VIII and the Remaking of the English Church* (New Haven: Yale University Press, 2007), 412.

33. Sharon L. Jansen, *Dangerous Talk and Strange Behavior: Women and Popular Resistance to the Reforms of Henry VIII* (New York: St. Martin's, 1996), 3.

34. Jansen, *Dangerous Talk and Strange Behavior*, 13–15.

35. The new law also lacked limits upon what was considered treasonable speech, permitting the government to charge those who were merely critical of the regime as equivalent to those who were outright seditious. Christopher Randall Duggan, *The Advent of Political Thought-Control in England: Seditious and Treasonable Speech, 1485–1547* (PhD diss., Northwestern University, 1993), 200.

36. Jansen, *Dangerous Talk and Strange Behavior*, 54.

37. Jansen, *Dangerous Talk and Strange Behavior*, 60–64.

38. Jansen, *Dangerous Talk and Strange Behavior*, 75.

39. Crawford, "Public Duty," 67.

40. Jansen, *Dangerous Talk and Strange Behavior*, 57.

41. "The Countess of Salisbury's Examination," November 12 and 13, 1538, TNA SP 1/138, fol. 243r.

42. TNA SP 1/138, fol. 246r.

43. "Oliver Frankelyn's Examination," November 20, 1538. TNA SP1/139, fol. 154.

44. "W., Earl of Southampton to Cromwell," September 20, 1538, *L&P* XIII (2), no. 392.

45. Until the 1586 execution of Margaret Clitherow, the Countess was one of the few contemporary women martyrs in the Tudor experience. Anne Dillon, *The Construction of Martyrdom in the English Catholic Community, 1535–1603* (Aldershot, UK: Ashgate, 2002), 278.

46. A short while later, Marian female Protestants were similarly characterized as unwomanly by Catholic interrogators. See Susannah Brietz Monta, "Foxe's Female Martyrs and the Sanctity of Transgression," *Renaissance and Reformation/ Renaissance et Réforme*, 25.1 (Winter, 2000): 4–6.

47. "The Countess of Salisbury's Examination," TNA SP 1/138, fols. 243–44.

48. Megan L. Hickerson, "'Ways of Lying': Anne Askew and the *Examinations*," *Gender and History*, 18.1 (April 2006): 57–61.

49. Tracey Sowerby, *Renaissance and Reform in Tudor England: The Careers of Sir Richard Morison, c. 1513–1536* (Oxford: Oxford University Press, 2010), 92–94.

50. Richard Morison, *An invective ayenste that great and detestable vice, treason* (London: Thomas Berthelet, 1539), B.viii.r.

51. Morison, *An invective*, C.vi.r–v.

52. Morison, *An invective*, C.vii.v–C.viii.r.

53. John Worth to Lord Lisle, *The Lisle Letters*, ed. Muriel St. Clare Byrne (Chicago: University of Chicago Press, 1981), Volume 5, #1419, 480–81.

54. "Immediate post cujus Bille Lectionem, Dominus Crumwell, Vicegerens Domini Regis in Spiritualibus, palam ostendit quandam Tunicam, ex albo Serico consectam, inventam per Dominum Admirallum, inter Linteamina Comitisse Sarum, in cujus parte anteriore existebant sola Arma Anglie, viz. Tres Leones circumdata serto ex duobus s[f]loribus, Anglice vocat. Paunses et Marigolds, confect. in parte vero posteriore suere Insignia illa, quibus nuper Rebelles in Aquilonari parte Anglie in Commotione sua utebantur." May 12, 1539, *Journal of the House of Lords: Volume 1: 1509–1577* (1802): 107–08. My translation.

55. "Warblington," *A History of the County of Hampshire: Volume 3* (1908), 134–39.

CHAPTER 3

Religious Intent and the Art of Courteous Pleasantry: A Few Letters from Englishwomen to Heinrich Bullinger (1543–1562)

Rebecca A. Giselbrecht

Queen Elizabeth I is no monster because it is permitted that women may also rule; according to its fundamental conviction, the highest political power is also allowed to make decisions in affairs of the church, for example, to depose bad Bishops and to replace them with better.[1]

Mapping the correspondence between a few Englishwomen and the Zurich *Antistes*, Heinrich Bullinger (1504–1575), may seem to be a rather trivial pursuit. As a matter of fact, it would be less fraught with danger to add an anecdote or two about these women to an essay on their husbands and fathers, who were leading figures either in the evangelical reform of England or the European commercial trade system, than to risk making assertions based on a handful of women's letters. While contemporary research on the relationship between the English reformers and Zurich depicts lively interaction between Bullinger and Englishmen and illustrates how their communications served as an international network for transmitting religious ideas and literature from Zurich to England during King Edward VI's (1537–1553) reign and the Marian Exile (1553–1558),[2] whether women played any significant role in the network, or even participated in it, has never been investigated.[3]

The reason for this void can be attributed to the scant sources available. To be exact, just thirteen letters written by Englishwomen to Bullinger have been preserved. The *Heinrich Bullinger Briefwechsel* has identified exchanges with thirty different women, including seventy-six of Bullinger's own writings, whereby, only a few of these letters have been published to date.[4] In comparison to the Genevan reformer John Calvin (1509–1564), who corresponded with eighteen women all of whom were noblewomen, and Oswald Myconius (1488–1552), who had two exchanges with women, Bullinger's correspondence is noteworthy because he wrote to and saved letters from noble ladies, common and merchant women, wives, and mothers from his own circle of family and friends.[5] Four exchanges with women from England, including Anna Hilles, Lady Jane Grey (1537–1554), Anne Hooper, and Margaret Parkhurst, are available in manuscript form, while a few have been transcribed and published. Putting this into perspective, the burgeoning Bullinger correspondence of twelve thousand letters contains thirteen letters from Englishwomen and eighty-two exchanges with the heads of these women's households—namely Richard Hilles (1514–1587); Henry Grey, Duke of Suffolk (1537–1554); John Hooper (1495–1555); and John Parkhurst (1511–1575).[6]

Limited documentation and mere historical traces do pose a challenge here; nevertheless, in the spirit of contemporary scholarship,[7] the following pages will probe the extant letters written by Englishwomen to Heinrich Bullinger in Zurich to determine how they might contribute to our understanding of this correspondence.[8] From a literary standpoint, the letters belong to the *familiares* genre,[9] and the rhetorical use of courteous and artful pleasantries, common in written exchanges of both women and men during the early modern period, constitutes the stylistic framework for most of the letters.[10] In particular the often-religious flowers of speech gracing these letters will be examined in view of the sixteenth-century epistolary tradition for semantic clues to the women's intent.

As vital as genre and styles may be, each letter in its historical context also holds the personal story and motivation for the individual woman's contact with the reformer. In order to discover to what extent these women were active members of Bullinger's evangelical network and to forge an understanding of the individual and communal identities that were unique to the Protestant Reformed women of England, their words must be found and assessed. Indeed, a little information has the capacity to inform the present superficial knowledge of Zurich's influence on the lives of Englishwomen in the evangelical wing of the Reformation. Even if distilling the information from the letters results in a coherent picture of this small group of women— Anna Hilles, Lady Jane Grey, Anne Hooper, and Margaret Parkhurst—one spirited question remains: How might these ladies have informed Heinrich Bullinger's own political action or stance toward England and the Protestant Church of England?

Our image of the Reformation context has evolved. Who influenced what five hundred years ago has taken five hundred years to determine. Currently church historians conclude that the Zurich reform began to formally influence the religious and political environment of England around 1526, when the Archbishop of Canterbury, Thomas Cranmer (1489–1556), added an unnamed work written by Huldrych Zwingli (1484–1531) concerning the Anabaptists to the official catalogue of banned books.[11] Although some of Huldrych Zwingli's works found immediate approval in England, research has identified the earliest formal connection between Zurich and the reform movement in England to be "Bullinger and Joachim Vadian's Letters to Archbishop Cranmer in January 1537"[12] and the "English students in Zurich."[13]

Although the mayor of St. Gallen, a town of about five thousand citizens located on the eastern border of modern Switzerland, Joachim Vadian (1484–1551), humanist and scholar, began corresponding with Cranmer in 1536 using the German theologian and humanist scholar Simon Grynäus (1493–1541) as an intermediary,[14] Bullinger's first letter was mediated by Rudolf Gwalther (1519–1586) and the reform sympathizer Nicolas Partridge (d. 1540) of Lenham in Kent.[15] The reformer chose Gwalther and Partridge to carry his letter across the English Channel to Thomas Cranmer.[16] More than likely, young Rudolf, who had been raised by Bullinger, was like a son to him, and eventually succeeded him as *Antistes*, delivered the letter to Thomas Cranmer along with some books.

At approximately the same time, between August 1536 and the end of 1537, various students were sent from England to Zurich and entrusted to the Helvetic theologians. The young men spent months at a time in Zurich, Berne, Geneva, and Strasbourg. Mingling with these cities' reformers and their students, these English gentlemen finally shaped the extensive network that spanned Europe, connecting England to the Swiss Confederation.[17] The lasting bonds between the Swiss Confederation and England were of a political, religious, and personal nature, the stuff of friendships connecting people together to build the "true church."

Although books and treaties by the Zurich reformers in both Latin and Early Modern High German had circulated in England for some time, the first book published in England by Zwingli's successor, Heinrich Bullinger, was his commentary on Paul's Letter to the Thessalonians, translated into English by R. H. (perhaps Richard Hilles[18]) and published in 1538 by James Nicholson.[19] That Zwingli's theology arrived in England first is not to be underestimated, but all too frequently, both Zwinglian and Calvinist streams are regarded without including Bullinger, who was *Antistes*, the chief pastor in Zurich from 1531 to 1574, and who outlived Calvin by eleven years.[20] In fact, between 1538 and 1556, thirty-three editions of Bullinger's works were published in England in English, that is, twenty-two influential books and treatises, often best sellers, including his handbook on marriage.[21] Bullinger's final work addressing England was his defense of Queen Elizabeth in 1571. In contrast, Calvin's publications peaked in England between 1578 and 1581. That the Zurich reform had substantial influence on British politics and the Church of England is certain. Less clear, however, is how the bonds of friendship and faith that the reformers shared with women may have potentially influenced and inspired the reformation effort.[22] The window of a few letters may shed some light on this.

Anna Hilles wrote one letter to Bullinger. Richard Hilles and his wife Anna were friends with Bullinger from the reign of Henry VIII to that of Henry's daughter Elizabeth I.[23] Richard Hilles was a Merchant Taylor, the first Anglo-Swiss trader.[24] Hilles kept Bullinger informed with details on Continental news, reporting mostly the tragic events of the evangelical reformation in England. He also presented the Bullingers with fabric and other gifts.[25] Due to his Protestant sympathies, Hilles was forced to take his family and flee to a safe haven in Strasbourg between 1541 and 1548. The Hilles visited the Bullingers in Zurich at least twice during their exile. The network of Strasbourg reformers—Mathew Zell (1477–1548) and his wife Katharina Zell (1497/98–1562) and Martin Bucer (1491–1551), who was exiled to England in 1549, among others—was in close contact with Zurich alongside the Hilles. After the Church achieved a Protestant identity under Edward VI, the Hilles returned to England. Under Mary I, the Merchant Taylor Society, which Richard belonged to, did not openly support Lady Jane Grey's claim to the throne. Despite imminent danger for reformation supporters, the Hilles spent the Marian Exile in England. The sources are ambivalent as to their Protestant loyalties at that time.[26]

Extant evidence suggests that Richard's wife, Anna Hilles, was the least prolific of the four women under consideration here. Her only preserved letter was sent from Strasbourg on May 9, 1543. The daughter of the well-situated Christopher Lacey of Yorkshire, Anna married Richard Hilles sometime before 1538, when their first son John was born. Between 1540 and 1548, she gave birth to Gerson, Barnabas, and Daniel. Anna is not mentioned in her husband's will of 1586, so it can be assumed that she had already passed away by then.

Anna begins her letter, which was written in Latin, with a biblical reference wishing Bullinger "health and success in the vineyard of the Lord."[27] Her tone is modest, and in step with the epistolary practices of her day, she apologizes profusely for bothering Bullinger, "a very busy man." Two-thirds of her letter describes her reason for writing and is peppered with apologies for diverting Bullinger's attention from greater things. Basically, after declaring that she maintains the positional status of Richard Hilles' wife, and although she is "not worthy," Anna tells Bullinger that she would be irreverent and ignorant to keep what she has to say to herself. "Therefore, trusting in your kindness and faithful service, and unaided by my husband," she considers it her duty to negotiate a financial issue in her husband's absence. John Burcher had requested that thirty gulden be sent to Bullinger for safe keeping, until he could claim them. Anna is sending twenty-one kronen as well as a gift to the Bullingers. Her gift may well have been cloth, since her husband was one of the leading cloth merchants on the Continent, and many of his thirty-one surviving letters addressed to Bullinger include comments on gifts of fabric and cheese. Anne's letter was a business letter; yet she ends her letter by sending her best greetings to Bullinger's wife, Anna. Anna corresponded with the help of her servant Francis Warner, who also sent his greetings to the Bullingers. One may assume that given Anna Hilles privileged social standing from birth, she was educated enough to have written the letter herself, but chose not to.

Anna greets Bullinger with, "*Salutem atque in vinea domini profectum.*" She resolutely announces her piety using an insider biblical reference, a Reformed salutation for those reforming and harvesting the "true church." For the wife of a businessman interested in a monetary transaction, there would be no reason to be religious, unless it was part of her self-identity and meaningful to both herself and her addressee. Richard Hilles was not a pastor or theologian, but he was a man interested in theology on the evangelical side. Thus, it must be assumed that Anna was involved in Protestantism by choice. The apologetic tone, yet firm request, is the sign of a woman who understands her relative positional power as a businesswoman in a hierarchical system. Familiarity and trust fill the space between the lines of her letter, yet her independent ability to get the task done belies her excessive apologies and references to her husband, whom she comfortably substituted by proxy. Richard had obviously empowered her to be his surrogate. Without expecting too much from around thirty lines of writing, the letter does give us a peek into the warmth and mutuality between the two families who shared a transnational relationship for years, "*Saluta te ex familia nostra famulus meus.*" Anna mentions her small gift and signs off "*Tua in Christo soror Anna*"

The exchange sheds light on a functional network and shared religiosity with practical everyday applications. Bullinger kept the rather ordinary letter, which lends weight to the assumption that he respected and honored Anna Hilles with his friendship. Politically speaking, Anna's and Bullinger's letters are reminders of the tight-knit network, the biblically coded language, and a subversive common purpose of reform that politics was unable to sabotage and that eventually transformed the church and state of England.

Lady Jane Grey's exchanges with Bullinger are more theological and zealous. The politics of reform extracted the highest price from Lady Jane Grey, the author of three letters to Bullinger in Latin between 1551 and 1553. In his biography of Lady Jane Grey's life, Eric Ives contends that, "Immediately on her death she became a martyr for the Protestant faith so that hagiography colors nearly every recollection of her and very many subsequent assessments."[28] The original exchange between Lady Jane Grey and Bullinger has been reprinted at least eight times and is literally what myths are made of. One story, passed down to many generations in Switzerland and representing the strong bonds between Zurich and the lady, claims that Jane Grey took off her gloves at the scaffold before her execution and asked for them to be sent to Bullinger.[29] David J. Keep traces the narrative of Lady Jane's gloves in key historical books on Bullinger's life through the eighteenth and nineteenth centuries but proves that they arrived in Zurich as a gift to Heinrich Bullinger's wife, Anna, between the autumn of 1552 and May 1553—at least half a year before Lady Jane was executed. Lady Jane Grey's letters reveal a close relationship and her ultimate influence within the Zurich-England network.

In her first letter to Bullinger in 1551, Lady Jane exclaimed, "Oh, happy me, to be possessed by such a friend and so wise a counselor." Jane was between fourteen and fifteen years old.[30] Her intentions are precisely to gain a friend and counselor in her new acquaintance. This first letter lends a profile to Lady Jane's voice, one resounding with the rhetoric of a religiously devout intellectual and an individual sharpening her own wit as she boldly practiced theology and politics. Her intention is no doubt to enter the domain of male reformers. Her letter to Bullinger in Zurich was sent from Bradgate, on July 12, 1551, inside a letter to Bullinger from John of Ulm, a German scholar at Oxford, who had already received a pension from Lady Jane's father promising Henry Grey that Bullinger would dedicate a book to him.[31] Ulm had previously negotiated with Bullinger concerning the dedication since his promise to Henry Grey had gone far beyond the boundaries of his own authority and friendship with Bullinger.[32] After Bullinger accommodated Ulm's requests by dedicating his fifth installment of the *Decades*[33] to Henry Grey, Ulm then introduced Lady Jane to Bullinger in a letter to Bullinger in April 1550.[34]

Lady Jane's literary prowess speaks volumes about her exquisite education and free spirit. Her first letter to Bullinger certainly did not include the commonplace, as did Anna Hilles' letter. Exercising her keen mind, Lady Jane upheld the traditions and protocol of a courteous and artful epistolary style practiced by noblewomen throughout early modern Europe. Her self-assured intentions are embedded in apologetic words, not oxymoronic in the context of this letter.[35] Lady Jane claims to be "unworthy of the correspondence of so distinguished a personage" and calls Bullinger her "godly counselor," flattering him as she proclaims her joy "to be connected by the ties of friendship and intimacy with so learned a man, so pious a divine, and so intrepid a champion of true religion!"[36]

In the same text, Lady Jane's impressive grasp of the Bible, church history, and her attempt at feminine theology evidence her intellectual prowess, which is astounding considering her tender age:

> For no better fortune can await me than to be thought worthy of the correspondence and most wholesome admonitions of men so renowned, whose virtues cannot be sufficiently eulogized; and to experience the same happiness as was enjoyed by Blesilla, Paula, and Eustochium, to whom, as it is recorded, Saint Jerome imparted instruction, and brought them by his discourses to the knowledge of divine truths; or, the happiness of that venerable matron, to whom St John addressed an exhortatory and evangelical epistle; or that, lastly, of the mother of Severus, who profited by the counsels of Origen, and was obedient to his precepts.[37]

Although Lady Jane Grey counts herself among great women of church history, she includes Bullinger in the company of the Church Fathers. Doing this is both frolicsome and bold. Yet within this playful display of knowledge, her ultimate intent is to take her place as a member of the evangelical network with Bullinger as her counselor.

Lady Jane owns her boldness (*audacula*) for writing to Bullinger before she actually tells him that the formal reason for her letter is to thank him in her father's name for sending the volume *Christian Perfection* to them.[38] The book had been dedicated to Henry II of France in 1551. Lady Jane continues writing with the demure claim that all of the good in her is a result of divine goodness bestowed on her by God. She entreats Bullinger to offer prayers on her behalf, "that he may so direct me and all my actions, that I may not be found unworthy of his so great goodness."[39] Amidst respectful flattery, she explains that her father was in a distant area of England on business, but that he would certainly write back to Bullinger himself upon his return. The religious intent and courteous pleasantries in Lady Jane's first letter are light-spirited but in an uncanny way also a solemn introduction to Reformation politics that destroyed her.

Although his letters to her are lost, Lady Jane's second communication with Bullinger from Bradgate on July 7, 1552, is an expression of thanks to Bullinger for his kindness toward her. She asserts to Bullinger that she is "undeserving" and "unfit to address a letter to a person of your eminence." After reading Bullinger's letter twice, Lady Jane writes,

I seemed to have derived as much benefit from your excellence and truly divine precepts, as I have scarcely obtained from the daily perusal of the best authors. You exhort me to embrace a genuine and sincere faith in Christ my Saviour. I will endeavor to satisfy you in this respect, as far as God shall enable me to do; but as I acknowledge faith to be his gift, I ought therefore only to promise so far as he may see fit to bestow it upon me. And to this I will add, as you exhort me, and with the divine blessing such holiness of life, as my (alas!) too feeble powers may enable me to practice. Do you, meanwhile, with your wonted kindness, make daily mention of me in your prayers.[40]

Like Anna Hilles, Lady Jane does not want "to disturb your important labours with my trifles."[41] The lost letter from Bullinger must have been instructional, encouraging, and supportive—he had become Lady Jane's counselor and friend. In conclusion, she begs him to pray for her and commits to using his method for her Hebrew studies.[42]

Before June 1553, Lady Jane Grey wrote her final letter to Heinrich Bullinger. By then she had been married to Lord Guilford Dudley (c. 1535–1554) since May 21, 1553, and her cousin, King Edward VI, had already fallen ill in January of that year. Although she does not mention it in her letter, Lady Jane was certainly aware that Edward had plans for her succession to the throne of England, as she wrote to Bullinger shortly after her marriage. Despite all of the changes in her life, Lady Jane begins her letter as usual with praises for Bullinger's "authority with all men," his solidity of preaching, the great integrity of his conduct, "that foreign and remote nations, as well as your own countrymen are excited not only by your words, but by your actions." Lady Jane's passion for Bullinger's piety continues with an allusion to the Greek mythological figure Narcissus, which, along with the spattering of Greek phrases throughout her Latin text, is once more a reminder of Lady Jane Grey's humanist education as well as her intellectual intent:

Neither, indeed, do you resemble those who behold their natural face in a glass, and, as soon as they have gone away, forget the form of it; but you preach true and sound doctrine, and by your manner of life afford an example and pattern for others to follow what you both enjoin and practice.[43]

She then commits to pray for Bullinger, but once again refers to her boldness, "I have exhibited more boldness than prudence."[44] A few lines later she refers again to boldness, "*Magnaque praeterea mihi spes est, te huic meae plusquam muliebri audaciae, quae virgo ad virum et indocta ad eruditionis patrem scribere audeam.*"[45]

Lady Jane's pleasantries, submission, and eloquently planted flowers of speech continue, "a boldness which ought not at all to exist in our sex." In the final paragraphs of her letter, after explaining that she considers her "age, sex, and mediocrity," in light of his "favours" toward her but writes out of respect to him, she sends greetings to Bibliander.[46] Contact with Theodore Bibliander, the Swiss orientalist, publisher, linguist, theologian, and another member of the Zurich evangelical network must have been one of Lady Jane Grey's reasons for writing given that this letter reads like a dedicatory epistle with a near hyperbolic *topos of humility* and no other clear purpose. She was obviously networking in order to gain contact to yet another learned man of Switzerland. Finally, she wishes both Bullinger and Bibliander good health and promises that she will pray for their welfare.[47]

Her letters suggest that Lady Jane was enthralled with intellectual and theological pursuits. However, due to her Protestant stance and proximity to the throne by birth, she became embroiled in Reformation politics and was imprisoned in the Tower of London on July 10, 1553. Edward VI died on July 6, and Lady Jane's execution followed on July 19. Nonetheless, Zurich retained its interest in the English religious reform, even after Bullinger received a translation of Lady Jane Grey's scaffold speech, as well as a letter from Lady Jane's sister, Catherine Grey (1540–1568).[48] Although others pushed Bullinger to publish Lady Jane's speech, the wise reformer insisted that it not be made available for the larger public so as not to exacerbate the English government at such a tender moment in reform politics. Bullinger was present at a crucial turning point in the developing Protestant Church of England even supporting and counseling Lady Jane Grey, coaching her spiritual progress.

By July 25, 1553, Mary I ruled England. She broke the reform thrust and ushered the Church of England back to its Roman traditions. As Frank Gulley asserted, "The fact that Zurich was the sole exception and that it received one of the first exile groups lends credence to the fact that it held a place of importance in the minds and hearts of English reformers."[49] The English reformers, who fled England and spent the years of Queen Mary's reign as refugees in Zurich, learned to share both the theology and the Zurich theologian's understanding of church and state. Bullinger's theological rhetoric and methods of reformation that first appeared in his writings, his covenant theology, understanding of the Eucharist and vestments, as well as his stance on the Anabaptists and other radical reformers were carried back to England by several men, who became powerful leaders in the Church of England supported by their wives, some of whom corresponded with Bullinger.[50]

Anne de Tserclaes met John Hooper at Richard and Anna Hilles' house in Strasbourg.[51] Anne Tserclaes was a Belgian woman, who had more than likely escaped from persecution in Antwerp to the house of Jacque de Bourgonge, seigneur de Falais in Strasbourg.[52] After meeting Anne and while in England making financial arrangements for returning to Zurich, John Hooper wrote to Bullinger that his future wife Anne is "a woman exceedingly favorable to true religion."[53] The couple married in 1547 in Basel where John was matriculated at the University of Basel from 1545 to 1546.[54] Hooper was an English churchman and later served as the Reformed Bishop of Gloucester and Worcester. Although Anne Hooper was not a native of England, given her transnational marriage to an Englishman and the time that she spent in England, she serves here as a representative connection between Englishwomen and Heinrich Bullinger. Like Anna Hilles and Lady Jane Grey, Anne Hooper was Bullinger's friend. Anne Hooper's loyalties were primarily to the reformation of religion with a passion for the English; she corresponded with Bullinger from London and Gloucester and later from Frankfurt, where she fled during the reign of Queen Mary I during which her husband was martyred.

The interconnectivity between the Hooper and Bullinger families is noteworthy. According to Bullinger's *Diarium,* "From England came to me John Hooper with his noble wife Anne von Tserclas on March 29, 1547, and stayed in my house for several days. He became bishop of Gloucester in England on May 15, 1550."[55] The Baptismal Book from the Grossmünster Church for March 29, 1548, documents that Rachel Hooper was baptized on that day.[56] Her godparents were Heinrich Bullinger and Rosilla Buchmann Bibliander, the wife of the Zurich theologian and orientalist Theodore Bibliander, whom Lady Jane desired to know. Later in his *Diarium*, Bullinger wrote, "On March 24, 1549 Doctor John Hooper left for England with his wife and his daughter Rachel, whose godfather I was."[57]

On May 3, 1549, John Hooper wrote to Bullinger with details concerning his wife. Anne had left home near Antwerp because her family did not share her strong Protestant religious convictions. Because they were close to her home, Anne had written to her mother. Hooper writes, "The messenger found her father dead. Her mother received the letter and gave it to my wife's brother to read, who immediately threw it into the fire without reading it. You see the words of Christ are true, that the brother shall persecute the brother for the sake of the Word of God."[58] John Hooper then wrote to Bullinger after the family arrived safely in England, on May 31, 1549, "My wife always makes mention of you in her prayers, she salutes you with your dear wife and all her family."[59] In June of 1550, Bullinger comments in his *Diarium* that "it was announced that John Hooper had become Bishop of Gloucester."[60]

Anne Hooper corresponded with Bullinger in Latin between 1551 and 1555.[61] Her first letter was sent from London on April 3, 1551, and begins by thanking Bullinger for the attention that he has given to her: "I heartily pray God and the Father of our Lord Jesus Christ, that he may abundantly recompense you, as I am unable to do myself."[62] Anne shares the news and local gossip with Bullinger. First, she speaks of her husband John's imprisonment for objecting to the prescribed vestments by order of the Privy Council on January 27, 1551.[63] By the time that she was writing, John Hooper was out of prison again and had immediately traveled to take care of the needs of his see.

Although Anne herself and several of her staff had been ill with the sweating sickness, Anne proceeds to tell Bullinger about the intellectual and spiritual progress of his goddaughter Rachel. Rachel Hooper was about four years old when Anne told Bullinger about the child's outstanding achievements:

> First then, you must know that she is well acquainted with English, and that she has learned by heart within these three months the form of giving thanks, the ten commandments, the Lord's prayer, the Apostles' Creed, together with the first and second Psalm of David. And now, as she knows her letters, she is instructed in the catechism.[64]

Anne's letter continues with a political discussion of Ireland and the French King who is reported to "have prepared a fleet for the purpose of invading and taking possession of it." She then requests that Bullinger tell her husband to be more moderate in his preaching program, although "very many people are hungering for the Word of God," preaching three to four times a day is apt to kill him so that "they will be deprived of their teacher and their doctrine."[65] She also ends this letter with greetings to Bibliander, his wife, the young Zwingli, Gwalther, Pellican, and their wives. A gold coin from Rachel with the Protestant King Edward of England on it was included for Bullinger and another to the younger Zwingli and his wife. Finally, even Anne's maid and her husband greet Bullinger. Almost as a premonition of the difficult times to come, Anne warns that letters must be sealed well because busybodies are opening and reading letters.[66]

The courteous pleasantries that fill Lady Jane Grey's letters are a lesser feature in Anne Hooper's correspondence. The tone belies an already secured position in the network; her intentions are to share religious, political, and personal news related to the evangelical reform. Part of the familiarity can be attributed to the interconnection between Bullinger and John Hooper, with twenty-eight letters sent by Hooper from seven different locations. Anne's first letter persuades us to assume that she was at least emotionally involved in church politics and also in one of the most profound strategies of the evangelical reformation: Anne Hooper was educating her daughter using the Bible as a foundation for learning.

The letter that followed from Gloucester on October 27, 1551, does not provide particularly new information, but it is interesting that Anne does not apologize for disturbing Bullinger, as Lady Jane Grey did. Instead, she explains that she took time from her own busy schedule to write him. The letter is friendly and familiar; indeed, she calls her words "most insignificant" in the already established style of the day. Bullinger is her "friend" and "patron," whom she will never be able to repay for all of his kindness. She completes her letter with salutations to Bullinger her "father" and his wife, Anna, whom she calls her "mother," as well as to all of her friends in Zurich, with a special note on Rachel's health. Rachel "begs your blessing, and prays that in your blessing God may deign to bless me too."[67]

The usual leisurely, self-assured nature of Anne Hooper's letters changes in her letter to Bullinger from Frankfurt/Main on April 20, 1554. Anne laments the condition of the church at large and in her own situation in general. She questions the strength of her "woman's mind" and whether or not it is about to give way.[68] Anne mentions that Bullinger had written to her in Frankfurt to console her and ask her to come to Zurich and stay with him. His letter is lost. She replies to that letter telling him that her husband and their friends had bidden her to leave England for Antwerp, after which she joined a family member in Frankfurt "where, by the mercy of God, the senate has granted liberty to the foreign church for their whole ecclesiastical ministry both of the word and sacraments." She asserts her will and announces that she will remain in Frankfurt in her "own hired house."[69]

The final section of her letter is dedicated to theology and God's foresight, care, the usefulness of prayer, and the Word of God.[70] Here, she asserts, "Although this widowhood is very painful, yet I comfort myself as far as I am able by prayer and the word of God."[71] Anne is obviously cleaving to her faith and upholding her cherished doctrines. She greets a long list of people from Switzerland and mentions several times that she prays to God and wishes that God might give Bullinger an increase in spirit. Almost as an afterthought, she comes to the business at hand and introduces her pastor, Valérandus Pollanus, a relative of hers, to her patron. She tells Bullinger about Rachel, who is prospering; yet Anna laments that her son Daniel is still in England. In conclusion, she entreats Bullinger to pray for her husband Bishop John Hooper.

On September 22, 1554, Anne replied to Bullinger reporting on her husband John's fortitude in prison. She mentions that Master Burcher is able to deliver mail to John Garner, the pastor of the French Church in Strasbourg, who somehow smuggles it to England. Anne's intention is to use the network with her friends in Zurich to further Valérandus Pollanus,[72] "who sends you this little book, from which you may know the constitution and general order of our little church: in which should there be anything which you think requires correction, you will exceedingly oblige him by letting him know."[73] Again Anne begs Bullinger's prayers.

Remarkably independent, by fleeing to Frankfurt, Anne demonstrated that she was embedded in the larger evangelical circle, a system of relationships clearly comparable in many ways to the cohesive qualities of other persecuted communities. She is astonishingly well-informed about the struggle within the Reformed Church to achieve a common understanding of the Eucharist and has clearly taken the side of Zurich instead of Luther. The intermediary function that she served between the Frankfurt Church and Zurich helped shape the Frankfurt exile church and Pollanus' influence on Reformed liturgy.[74] The fact that Anne asks Bullinger to help a friend, without any qualms, is yet another example of the freedom that wives had as participating and influential members of the evangelical reformation, something that is left unsaid in most historical accounts of the reforming movements.

In November of 1554, Anne's writing projects vexation, and her anxiety is evident. God is faithful, she says; however, in her condition, she needs prayer. She provides morose news of the "Spaniard's" coronation and how "the hand of an individual had been burnt off, because he refused to hear mass and chose rather to be brought to the stake."[75] The letter continues with information about the German situation, which, according to Anne, has little to do with religion. Anne salutes Bullinger's wife, Anna, from herself, Rachel, Daniel, and Valérandus Pollanus. Once again, she asks for Bullinger's prayers.

John Hooper was executed on February 9, 1555. On April 11, 1555, Anne Hooper wrote a brief letter to Bullinger from Frankfurt. The letter begins straight up with the discussion of John Hooper's book, which she had sent to Peter Martyr in Strasbourg for publication: "He excused himself on account of the doctrine of the Eucharist, which is not received there."[76] She suggests that Bullinger should revise the book and have it published in Switzerland. She concludes:

> But as I am well aware that his memory is most precious to you, I do not doubt but that you will be equally ready to oblige him in this matter, as if he were not alive: indeed, he is alive with all the holy martyrs and with his Christ the head of the martyrs; and I am dead here till God shall again unite me to him.

Anne expresses her thanks to Bullinger, begging for consolation, and requests Bullinger's prayers. In return for a gift that Bullinger sent to her for New Year's, Rachel includes an English gold coin as a gift to the Bullingers, "on which are the effigies of Ahab and Jezebel," that is, the Spaniard King Philip and Queen Mary, were embossed.[77] Anne and her daughter, Rachel, died of the plague later in 1555.

Volumes have been written about John Hooper and his political ecclesiological contributions to the evangelical reform, and how he defined the

Puritan wing of the church. Anne is seldom mentioned. Nevertheless, the letters she wrote do provide a window into the life of a woman who participated in the events and influenced them, even if she did not author books. Anne's self identity was defined by her position as mother, wife, church member, and friend. Her significance is difficult to comprehend without understanding the concept of community in the Reformation.[78]

The final direct correspondence between an Englishwoman and Bullinger are the three letters signed by Margaret Parkhurst and written between 1561 and 1562.[79] Margaret has rated little interest in the chronicles of history—her letters are unpublished. I transcribed two for the first time in preparation for this essay. In most references, including Euler, scholars tell us that John Parkhurst married a Swiss woman.[80] The British Isle Genealogy records that "John Parkhurst, D.D., Bishop of Norwich, married Margaret, daughter of Thomas Garnish, of this parish, Esq., and Margaret his wife, daughter of Sir Hugh Francys, of Giffard's Hall, in Wickhambrook, in this county, Knt."[81] The letters attributed to Margaret were written in Early Modern High German, but not all of them in the Swiss dialect, with a bit of Latin and some English words. The handwriting of the first letter is not the same as that of the signature.[82] The second letter displays a completely different script and appears to have been written by a scribe with a Swiss dialect. The initials M. P. are written in a different hand at the bottom of this second letter.[83] The third letter carries yet another hand; the initials on it are identical to the second letter.[84] More than likely, Margaret Parkhurst's own initials grace both the second and third letters; however, the signature remains uncertain. Although Margaret Parkhurst was the wife of the great John Parkhurst, her person is poorly documented.

John Parkhurst began as a poet, served as Katherine Parr's chaplain and also chaplain to the dowager Duchess of Suffolk, worked against the Catholics, and later translated parts of the Bible for Queen Elizabeth I.[85] John joined the Marian Exiles in Zurich at John Hooper's insistence. He escaped to Zurich with a group of thirteen other clergy members in order to further his education under the guidance of the Zurich Reformers; the students lived in Tigurine, studied at the *prophezei*, and worshipped together with the people of Zurich in Grossmünster.[86] John was Rudolph Gwalther's good friend, wrote twenty letters to Bullinger, and became Bishop of Norwich in 1560.[87] He ended his career as a Doctor of Divinity at Oxford in 1566—John Parkhurst is relatively well represented in English archives from this period.

In her letters, John's wife Margaret exercises little of the demure that is typical in the writing of her contemporaries. In this respect, her first letter from 1561 is striking, but the aberration may be due to the fact that she was dictating to a male scribe, who was translating her words into a foreign language. Margaret does not employ any specific niceties or courteous pleasantries in her letter, which has the stated purpose of being a reply to a missive sent by Bullinger to the Parkhursts on May 28, 1560. Margaret Parkhurst seems most interested in congratulating Rudolph Gwalther, her husband's friend, on his marriage to Susana Keller; blessings are sent, and she wishes them "many gifted and godly children." After a good report on her husband's health—he is at least ten years Margaret's senior—she tells Bullinger that times are not easy in the church, but in the wake of much hard work, the situation seems to be getting better: the "papists" are finding it very uncomfortable. John is aware that he must be wise and tread lightly in the present dangers of his opponents evil and false tongues. Margaret promises to pray for Bullinger and his work; she asks Bullinger to do the same for her family. Finally, she sends her greetings to their common friends as well as the Bullinger family and informs the *Antistes* that some spoons are on their way from England to his Bullinger's wife, Anna. The letter ends and is dated; whereby, the month of May is written in English rather than German.[88]

In her second letter to Bullinger, as already mentioned, Margaret's handwriting and articulation completely change. She informs Bullinger how happy she is that Hans Heinrich Schmid is spending time with the Parkhursts. Perhaps Schmid is writing the letter that she is dictating in German? The rest of the text provides greetings and blessings to Bullinger and friends.[89]

Margaret Parkhurst's final letter starts by thanking Bullinger, his wife, and their children for not forgetting her people (the English) and the difficulties that they, as well as their queen face. She tells Bullinger that her husband, John, has been ill. Margaret then turns to politics, sharing with Bullinger that she and her husband's people did not partake in the Council of Trent because the Pope was involved. Finally, she prays that, "God the almighty gives us all mercy and support to Bullinger, that all of us live according to his godly will and goodness, and that we avoid all evil and badness, which might move God to wrath against us." Then Margaret greets Anna Bullinger, all good men, and her friends in Zurich.[90] Margaret's letters may seem trite next to the missives of other women; nevertheless, an analysis of what she wrote demonstrates the trust and familiarity of twenty-odd years of correspondence for a common cause.

How are thirteen letters from Englishwomen relevant to the larger reform landscape? As we know, sixteenth-century women were situated in the private sphere, filling conventional female roles as wives, daughters, and mothers in-line with sixteenth-century domestic customs.[91] At the same time, the featured women shared their religious conviction, which comprises the substance of their letters. Religious language and doctrine is the common thread between the letters and the glue, so to speak, in each of the women's epistles. The female authors were able to step, with more or less ease, from the private sphere and to enter the public domain when duty called. Yet their intentions were usually to assist the leaders of the Reformed movement to install an evangelical, Puritan church in England. The religious language, Bible texts, allusions to prayer and blessings were not empty phrases or clichés but expressions of the women's self-identity as pious Christians. Radical evangelicalism with underlying militant tones echo in Anna Hilles' declaration of "harvest"; Lady Jane Grey's feminist thoughts, and her attempt to enter the masculine world of evangelical theology; Anne Hooper's gift of coins embossed with "Ahab and Jezebel"; and Margaret Parkhurst's decrying of the "papists." These women were convicted in their faith and capable of carrying on men's work when necessary.

No sound response to the larger question of whether Englishwomen influenced Bullinger can be made based on a quantitative assessment of archival data. In light of the letters he saved and Bullinger's own writings, there is reason to believe that he upheld the Protestant women of England as capable members of the Reformed network, rightfully participating in reforming the English church, as partners in reshaping a "true" Christian community. One of Bullinger's final reformation efforts before he passed away was to support Queen Elizabeth as the rightful Queen of England. His treaties *Bullae papisticae contra Angliae Regnum Eliabetham* published in 1571 in defense of Queen Elizabeth's right to govern against the bull of excommunication of Pope Pius V is nothing more than the logical consequence of his acceptance of women as coworkers in his network and the church.[92] Bullinger's treaties defended Queen Elizabeth of England against Pope Pius V, who condemned Elizabeth, denied her the right to be supreme governor of the Church of England, accused her of schism, called her a heretic, and proclaimed that the people of England were no longer subject to her rule. John Parkhurst wrote on March 10, 1572: "Your most learned refutation is in the hands of everyone; for it is translated into English, and is printed in London," and Richard Cox (1500–1581) wrote on February 17, 1572, "Moreover, the Queen herself has also read your book, and is much gratified."[93] Not a few reformers cried that it was unnatural for women to lead men; and although Bullinger did not put women in the pulpit to preach to the people of Zurich, Bullinger supported a female governor of the English church and state.[94]

Although the results of a comprehensive study of Bullinger's written exchanges with women remains outstanding, in light of the correspondence of Anna Hilles, Lady Jane Grey, Anne Hooper, and Margaret Parkhurst, a tentative conclusion may be that women played a more significant role and influenced the Protestant network more than is currently assumed. Probably only unconventional, bold, and risky strategies and methods for capturing and recording the traces of these Reformation women will contribute to a gender inclusive narrative of the complex, encrusted, and extended history of the reformations.[95]

Notes

1. Heinrich Bullinger, *Bullae Papisticae Ante Biennium Contra Sereniss, Angliae, Franciae & Hyberniae Elizabetham: & Contra Inclytum Angliae Regnum Promulgatae, Refutatio* (London: Joha[n]nem Dayum, 1571), intro. Note that all translations are the author's own unless otherwise noted.
2. Bruce Gordon, *The Swiss Reformation* (Manchester: Manchester University Press, 2002), 299–304. For insights into Bullinger's relations with England, also see Diarmaid MacCulloch, "Heinrich Bullinger in the English-Speaking World," in *Heinrich Bullinger Life-Thought-Influence* (Zurich: Theologischer Verlag, 2007), 891–934; Torrance Kerby, *The Zurich Connection and Tudor Political Theology* (Leiden: Brill, 2007); Carrie Euler, *Couriers of the Gospel: England and Zurich, 1531–1558* (Zurich: Theologischer Verlag, 2006), 267, 307–14. "The heavily pastoral and practical flavor of the Zurich Reformation attracted English evangelicals to Zurich writings and played a central role in the evangelization of England, particularly during the reign of Edward VI. The number of translations of Zurich writings in circulation in England by 1558 exceeded those coming from Geneva and Strasbourg. One reason for this is the high number of popular books written by Zurich reformers in this period, books that skillfully blended theology with education and practical advice" (267).
3. Women's letters to and from Bullinger have not been the subject of any in-depth research. The only essay concerning the exchanges Bullinger had with women is a comprehensive survey of the letters in Hans Ulrich Bächtold, "Frauen schreiben Bullinger—Bullinger schreibt Frauen: Heinrich Bullinger in Briefwechsel mit Frauen, Insbesondere mit Anna Alexandria zu Rappolstein," in *Die Zürcher Reformation: Ausstrahlungen und Rückwirkungen*, ed. Alfred Schindler and Hans Stickelberger (Zurich: Peter Lang, 2001), 143–60.
4. The letters to and from Bullinger have been edited up to 1544, vol. 14, by the Heinrich Bullinger Briefwechsel at the University of Zurich, funded by the Nationalfonds zur Förderung der wissenschaftlichen Forschung. Two volumes are of interest for this essay: *Heinrich Bullinger Briefwechsel*, vol. 1, Briefe der Jahre 1524–1531, ed. Ulrich Gäbler and Endre Zsindely (Zurich: Theologischer Verlag, 1973) and *Heinrich Bullinger Briefwechsel*, vol. 13, Briefe des Jahres 1543, ed. Rainer Henrich, Alexandra Kess, and Christian Moser (Zurich: Theologischer Verlag, 2008) (henceforth referred to respectively as HBBW 1 and HBBW 13).
5. See Charmarie Jenkins Blaisdell, "Calvin's Letters to Women: The Courting of Ladies in High Places," *The Sixteenth Century Journal* 13, no. 3 (1982): 69 [67–84]. Many thanks to Rainer Henrich who is currently editing the Myconius correspondence and has kindly provided this information; the women that

Myconius wrote to were Elisabeth Hoecklin von Steineck in 1545 and Eva von Schönau in 1546.

6. I am grateful for all of the assistance that Dr. Judith Steiniger, from the Bullinger Briefwechsel team at the University of Zurich, Institute for Reformation Studies, has provided for understanding Bullinger and his correspondence.

7. An effort to include women and minorities in history has opened a door to methodological experimentation since the 1980s; see the classic example of Elisabeth Schüssler Fiorenza, *In Memory of Her: A Feminist Theological Reconstruction of Christian Origins* (New York: Crossroad Publishing Company, 1982), 167: "Yet women's actual contribution to the early Christian missionary movement largely remains lost because of the scarcity and androcentric character of our sources. It must be rescued through historical imagination as well as in and through a reconstruction of this movement which fills out and contextualizes the fragmentary information still available to us." Also consider Carlo Ginzburg, *The Cheese and the Worms: The Cosmos of a Sixteenth-Century Miller* (Baltimore, MD: Johns Hopkins University Press, 1980), xvii: "In short, even meager, scattered, and obscure documentation can be put to good use."

8. The letters from Anna Hilles, Jane Grey, and Anne Hooper were originally written in eloquent Latin. Later, these were translated into English and published by the Parker Society as *The Zurich Letters*; see Hastings Robinson, *Original Letters Relative to the English Reformation, Written during the Reigns of King Henry VIII., King Edward VI., and Queen Mary: Chiefly from the Archives of Zurich* (Cambridge: Cambridge University Press, 1846). Margaret Parkhurst wrote to Bullinger in German.

9. The same style is used in women's letters to John Calvin; see Blaisdell, *Calvin's Letters to Women*, 69: "They are spontaneous and reveal concrete issues that were of direct concern to the writer and the recipient."

10. For recent interest in women's modes of writing letters in sixteenth-century Europe, see Jane Couchman and Ann Crabb, *Women's Letters Across Europe, 1400–1700: Form and Persuasion* (Aldershot, UK: Ashgate, 2005); Katherine R. Larson, *Early Modern Women in Conversation* (Basingstoke, UK: Palgrave Macmillan, 2011); Julie D. Campbell and Anne R. Larsen, eds., *Early Modern Women and Transnational Communities of Letters* (Aldershot, UK: Ashgate, 2009).

11. Gordon, *The Swiss Reformation*, 299; W. Ian P. Hazlett, *The Reformation in Britain and Ireland: An Introduction* (London: T&T Clark, 2003), 37–38.

12. "Archbishop Cranmer to Joachim Vadian, 1537," in Robinson, 11–14.

13. Euler, *Couriers of the Gospel*, 58–59.

14. Euler, *Couriers of the Gospel*, 58–59.

15. Robinson, 608.

16. See Paul Boesch, "Rudolph Gwalthers Reise nach England im Jahr 1537," *Zwingliana* 8, no. 2 (1947): 432–71. The travel log that Rudolf Gwalther kept is a lilting Latin text, which gives an overview of what fascinated the young man and a feeling for the mentality of his generation. Also see Heinrich Bullinger's "Letter to Vadian," from August 22, 1536, E. Arbenz, ed., *Die Vadianische Briefsammlung*, vol. 5 (St. Gallen: Fehr, 1891–1913), 351–52.

17. William M. S. West, *A Study of John Hooper with Special Reference to His Contact with Henry Bullinger*, (PhD diss., University of Zurich, 1953). The strong influence of Zurich on the English reformers, who fled England and spent the years of Mary I's reign as refugees in Zurich, is easily recognizable in these men's works in which they often assumed theological rhetoric, ideas, and methods of reformation that first appeared in Heinrich Bullinger's writings. Many of this group eventually became powerful leaders in the Church of England. Despite Bullinger's influence, it is noteworthy that research on the evangelical reformation often attributes the theological mindset of them to John Calvin of Geneva rather than Bullinger in Zurich.

18. Euler, *Couriers of the Gospel*, 169.

19. Heinrich Bullinger, *In d. Apostoli Pauli ad Thessalonicenses . . . Heinriychi Bullingeri Commentarij*, (Zurich: Christoff Froschauer, 1536). For the complete list of literature from Zurich published in English between 1541 and 1558, see "Appendix II: The Translations" in Carrie Euler, *Couriers of the Gospel*, 307–14.

20. See Philip Benedict, *Christ's Churches Purely Reformed: A Social History of Calvinism* (New Haven & London: Yale University Press, 2002), 245–55.

21. Heinrich Bullinger, *The Christian State of Refutation Bullae Matrimony: Wherein Husbandes [and] Wyues May Learne to Keepe House Together wyth Loue. The Contentes. The Originall of Holy Wedlocke, When, Where, How, and of Whom It Was Instituted and Ordayned . . . And How Maryed Folkes Should Bring vp Their Chyldren in the Feare of God* (trans. Myles Couerdale (London, 1575), with reprints in English in 1541, 1542, 1543, 1548, and 1552 published in Antwerp and London. In his presentation of marriage, Bullinger takes a biblical view of relationships between men and women much like that of Erasmus of Rotterdam, including the ideas and disputes about the role of women discussed by the Church Fathers. He presents suggestions for men and women in relationships, in marriage, and in the home, proposing a gender equality with emphasis on biblical mutuality. The social structure and hierarchy of sixteenth-century, middle Europe are also present but do not comprise the core of his ideas. See the edited volume with both Bullinger's first tract on marriage from 1527, *Volkommne underrichturn desz christlichenn eesstands*, and the *Der christlich eestand* from 1540 in Heinrich Bullinger, *Pastoraltheologische Schriften*, ed. Detlef Roth, HBTS (Zurich: Theologischer Verlag, 2009).

22. See West, where he argues throughout his dissertation that Bullinger intended to influence the English Reformation through friends like Hooper, Hilles, Parkhurst, and so on, almost lending Bullinger a premeditated subversive nature; Bruce Gordon, *The Swiss Reformation*, 299–304; see also Diarmaid MacCulloch, "Heinrich Bullinger in the English-Speaking World."

23. Bullinger, *Pastoraltheologische Schriften*.

24. Robinson, *Original Letters*, 196–271.

25. Many thanks to Dr. Alexandra Kess from the Heinrich Bullinger Brief Edition at the Institute for Swiss Reformation Studies at the University of Zurich for sharing her notes on the English Reformers with me.

26. "Rudolf Gwalther to Heinrich Bullinger," Frankfurt am Main, September 15, 1540, in HBBW, vol. 10, no. 1420, 159–65, n60.

27. "Anna Hilles to Heinrich Bullinger," Strasbourg, May 9, 1543, in HBBW, vol. 13, no. 1744, 131–32. All subsequent quotations are from this single missive. Here, Anna Hilles illustrates her biblical knowledge conjuring its more than one hundred references to harvest.

28. Ives, *Lady Jane Grey*, 60.

29. See the article by David J. Keep, "Die Handschuhe der Lady Jane Grey," *Zwingliana* 11 (1963): 663–68.

30. Robinson, 5. The English translations of Lady Jane's letters are taken from Robinson. The original letters have not yet been printed in HBBW. For the Latin see Staatsarchiv Zurich, StA, E II 335, 2174f. Lady Jane Grey's letters are also published in the original Latin in Parker Society, *Epistoloae Tigurinae de Rebus Potissimum Ad Ecclesiae Anglicanae Reformationem Pertinentibus Conscriptae A.D. 1531–1558* (Cambridge: J. Gul. Parker, 1848) (henceforth Ep. Tig.), 3–7.

31. Robinson, 4, n1.

32. For the provocative and entertaining story on the relationship between the Greys, Bullinger, and the somewhat rogue John of Ulm, see Ives, *Lady Jane Grey*, 59–64.

33. Heinrich Bullinger, *Cinq Decades, Qui Sont Cinqvante Sermons: Contenans Les Principavx Poincts & Lieux Communs De La Religion Chrestienne, Nouuellement Reueus & Corrigez Sur L'Exemplaire Latin* (Geneve: M. Blanchier, 1564).

34. See Jane Couchman and Ann Crabb, *Women's Letters Across Europe*; see also Katherine R. Larson, *Early Modern Women in Conversation* and Julie D. Campbell and Anne R. Larsen, eds., *Early Modern Women and Transnational Communities of Letters*.

35. Robinson, 4.

36. Robinson, 5.

37. Robinson, 5–6.

38. Robinson, 5, 7. Boldness is a theme in Jane Grey's first letter from July 12, 1551, where she writes, "my unreserved requests may carry with them an appearance of boldness" [*Audacula tibi videar oportet que tam audactor hoc efflagito*]. See also "Letter from Lady Jane Grey to Bullinger," StA, E II 335, 2174f; Ep. Tig., 4; Heinrich Bullinger, *Perfectio Christianorum, sive de Jesus Christo, Christianorum perfectione unico, demonstratio*, (Tigurino: Gesnerus & Wyssenbachius, 1551), 8 vol.

39. Robinson, 7.

40. Robinson, 8.

41. Robinson, 8.

42. Robinson, 9–11.

43. Robinson, 9.

44. Robinson, 10.

45. Ep. Tig. III, 6; Robinson, 10, translates this: "Besides, I entertain the hope that you will excuse the more than feminine boldness of me, who, girlish and unlearned as I am, presume to write to a man who is the father of learning."

46. Robinson, 10–11.

47. Robinson, 11.

48. Robinson, 303–5.

49. Frank Gulley, Jr., *The Influence of Heinrich Bullinger and the Tigurine Tradition upon the English Church in the Sixteenth Century* (PhD diss., Vanderbilt University, 1961), 211.
50. Paul Boesch, "Die english Flüchtlinge in Zürich unter Königin Elisabeth I," *Zwingliana* 9 (1953): 531–35. Boesch lists a few prominent members of this group, including Robert Beaumont, the Vice Chancellor in Cambridge; Thomas Bentham, Bishop of Coventry; Robert Horn, Bishop of Winchester; John Jewel, Bishop of Salisbury; John Parkhurst, Bishop of Norwich; James Pilkington, Bishop of Durham; Edwin Sandys, Bishop of Worcester and later Archbishop of York.
51. See Edwin Clyde Deibler, Jr., *Bishop John Hooper: A Link Connecting the Reformation Thought of Ulrich Zwingli and the Zurich Tradition With the Earliest English Pietistic,* (PhD diss., Temple University, 1970), 272–73, esp. 272; see also D. G. Newcombe, *John Hooper: Tudor Bishop and Martyr (c.1495–1555), Monographs Medieval and Modern,* (Oxford: The Devenant Press, 2009).
52. Diebler, 272.
53. "John Hooper to Heinrich Bullinger," Strasbourg, January 27, 1546, in Robinson, 38.
54. Hans George Wackernagel, ed., *Matrikel der Universität Basel,* vol. 2, 1532–1601 (Basel, Verlag der Universitätsbibliothek, 1951), 44.
55. Heinrich Bullinger, *Diarium (Annales Vitae) Der Jahre 1504–1574,* ed. Emil Egli (1904; repr. Zurich: Theologische Buchhandlung, 1985), 35.
56. Entry in the baptismal book from the Grossmünster Church, Zurich, March 29, 1548: "Ionnes Hopperus ex Anglia: Rachael: M. Heinrich Bullinger und Rosilla Buchmann."
57. Bullinger, *Diarium,* 37.
58. Ep. Tig., 40 and Robinson, 63.
59. Ep. Tig., 41 and Robinson, 64.
60. Bullinger, *Diarium,* 38.
61. Anne Hooper's six letters to Bullinger are published in Robinson, 107–15; Ep. Tig., 68–74. Anne Hooper signs her letters as "Anne." The titles in the Ep. Tig. give "Anna," and the sources all vary in spelling her name. The original Latin has not been edited for the *Heinrich Bullinger Briefwechsel.* The original documents are available at the Zurich Staatsarchiv: Zurich StA, E II, 343, 478.
62. Robinson, 107, n.2.
63. Robinson, 107.
64. Robinson, 107.
65. Robinson, 108.
66. Robinson, 109.
67. Robinson, 109.
68. Robinson, 110.
69. Robinson, 110.
70. Anne Hooper's understanding of the Lord's Supper appears to follow what Bullinger and Calvin agreed on when they signed the *Consensus Tigurinus* in 1549, which John Hooper also supported. See the introductory article with

documentation of the agreement in *Consensus Tigurinus: Heinrich Bullinger Und Johannes Calvin Über Das Abendmal*, ed. Emidio Campi and Ruedi Reich (Zurich: Theologischer Verlag, 2009), 1–33; for John Hooper's theology and for the ways in which Zurich influenced English Pietism, see Diebler, 337–563.
71. Robinson, 111.
72. "Valérand Poullain [was] one of the foreign ministers and theologians who found employment in England during Edward's reign and who were not forced to return to the Continent. Their writings made a significant contribution to the literature of the exile. In addition to his translation of Philpot, Poullain was responsible for the publication of two editions of the liturgy used by the Frankfurt exile community." Andrew Pettegree, *Marian Protestantism: Six Studies*, (Aldershot, UK: Scolar Press, 1996), 120.
73. Robinson, 111–12.
74. Robinson, 112–14, esp. 113; also see n70 above.
75. Robinson, 113.
76. Robinson, 114.
77. Robinson, 114.
78. The nature of community in the reform movements of this period is not under discussion in this chapter.
79. See Zurich StA, E II 375, 648; StA, E II 375, 647; StA, E II 377, 2322.
80. Carrie Euler asserts that "John Parkhurst, future bishop of Norwich, lived in Zurich for more years than any other Marian Exile. He arrived in July 1554, eventually married a woman from Zurich, and stayed until his departure for England in January 1559, residing all of this time in a small room in Gwalther's house" (102).
81. British Isle Genealogy: England, Scotland, Ireland, Isle of Man, Wales, Channel Island, Isle of Wight: Kenton Parish, http://www.bigenealogy.com/suffolk/kenton_parish.htm.
82. "Margareta Parkhurst to Heinrich Bullinger," Ludham, May 14, 1561, Orig.: Zurich StA, E II 375, 648.
83. "Margareta Parkhurst to Heinrich Bullinger," Ludham, April 24, 1562, Orig.: Zurich StA, E II 377, 2372.
84. "Margareta Parkhurst to Bullinger," Ludham, May 30, 1562, Orig.: Zurich StA, E II 375, 647.
85. John Parkhurst translated the Apocrypha from Wisdom to the end for Queen Elizabeth's Bible. His Latin poems were prepared for translation in Zurich in 1558. See *The History and Description of Guildford, the County-Town of Surrey*, (Andover, Hants: Gale Ecco, Print Editions, 2010).
86. Gulley, 211–27.
87. Francis J. Bremer and Tom Webster, eds., *Puritans and Puritanism in Europe and America: A Comprehensive Encyclopedia* (Santa Barbara, CA: ABC CLIO, 2006), 494.
88. Parkhurst, May 14, 1561. Orig.: Zurich StA, E II 375, 648.
89. Parkhurst, April 24, 1562. Orig.: Zurich StA, E II 377, 2372.

90. Parkhurst, May 30, 1562. Orig.: Zurich StA, E II 375, 647.
91. For a cogent explanation of the historical reality of the public and private sphere in gender questions, see Jean Bethke Elshtain, *Public Man, Private Woman: Women in Social and Political Thought* (Princeton, NJ: Princeton University Press, 1981).
92. Bullinger, *Bullae Papisticae Ante Biennium Contra Sereniss . . . Refutatio.*
93. "John Parkhurst to Heinrich Bullinger," Ludham, March 10, 1572, Robinson, 102; "Richard Cox to Heinrich Bullinger," London, February 19, 1572, Robinson, 192.
94. For the antifeminist view, see esp. John Knox, *The First Blast of the Trumpet against the Monstrous Regiment of Women* (Edinburgh, 1571).
95. G. R. Elton has proclaimed: "A better example of a purely spiritual power could hardly be found than the influence that was exercised in England by Zwingli's successor Henry Bullinger. Bishops and Puritans argue their causes before him as if he were the judge. . . . And then when the bad day came and the Pope hurled his thunderbolt, it was Bullinger that the Elizabethan Bishops looked to for a learned defense of their Queen and their creed." *The New Cambridge Modern History: The Reformation Vol. II, 1520–1559*, second edn. (Cambridge: Cambridge University Press, 1990), 597.

CHAPTER 4

Elizabeth Cary and Intersections of Catholicism and Gender in Early Modern England

Lisa McClain

Historians have analyzed the life of Elizabeth Cary, Lady Falkland, primarily in the context of her highly publicized conversion to Catholicism and her equally public separation from her Protestant husband, Henry Cary. Through this scrutiny, she has become one among many English Catholic recusant heroines. Literary critics, in contrast, have celebrated Cary's literary corpus both for its challenge to traditional ideals of early modern women as chaste, silent, and obedient and for its reevaluation of women's roles within marriage.[1] To circumscribe our understanding of Cary in such ways obscures one of her greatest contributions. Elizabeth Cary, albeit unintentionally, provided an alternative model of Catholic womanhood that sought to negotiate a new balance between religion and gender, thus challenging assumptions about women's roles in English Catholic communities and about the rigid character of Catholicism in the Reformation era.

Her writings and life choices reveal the trajectory of Elizabeth Cary's willingness to question traditional understandings of masculinity and femininity and the centrality of her faith to her understanding of the relationship between the two. Shortly after her marriage to Henry Cary, she interrogated male and female roles in *The Tragedy of Mariam*. Although one character, Salome, is willing to be the "custom-breaker," the play ends with Mariam's apparent acceptance of her fate and her submission to male authority. In the 1620s, with *The History of the Life, Reign and Death of Edward II*, Cary again questioned gender but with a character, Isabel, who was not only willing to be the custom-breaker but who also shaped her own fate in the midst of upheaval and controversy, just as Cary was doing through her conversion and struggle to live independently. By the 1630s, it was not Cary's characters questioning assumptions but Cary herself, and by this point, her challenges were open and public. Throughout her life and career, Cary explored the relationships between gender and religious identities; the connections are evident in both her published work and her involvement in public controversies. The fluctuating relationship between faith and gender, rather than one or the other, inspired many of Cary's writings and actions, opening up new sets of opportunities and challenges for Catholic women.

Throughout her life and writings, overlaps and conflicts between the demands of gender and faith are often present but unresolved. Cary often raised more issues than she settled, but this is understandable given the confusion over how gender and religion layered over the political controversies of the time.[2] Religious lines between Protestants and Catholics often blurred, as Puritans proved more than willing to point out;[3] so did the lines between masculine authority and expected feminine obedience. These unstable intersections between religion and gender created opportunities for women like Elizabeth Cary to occupy unusual social spaces. Had Elizabeth Cary been a Catholic woman living in a predominantly Catholic society, her independence and boldness would hardly have been condoned. She would likely have been less willing to push the boundaries of gender as she did without the driving force of her faith. Had Henry Cary been dealing with an independent Protestant wife, he probably would not have felt compelled to cut himself off from her and thus leave her with greater freedom to act without his authority. What we see are the Carys and, more broadly, Stuart society working through these issues, asking questions, and testing or reinforcing boundaries, effectively using intersections of gender and faith to try various options.

By examining Elizabeth Cary's written work in conjunction with the event and the aftermath of her conversion to Catholicism, we can identify more clearly how Cary negotiated such options over time. Prior to her conversion, she was known for her closet drama, *The Tragedy of Mariam*, which is recognized as the first tragedy written by an Englishwoman. After her conversion in 1626, her literary output increased substantially. In 1627 she wrote *The History of the Life, Reign and Death of Edward II,* becoming the first Englishwoman to write and publish a full-length historical biography, and she inserted herself into confessional controversy with her 1630 translation from the French of a polemical treatise written by Cardinal Jacques Davy du Perron.[4] Additionally, with Henry Cary, Elizabeth participated in a lively correspondence with friends and patrons, vying for the support of king, queen, and court officials. These letters provide insight into the changes taking place among gender and religious roles during this period in English history, and according to Heather Wolfe, they are the most overlooked of Cary's writings.[5]

Scholars typically interpret *The Tragedy of Mariam* and *Edward II*—both of which feature strong heroines who challenge their husbands' dominance—as reflections of Cary's challenges within her own marriage. Yet two decades and a religious conversion occurred between the writing of the two texts. Cary's evolving religious beliefs—which would certainly have affected her understanding of her role as a wife—must have affected her perceptions of gender roles more broadly. This changing prospect remains an aspect of evolution in Cary's writing that scholars have yet to investigate.

Cary wrote *Mariam* between 1603 and 1604 as a young bride and as a Protestant.[6] She would not convert for twenty-three years. Yet even then, Cary raised questions about the fluidity of gender roles and female obedience to male authority. Within the verses, Constabarus criticizes his wife for taking a lover and proposing to divorce him:

> Are Hebrew women now transform'd to men?
> Why do you not as well our battels fight,
> And weare our armour? Suffer this, and then
> Let all the world be topsie turved quite.[7]

Only men took lovers and could divorce, yet here a woman assumed these privileges for herself. Cary understood widespread fears about social disorder if women acted outside their traditional gender roles, but she nonetheless allowed Salome, the wife in question, to voice her opinion. Salome eloquently expresses a willingness to be the "custom-breaker and beginner" for all women. Of Constabarus, Salome reasoned:

> If he to me did beare as Earnest hate,
> As I to him, for him there were an ease,
> A separating bill might free his fate:
> From such a yoke that did so much displease.
> Why should such a priviledge to man be given?
> Or given to them, why bard from women then?
> Are men then we in greater grace with Heaven?
> Or cannot women hate as well as men?
> Ile be the custome-breaker: and beginner
> To shew my Sexe the way to freedoms doore.[8]

Mariam, the sympathetic protagonist, also adopts male roles and privileges, as a ruler, after she believes her husband, Herod, dead. She speaks publicly and forcefully to her subjects, yet she claims there was no unchastity in it. She even likened herself to a male ruler, Caesar, in the opening scene of the play.[9] Yet in the end, Herod returns and sentences Mariam to death. In spite of her earlier convictions about women's equality, Mariam accepts her fate with heroic silence and obedience to her husband's authority.

By the time she wrote *Edward II* over twenty years later in 1627, Cary had considerably longer experience as a wife and was a convert to Catholicism. In 1622, Henry Cary, Viscount Falkland, had been appointed Lord Deputy of Ireland, and he and Elizabeth, both Protestants, resettled in Dublin. Through the exercise of his office, Henry enforced England's "harshly repressive policies toward the Catholics in Ireland."[10] Elizabeth, on the other hand, met her first open Catholics. She started a workhouse for Irish Catholic children, entertained Catholic clerics, and otherwise immersed herself willingly in Irish and Catholic cultures.[11] After four years, Elizabeth Cary converted to Catholicism while on a visit home to England in 1626. Unfortunately, reports of her conversion reached her sovereign and her husband before she could break the news herself. King Charles I asked her to recant, which she refused to do based on freedom of conscience; as a result, Charles ordered her confined to her household in London. The news reached Henry in Ireland shortly thereafter, provoking his great displeasure. Husbands of recusant women were not allowed to hold public office, thus her conversion endangered his career.[12] Attempting to minimize the damage, Henry distanced himself from his wife. He immediately cut Elizabeth off financially and seized the majority of the household goods from their home in England.[13]

Elizabeth Cary now found herself in a situation familiar to many English Catholic women married to Protestant husbands. She had to mediate between the demands of her faith and the obedience she owed her husband, renegotiating accepted gender and religious roles. But this is a two-sided story. Protestant husbands like Henry Cary faced a similar challenge. Such men could not condone or support Catholicism, yet their duties as male heads of household to govern and provide for their families meant they were expected to support Catholic family members who openly and publicly defied them. No party could simply both follow the dictates of their faith *and* fulfill the gender role society expected of them. The nature of this tension was also such that it did not require a conscious effort on anyone's part to reshape ideas about religion and gender. The struggle to reconcile oneself to the demands of competing desires could produce such change as a byproduct.

Once Elizabeth, the repudiated wife, lived independently, she displayed a progressively greater willingness to engage in gender and religious controversy in her written and published work, as well as her life choices.[14] In doing so, she created a new model for Catholic women's behavior that contrasts with scholars' previous depictions of Catholic recusant women as conforming to traditional, pre-reform ideals of women's piety, wifely obedience, and mother-hood.[15] When the dictates of her faith conflicted with the dictates of her gen-der, Elizabeth Cary was inspired to work through the contradictions, at times privileging faith and at others, gender. As Gwynne Kennedy has argued, Cary wanted "to 're-form' her situation while remaining obedient."[16] The deciding factor seems to have been whether doctrinal or salvific issues were involved. If they were, Elizabeth Cary openly privileged Catholicism over gender. If no such issues were at stake, she appears to place her expectations as a woman and wife over other considerations. There were, however, more ambiguous issues, such as her decision to write. In most situations, both religious and gender considerations are present, and we can see Cary's attempts to balance and reconcile the competing demands of each changing over time.

In the first years after her conversion, her emphasis appears to favor gen-dered concerns, although religious issues are always present and part of the language through which she discusses women's needs, both her characters' and her own. Her sympathetic treatment of the disobedient and treasonous Queen Isabel in *Edward II*, for example, weaves Cary's earlier questions about feminine and masculine roles from *The Tragedy of Mariam* together with new concerns about the fate of the state. In prose that echoes English Catholic concerns over the future of the now-Protestant England, Isabel laments:

> My burthen is grown greater than my patience
> Yet 'tis not I alone unjustly suffer;
> My tears speak those of a distressed Kingdom,
> Which, long time glorious, now is almost ruin'd.[17]

By invoking conventions and issues of historical and political writing, Cary transformed safe, private, female-friendly closet drama into public, contro-versial, male-dominated literary genres, which Mihoko Suzuki maintains were considered the least welcoming to women writers in the early modern era.[18]

In addition to *Edward II*, she and Lord Falkland produced a substantial body of correspondence during the years between her conversion in 1626 and Henry's death in 1633. Both Carys wrote numerous letters to friends and patrons, which have been preserved in the public record, engaging sup-port for their parts in their marital and familial conflict. Additional letters written by external observers referring to the conflict within the family are also extant, as are examinations of Elizabeth Cary before the King's Bench and Star Chamber. The interaction between all parties involved in these events and exchanges opens a window into the active, participatory—though often unconscious—process of renegotiating what it meant to be men and women, as well as Catholic or Protestant, in seventeenth-century England. The struggle among the Cary family is significant not because their relationship was unique (though their circumstances were exceptional in some ways) but because the elements that drove it—the fundamentally incompatible demands of feminine and masculine social roles and competing religious faiths—were replicated in many other households throughout England. The record itself is special for the literary and epistolary insight it offers into these private and public negotiations of identity and faith.

Henry Cary challenged his wife's actions in a series of scathing letters. As a husband and father, Henry Cary had a right to rule over his wife and household. A man's reputation, his sense of manhood, indeed the very order of society, all depended upon his ability to "husband," to manage and govern his "substance." Pastor Justus Menius reinforced this generally accepted understanding in a declaration of 1528: "A husband has two functions: first, he should rule over his wife, his children, and servants and be head and master of the entire house; second, he should work and produce enough to support and feed his household."[19] Given these personal and social expectations of authority, it is understandable that in his letters Henry Cary claimed he had the natural right to mastery over his wife and that she was overstepping her capabilities and her station in ways that he eventually interpreted as embarrassing and indecent. Following Elizabeth's conversion, Lord Falkland's epistolary descriptions of his wife's character referred to her "feminine wily pretenses . . . assisted by feminine mediation," her "serpentyne subtlety," and her "violent contestation with him, against duty and the Lawe Matrimoniall."[20] Such comments are consistent with popular views about women contained in the highly publicized debate that centered on the capabilities, nature, and proper roles of women; most previous scholars have framed the Cary debate within this context.[21] The terms of this debate had long been public and all classes of people were exposed to various sides and opinions through popular pamphlets that both criticized women's nature—from the low brow pamphlets of Joseph Swetnam to the high brow tracts of John Knox—and defended it in such treatises as those by Jane Anger, Rachel Speght, and Constantia Munda.[22]

The propagandist face of the conflict only provides one side of the story, however, and Henry's letters reveal as much about masculinity and its relationship to female behaviors as they do about popular views on femininity, and they do so within the context of Catholic-Protestant controversy. Not only could Henry Cary *not* control his wife, his protestations about her insubordination served to advertise this fact. His accusations of Elizabeth's incompetence rang hollow the more they were repeated, for she was clearly competent enough to sidestep the customs and laws relating to both gender and faith that stood in the way of what she wanted to accomplish as both a woman and a Catholic. For example, following announcement of her conversion, Elizabeth refused Henry's order to go live with her mother, preferring instead to stay in London near her Catholic circle of supporters.[23] Her mother, Lady Tanfield, allegedly refused to take her in.[24] Henry accused Elizabeth of engineering this split with her mother in order to "remayen wheare shee is, as shee is, in despight of me, by the Power of hir popishe friends."[25] Elizabeth chose to live on Drury Lane, an area known for its high concentration of Catholics, and her friends included the French Ambassador, the Bishop of Chalcedon, Jesuits, and secular priests, as well as other London Catholics.[26] Elizabeth Cary thus participated in a very different type of Catholic household and community than the women-led households typically lauded in recusant literature. She chose where she would live and with whom she would live and associate, actively resisting pressure to conform her behavior to her husband's will.

Henry also demonstrated his understanding that gender roles and religion were intimately intertwined in this controversy. Elizabeth's defiance led him to petition Charles I's officials, decrying that "Surely her residency ought to be according to her husbands election and not her owne. Soe our religion teacheth. And if hir newe Profession teach contrary poincts of doctrine, in that as abhominable as in other things, let me first obtaine an vtter and absolute divorse."[27] He asked to be separated from his wife so that "dishonour and confusion of face, with ruine of fortune may not thereby assayle me and overwhelme me; and I shalbe contented then to quitt my clayme of superioritye, and being made free, leave hir free."[28] Henry clearly declared that Elizabeth's actions shamed him, and that both masculine and Protestant authority ought to be enforced. But at the same time he acknowledged that he could not rule over his wife as a Protestant husband was expected to do. He asked for his freedom, a legal separation, a similar type of marital separation that Elizabeth Cary had noted a husband might request to free himself "from such a yoke that did so much displease" in *The Tragedy of Mariam* decades earlier.[29] Henry recognized that he lacked the power associated with both his gender and his faith to force Elizabeth's conformity and that he found the burden of his responsibilities to be potentially ruinous.[30]

As Alexandra Shepard has noted, although wives received a good deal of criticism for any disobedience to their husbands' authority, it was husbands who bore the greatest stigma by allowing it. Shepard maintains that the majority of conduct writers denigrated men who had abdicated their mastery over both themselves and their subordinates. Manhood and the entire social order were at stake. Patricia Crawford describes how a husband's allowance of religious disorder within his household was perhaps the worst transgression: God would lay the sins of a wife's religious disobedience upon her husband.[31] But Henry went further in suggesting it was not only his honor at stake but also the king's and Protestantism's as well. In a separate entreaty to Edward Conway, Secretary of State, Henry appealed to a monarch's superiority above all subjects, both Catholic and Protestant. Charles I could make Elizabeth leave her Catholic friends and return to her mother's household. He could make a mother accept her daughter. Henry declared that "The honour of our religion, and of his Maiesty, in the Interest of his deputy, who is become notorious ouer all the Christian world for this defection of his Wiues, and hir preualent contestation with him, ageynst duty, and the lawe Matrimoniall . . . doeth require that he should remoue her."[32] Henry appealed directly to Charles I, saying that surely Charles's kingdom was big enough that some space away from London might be found for Elizabeth so that both he and Charles would be free of her and the "scandall and shame" she had brought upon them.[33] Yet Elizabeth remained in London. As mentioned earlier, the second responsibility of male heads of household was to support their dependents. Henry Cary also failed to do this, though no doubt with justification in his eyes. After her conversion, he promptly cut off his wife financially and continually refused to maintain her until his death in 1633.[34] Elizabeth used her alleged penury as an excuse to stay in London.[35] Referring to herself as a "woman distrest," she assured Lord Conway that she earnestly desired to leave London and that nothing kept her there "but sharp necessity."[36] She continued to live with her community of choice.

For her part, Elizabeth Cary's letters and published works are filled with declarations of her respect and obedience to both husband and king that are belied by her actions.[37] Cary was a married woman, living independently, who defied her husband's mandates and her sovereign's will. This is not to say that Elizabeth used her religion as a convenient pretext to disobey male authority. Instead, her situation as a Catholic wife living apart from her Protestant husband created an ultimately unresolvable situation based on current religious and gendered norms. In trying to work through the contradictions, at times privileging faith and at others, gender, Elizabeth Cary unintentionally participated in constructing new norms of religious and gendered behavior for Catholic women.

Most of Elizabeth Cary's surviving letters involve requests for financial support from male authority figures, functionally asking them to assume the masculine role Henry refused to fulfill, thus relying on traditional gender roles in her efforts to gain maintenance. This again reflects her apparent emphasis on gendered concerns in the immediate years following her conversion. Even at this early stage, religious concerns are subtly present. Beginning in 1627, Elizabeth petitioned Charles I, Conway, and the Privy Council, presenting herself as a "distressed lady" whose husband was not fulfilling his responsibilities as he should and appealing to their genteel masculinity—as gentlemen, soldiers, and courtiers—to aid a lady. Charles ordered his councilors to take an interest and get the matter settled.[38] The Privy Council repeatedly requested that Henry support his wife, detailing the number of servants he should provide, the level of obedience required of such servants, quality of meat and drink, healthfulness of the atmosphere, furniture, clothing, linens, horses, and a monetary allowance. In other words, this was more than a general formal request for maintenance. The Privy Council carefully prescribed the maintenance of Elizabeth's household, clearly outlining what a husband was expected to provide. In informing Henry of his obligations, the Privy Council ordered him "soe to apply your selfe to the effectuall performance thereof, as that the Lady your wife may haue no further Cause to Complaine neither to his Maiestie nor this Board."[39] Lord Falkland had been an ineffectual provider, and the interventions of the Privy Council explicitly chastised Henry's lack of properly masculine authority and critiqued his ability to enforce his will either publicly or privately. If a man's ability to support his family was in question, his worth as a man was also in doubt.[40] And when Henry still refused to maintain his wife, Charles upbraided Henry for his failure and ordered the early modern equivalent of garnishing Henry's wages.[41]

The gendered and religious identities of both Elizabeth and Henry Cary were thus evolving by the very words they wrote down and the actions they took up to defend them. The debate is interesting for the ways in which the proclamations made by each party are undermined by their actions. On the surface, each writer claimed to be upholding the gender role expected of them and to be following their religious convictions. Yet none of these claims ring true, for they are all venturing into unfamiliar territory as regards intersections of the ideals of masculinity, femininity, and faith in their age. Elizabeth placed her gendered identity as a distressed lady front and center as she petitioned men to step in and relieve her want. Yet she used this poverty as an excuse to stay put, immersed in London's network of powerful Catholics that gave her access to the sacraments and support she needed. Religious considerations intersected with her declarations of herself as an obedient wife and her portrayal of herself as needing the support of Protestant men. Henry was not only unable to exercise traditional masculine authority within the Cary family, but, as previously discussed, he could not effectively assert the authority of his religion either, and the two issues were intertwined in his mind and in those of his contemporaries. Perhaps recognizing the futility of fighting this battle and unwilling to stomach the compromises needed for a rapprochement, he sought to separate himself from Elizabeth. He tried without apparent success to carve out alternative masculine roles for himself that refuted the public challenge to his authority made by Elizabeth Cary's conversion and subsequent actions.

By the 1630s, after much of the marital controversy had exhausted itself, Elizabeth Cary's negotiations between gender and religion appeared to evolve in new directions, as she entered the polemical controversies of pre-Civil War England. In 1630, she published her translation of *The Reply of the Most Ill-vstriovs Cardinall of Perron, to the Answeare of the Most Excellent King of Great Britaine, the First Tome*, a response to the then-deceased Protestant King James I's claim that he belonged to the Catholic Church since he believed in the truths of the first Christians. In her dedication of the work to Henrietta Maria and epistle to her readers, she defined her identity proudly and unabashedly: "I desire to haue noe more guest at of me, but that I am a Catholique, and a Woman: the first serves for mine honour, and the second, for my excuse." Nonetheless, she professed that she thought the translation was done well and wanting nothing. Cary claimed she was inspired by God to undertake the work, yet she refused to ask for the traditional indulgence that authors hoped readers would allow a woman writer, rejecting such demureness as "worne out forme."[42] She forthrightly categorized her translation as a "Catholicke-worke," asserting that she "could have noe other end" in producing the translation other than to inform her readers "aright."[43] Elizabeth Cary, a Catholic woman, would teach the male Protestant intellectuals at universities and at court by proclaiming both her faith and her gender as central to her identity, willingly using her religious writing in negotiating her gender identity. But, although Cary attempted to balance considerations of both Catholicism and gender, the balance appears to tilt toward faith in how and what she wrote, particularly as she knew that she addressed a predominantly male Protestant readership.

Following Henry's death in 1633, Elizabeth Cary found herself in the midst of new religious debates with men in both her written work and her life choices. As with Cary's translation of Perron in 1630, these later controversies are distinguished from earlier ones by Cary's overt preference of religious considerations over gender expectations, particularly concerning salvific issues. For example, Lucius, as the eldest Cary son, assumed the role of head of household over his mother, brothers, and sisters after his father's death. Like his father, he was a staunch Protestant. He became best known as the leading figure of the Great Tew Circle, a group of Protestant activists and intellectuals that gathered informally at Lucius's home in Oxfordshire. In 1635, Walter Montague, a Cary family friend, publicly converted to Catholicism. He wrote a letter to his Protestant father, later published, explaining his reasons for embracing the Roman faith as the only means to salvation, against his father's and sovereign's wishes. Lucius Cary entered this public religious controversy by penning a rebuttal to Montague's explanatory letter. Elizabeth Cary decided to involve herself as well. She wrote a "letter of Controuersy" countering Lucius's arguments; the letter is unfortunately lost but her daughter said it "was thought the best thing shee euer writ."[44] Elizabeth assumed the privilege to involve herself authoritatively in this debate, despite the public embarrassment it would cause her son. Once again, her ostensible head of household could not control her. She again got away with defying male Protestant authority.

Among the situations in which Elizabeth Cary privileged religious concerns over gender norms, perhaps her most blatant provocations came in her efforts to convert her children. For Cary, her children's souls were at stake. Although men were expected to provide religious leadership within their families, Elizabeth Cary began actively converting her children to Catholicism after Henry's death and did not scruple to hide her efforts. Archbishop William Laud wrote directly to the king in July of 1634:

> The Lord Newburge hath latly acquainted me that Mrs Ann and Mrs Elizabeth Carye, two daughters of the late Lord Faulkland, are reconciled to the Church of Rome, not without the practice of the Ladye their Mother. Your Maiestye I presume remembers what sute the Lord Newburge made to you at Greenwitch; and what command you sent bye mr Secretarye Coke to that Ladye that she should forbeare working upon her daughters Consciences and suffer them to go to my Lord theire brother [Lucius Cary, a Protestant], or anye other safe place whear they might receive such instruction as was fit for them. The Lady trifled out all these Commands . . . I have taken hold of thiss and according to mye deutye done what I could think fittest for the present. But the greatest thing I feare is that the Mother will still be practicinge and doe all she can to hinder.[45]

In spite of these protests, no one seemed able to stop her. She later subverted the intent of the law in her attempts to have her children educated abroad as Catholics. She petitioned Henrietta Maria in autumn of 1635 to send her daughter, Mary, to the Spanish court of Philip IV. The queen agreed.[46] Elizabeth knew full well that Mary would live in a Catholic milieu and receive Catholic instruction at the Spanish court. Soon after Elizabeth successfully negotiated these arrangements, however, Mary declared her vocation as a nun and left England for a house of English nuns at Cambrai.[47]

In 1636, the government discovered her plan to spirit away two of her sons, Patrick and Henry, to receive Catholic educations in France. Even though she knew them to be still in London, Elizabeth equivocated, claiming not to know *exactly* where her sons were when she was brought before the King's Bench.[48] The officials of Star Chamber saw through this artifice and recommended she be committed to the Tower of London but to no avail.[49] When examined again, she was evasive: "beeinge againe demanded where her said sons now are, shee saith that shee thinketh they are in France, but in what parte of France she knoweth not."[50] Elizabeth broke the law and obstructed the investigation into her crime with little personal consequence.[51]

Because a salvific issue was involved in the education of her sons, she seems to have chosen her faith over her traditional woman's role in the family hierarchy. Yet as Mendelson and Crawford have observed, female networks, both intra- and extrafamilial, functioned as efficient transmitters for habits of women's piety, from parent to child, from mistress to servant.[52] Although husbands possessed official authority over matters of faith in the home, the day-to-day work of instructing children in the faith typically fell to mothers. As women worked and socialized together, often informally and with children present, they would discuss, challenge, reinforce, and pass on their religious beliefs to the next generations. And Elizabeth Cary was a Catholic mother who appears to have been successful at passing *her* faith on to her children. Although her eldest son, Lucius, was a Protestant, both younger sons—the ones sent to France—became Benedictine monks. Of her five daughters, four became Benedictine nuns at Cambrai.[53] Each child experienced their mother's efforts differently and negotiated issues of spiritual choice for themselves, but the lifelong importance of Cary's efforts is difficult to deny.[54] She tried to balance Catholic faith with a woman's responsibilities, although her inspiration seems to tilt more toward her identity as a Catholic.

As influential as her role in her family appears to have been, however, Elizabeth Cary's impact extended well beyond this intimate circle, creating new options for Catholic women's piety, behavior, and relations within Catholic communities. Certainly in some ways, Elizabeth Cary was exceptional. As a viscountess living in London, Cary enjoyed opportunities as a Catholic and as a woman that many lesser-born or rural Catholic women may have envied. Catholic women with access to Henrietta Maria's court enjoyed a degree of royal protection and patronage, as well as regular access to the Catholic sacraments.[55] In other ways, the Cary family was not unlike many English families challenged by religious nonconformity. Elizabeth and Henry Cary lived and wrote at a time in which the Stuart government hesitated to interfere in families over these issues. Although heads of household were theoretically responsible for the religious compliance of the entire household, Parliament acknowledged in 1601 that men were often powerless to change the religious views of their spouses. After 1620, the government became less involved in enforcing individual conformity within families and more interested in collecting fines and minimizing the political influence of nonconformists.[56] The courts seemed little concerned with prosecuting Henry or Elizabeth, despite the bad example their situation set. Both society and government still cared deeply about the religious and gender issues involved in the Cary conflict, but once the government ceased to intervene directly to enforce conformity, individuals and families like the Carys were left to work through the contradictions and tensions between gender and religion on their own, while neighbors and acquaintances watched, waited, and gossiped.

The Cary conflict became public in all its aspects: the news about Elizabeth's conversion, Henry's inability to enforce his authority and refusal to support his wife, and her willingness to write publicly and boldly in defense of her faith or more modestly in request of financial support. Because of this publicity, it became a family conflict with broader implications. Inevitably, the Carys provided a model that other individuals and families might emulate. Links between family authority and political stability were common in England, particularly prior to the Civil War. Protestant cleric and popular sermonizer William Gouge suggested in 1622 that the maintenance of proper authority and order within individual households should be a priority because families preceded other types of polities and were the foundation upon which others are built.[57] Henry feared for that foundation, thanks to his own family controversy. "In a short tyme," he wrote to John Coke, the new Secretary of State, "we shalle haue such vnhappy deuisions made in all the familyes of the kingdome as is now begun in myne, to the hazard of greate and manifest mischeefes and daungers." Again evincing his understanding of the intersections between gender and religion, he blamed priests—"hir seducers," "hir Popelings"—for these dangers rather than women. He believed it was through these religious men that women gained the ability to defy their husbands. Such men would be encouraged by the state's inability or unwillingness to force Elizabeth into obedience and conformity to her husband's will and begin to "prosecute theise attempts with bouldness euerywheare."[58]

Elizabeth saw the intersections between gender and religion differently, and as a noblewoman, her words and actions were seen and heard more broadly than those of other Catholic women.[59] They carried the authority and influence of her social rank, influencing what was thought possible for women, as individuals and as members of families. It was not men who gave her authority to defy her husband, practice her chosen faith, live independently as part of a larger community of London Catholics, and write. It was God. She turned to God for her spiritual inspiration and to other men to meet her worldly needs. Her writings reflect how she negotiated between her religious identity and her gender identity differently when doctrinal or salvific issues were at issue, such as in her Perron translation, the Montague controversy, and her efforts to convert and educate her children. She appears to give gender issues more prominence, as in *The Tragedy of Mariam* and her letters requesting financial support, when these were not at issue. Both religion and gender were always present, in tension with one another. Elizabeth Cary's balancing act between them was a continual process throughout her life and writings.

Cary's efforts to reconcile the competing demands of faith and gender reflect a different type of Catholic female agency and experience emerging in Protestant England than is typically discussed. Although Catholic women are well documented in this era, Catholic-authored documentation typically paints idealistic portraits of such women. Catholic writers of the time certainly praised Catholic women who adhered to expectations about womanhood, wifehood, and motherhood. Such women were usually wealthy and well connected, overseeing households far from London where Protestant authorities were less likely to bother them as they secretly welcomed and hid priests, provided a central meeting place for area Catholics to worship and receive the sacraments, and raised the next generation of Catholic children to join the mission or to marry other English Catholics.[60] Scholars investigating the contributions of Catholic women to upholding underground Catholic communities emphasize these stories and characterizations of women's conformity to traditional ideals of Catholic womanhood and heroism.[61] Catholic women have been described as "less conspicuous, retreating again into comparative invisibility in the records."[62]

Alternatively, Protestant-authored documentation within the public record generally criticizes Catholic women, and scholarship about Protestant women rarely allows them a voice. Discussions of seventeenth-century England, for example, frequently consider the initial expansion and subsequent contraction or evolution of women's roles tied to political events from the Civil War through the Glorious Revolution. Protestant women are frequently depicted as enjoying a variety of new opportunities to participate in politics, religion, and society, and their voices *as religious women* figure prominently in such discussions. Catholic women's voices, however, seldom appear. When a Catholic woman's writings or activities are included, scholars may identify the woman as a Catholic but rarely analyze her legacy or contributions through the intersections of her gender with her Catholicism.[63]

Elizabeth Cary fits neither mold. She was anything but inconspicuous and invisible in the public record.[64] And although well connected, she was no longer wealthy. She lived in London and openly visited or hosted priests and Jesuits. She enjoyed regular access to the sacraments at Henrietta Maria's chapel. Although she ultimately persuaded most of her children to convert to Catholicism and join religious orders, they did not reside with her growing up, and she was never allowed to raise them as Catholics in a traditional Catholic household. In contrast to modern assumptions about the somewhat rigid character of early modern Catholicism, there were a diversity of Catholic women's subcultures operating within England in the seventeenth century, some traditionally based and others testing or reinforcing boundaries, effectively using intersections of gender and faith to experiment with new ways to be both a Catholic and a woman. In subsequent decades of the seventeenth century, other English Catholic women, such as Mary Ward and the women of her Institute of English Ladies and the "Popish Midwife" Elizabeth Cellier, would continue to broaden the boundaries of traditional gender roles, inspired by both their Catholicism and their gender. They, too, would be simultaneously lauded and criticized for their activities. Such women's living situations look different. Their activities on behalf of Catholicism look different. Their participation in Catholic communities looks different.

Because the experiences of such women were so public, they provided, albeit unintentionally, an alternative model of Catholic womanhood that sought to negotiate new balances between religion and gender. Individuals and societies negotiate men's and women's gender roles within a web of other issues and concerns, including religion. Although sharing some similarities, Catholic women's piety is distinct from Protestant women's and Catholic men's, providing differing sets of priorities, choices, legitimations, expressions, and relationships to authority. Moreover, as a whole, English Catholic heads of households—male or female—exercised more authority over family religious life in the absence of regular priestly counsel than did heads of household in countries where Catholicism was legal.[65] Unexpected opportunities were opened to Catholic women such as Elizabeth Cary in the evolving, unstable environment in which Catholics practiced in Protestant England.

Nontraditional Catholic women such as Elizabeth Cary participated actively in the confessional controversies of their time and contributed to larger European-wide renegotiations of the rules of masculine and feminine behavior in the seventeenth century. As Elizabeth Cary gained experience as a woman, a wife, and a Catholic, her willingness to question traditional understandings of masculinity, femininity, and religious authority evolved and matured. The trajectory of Cary's life, literary accomplishments, and preserved correspondence provides scholars with an exceptional opportunity to view the process through which such changes can occur—from the early years of her marriage, with the closet drama *The Tragedy of Mariam*, through her conversion, and from her conflict with Henry Cary and willingness to appeal to accepted gender norms in the late 1620s to the 1630s, when her gender and religious identities intersected more visibly in her later provocative religious writings and in her efforts as a Catholic mother on behalf of her children. Her involvement in the evolution of gender roles was often inadvertent and changes slow, but each time situations such as Elizabeth Cary's were made known to the public, new paradigms for Catholic women's identity and participation in the English Catholic community became possible. As she stated in her translator's epistle of Perron, Elizabeth wished no more to be known of her but that she was a Catholic and a woman. She did not have to choose one or the other but was always both, blending religion and gender in a new type of re-formation.

Notes

1. Nandra Perry, "The Sound of Silence: Elizabeth Cary and the Christian Hero," *English Literary Renaissance* 38.1 (2008): 106–41; Frances Dolan, "Reading, Work, and Catholic Women's Biographies," *English Literary Renaissance* 33.3 (2003): 328–57; Stephanie Wright, "The Canonization of Elizabeth Cary," in *Voicing Women: Gender and Sexuality in Early Modern Writing*, ed. Kate Chedgzoy, Melanie Hansen, and Suzanne Trill (Keele, Staffordshire: Keele University Press, 1996), 55–68; Patricia Demers, *Women's Writing in English: Early Modern England* (Toronto: University of Toronto Press, 2005), 208–14; Danielle Clark, "The Tragedy of Miriam and the Politics of Marriage," in *Early Modern English Drama: A Critical Companion*, ed. Garrett A. Sullivan, Jr., Patrick Cheney, and Andrew Hatfield (New York: Oxford University Press, 2006), 248–59; Barbara Kiefer Lewalski, *Writing Women in Jacobean England* (Cambridge: Harvard University Press, 1993), 183–211.

2. Gender is increasingly politicized during the English Civil War and the next century. See Ann Hughes, *Gender and the English Civil War* (New York: Routledge, 2012); David Kuchta, *The Three-Piece Suit and Modern Masculinity: England 1550–1850* (Berkeley: University of California Press, 2002).

3. Henrietta Maria headed an openly Catholic community at court, while Laudian churchmen, such as Dr. John Cosin, tried to keep them within an "Anglo-Catholic community." Lewalski, *Writing Women*, 186.

4. Many other works written by Cary have been lost, such as hagiographies, letters of religious controversy, and so on. See Heather Wolfe, ed., *The Literary Career and Legacy of Elizabeth Cary, 1613–1680* (New York: Palgrave MacMillan, 2007), 3.

5. Heather Wolfe describes Cary as a master of the literary form of letter writing. *Literary Career*, 10, and *Elizabeth Cary, Lady Falkland: Life and Letters*, ed. Heather Wolfe (Cambridge: RTM Publishing, 2001), 226–27. One of Cary's daughters penned Elizabeth Cary's *Life* while a nun with the English Benedictine Order in Cambrai. Although its hagiographic elements must be taken into consideration, it is a valuable historical source as well.

6. The closet drama, based on Josephus's histories, was not published until 1613. Elizabeth Cary, *The Tragedie of Mariam, The Faire Queene of Jewry* (London: Thomas Creede for Richard Hawkins, 1613).

7. *Mariam*, I. vi.

8. *Mariam*, I, iv.

9. Cary also portrays Mariam's execution as an allegory of Christ's crucifixion. Kim Walker, *Women Writers of the English Renaissance*, English Authors Series (New York: Twayne/Simon Schuster Macmillan, 1996), 134, 139.

10. Lewalski, *Writing Women*, 184.

11. Deanna Rankin, "'A More Worthy Patronesse': Elizabeth Cary and Ireland," in Wolfe, *Literary Career*, 203–21.

12. "Lady Tanfield to Lady Falkland," May 6, 1627, in Wolfe, *Life and Letters*, 279; "Lord Falkland to Sir Edward Conway," July 5, 1627, in Wolfe, *Life and Letters*, 293–44; Walker, *Women Writers*, 131.

13. "Lord Falkland to Charles I," December 8, 1626, in Wolfe, *Life and Letters*, 268.

14. Catholic and Protestant women discussed conscience and its relationship to obedience and disobedience. See Katherine Gillespie, *Domesticity and Dissent in the Seventeenth Century: English Women's Writing and the Public Sphere* (Cambridge: Cambridge University Press, 2004); Susan Wiseman, *Conspiracy and Virtue: Women, Writing and Politics in Seventeenth Century England* (Oxford University Press, 2006), 108; Anthony Fletcher, *Gender, Sex and Subordination in England, 1500–1800* (New Haven: Yale University Press, 1999), 168; Sara Mendelson and Patricia Crawford, *Women in Early Modern England* (Oxford: Clarendon Press, 1998), 137–38, 253, 388.

15. Robert E. Scully, SJ, *Into the Lion's Den: The Jesuit Mission into Elizabethan England and Wales, 1580–1603* (St. Louis, MO: The Institute of Jesuit Sources, 2011), Scully, chapter 6; Dolan, "Reading, Work."

16. Gwynne Kennedy, "Reform or Rebellion: The Limits of Female Authority in Elizabeth Cary's *The History of the Life, Reign and Death of Edward II*," in *Political Rhetoric, Power, and Renaissance Women*, ed. Carole Levin and Patricia A. Sullivan (Albany: SUNY University Press, 1995), 212. See also Patricia Crawford, *Women and Religion in England, 1500–1720* (London: Routledge, 1993), 142–43.

17. Elizabeth Cary, *The History of the Life, Reign and Death of Edward II. King of England, and Lord of Ireland. With The Rise and Fall of his Great Favourites, Gaveston and Spenser* (London: J. C. for Charles Harper, 1680), 96. Originally written in 1627 but unpublished until 1680; two forms of the text exist.

18. Mihoko Suzuki, "'Fortune a Stepmother': Gender and Political Discourse in Elizabeth Cary's *History of Edward II*," in Wolfe, *Literary Career*, 89. A textual genre embraced by an increasing number of women to express their religious and political views, and one that was more consonant with women's traditional roles, was the stitched sampler. See Susan Frye, *Pens and Needles: Women's Textualities in Early Modern England* (Philadelphia: University of Pennsylvania Press, 2010), 159.

19. Justus Menius, *Erynnerung*, Biv, "Masculinity and Patriarchy in Reformation Germany," in *Masculinity in the Reformation Era*, Sixteenth Century Essays & Studies Series 83, ed. Scott H. Hendrix and Susan C. Karant-Nunn (Kirksville, MO: Truman State University Press, 2008), 71–91.

20. "Lord Falkland to Conway," July 5, 1627, in Wolfe, *Life and Letters*, 293.

21. For examples, see Lewalski, *Writing Women;* Walker, *Women Writers;* Mary E. Burke, Jane Donawerth, Linda L. Dove, and Karen Nelson, eds., *Women, Writing,*

and the Reproduction of Culture in Tudor-Stuart Britain (Syracuse: Syracuse University Press, 2000); Levin and Sullivan, *Political Rhetoric*; Demers, *Women's Writing.*

22. Joseph Swetnam, *The Araignment of Lewd, Idle, Forward, and Unconstant Women or the Vanity of Them, Choose You Whether, with a Commendation of Wise, Virtuous, and Honest Women, Pleasant for Married Men, Profitable for Young Men, and Hurtful to None* (1615); John Knox, *The First Blast of the Trumpet against the Monstrous Regiment of Women* (1558); Jane Anger, *Jane Anger Her Protection for Women, To Defend Them against the Scandalous Reportes of a Late Surfeiting Lover, and All Other Like Venerians that Complaine so To Bee Overcloyed with Women's Kindnesse* (1589); Rachel Speght, *A Mouzell for Melastomus* (1617); Constantia Munda, *The Worming of a Mad Dogge, or A Sop for Cerberus, the Jailer of Hell* (1617).

23. "Lady Falkland to Conway," March 24, 1627, in Wolfe, *Life and Letters*, 275; "Leonard Welstead to Lord Falkland," July 3, 1628, in Wolfe, *Life and Letters*, 320. Elizabeth Cary claimed she went home to her mother, as directed, but her mother refused to take her in so she returned to London. Protestant women and women of lower social class could also refuse to live where their male heads of household dictated. See Paula McDowell, *The Women of Grub Street: Press, Politics and Gender in the London Literary Marketplace 1678–1730* (Oxford: Clarendon Press, 1998), 169.

24. "Lady Tanfield to Lady Falkland," May 6, 1627, in Wolfe, *Life and Letters*, 278.

25. "Lord Falkland to Conway," July 5, 1627, in Wolfe, *Life and Letters*, 293–94.

26. "Statement of Benedicto Rollini, Master Gardener to the French Ambassador," 1630, in Wolfe, *Life and Letters*, 365–66; "Welstead to Lord Falkland," December 20, 1627, in Wolfe, *Life and Letters*, 307.

27. "Lord Falkland to Conway," April 4, 1627, in Wolfe, *Life and Letters*, 277. See also "Lord Falkland to Welstead," June 25, 1627, in Wolfe, *Life and Letters*, 290.

28. "Lord Falkland to Conway," April 4, 1627, in Wolfe, *Life and Letters*, 277.

29. *Mariam*, I, iv.

30. If his wife could not be made to bend to his will on this matter, then Henry Cary requested a legal separation so his wife could "liue howe and wheare shee liste." "Lord Falkland to Conway," July 5, 1627, in Wolfe, *Life and Letters*, 293–94.

31. Alexandra Shepard, *Meanings of Manhood in Early Modern England* (New York: Oxford University Press, 2003), 73, 83, 86; Crawford, *Women and Religion*, 126–27.

32. "Lord Falkland to Conway," July 5, 1627, in Wolfe, *Life and Letters*, 293–94.

33. "Lord Falkland to Charles I," June 27, 1628, in Wolfe, *Life and Letters*, 318–19.

34. It appears that for a time, Henry Cary did send maintenance to Elizabeth, but she refused to spend it, saying she did not wish to spend an allowance he gave against his will. "Welstead to Lord Falkland," April 18, 1628, in Wolfe, *Life and Letters*, 310. On the whole, he refused to support his wife, often claiming penury himself. See "Privy Council Order," April 12, 1630, in Wolfe, *Life and Letters*, 357; "Charles I to Lord Coventry," ca. January–March 1631, in Wolfe, *Life and Letters*, 366–67.

35. "Lady Falkland to Conway," March 24, 1627, in Wolfe, *Life and Letters*, 274.
36. "Lady Falkland to Conway," March 24, 1627, in Wolfe, *Life and Letters*, 274.
37. For examples, see the following in Wolfe, *Life and Letters*: "Lady Falkland to Conway," ca. October–December 1625 (250); "Lady Falkland's Petition to the Privy Council," April 1630 (357–58); "Lady Falkland to Charles I," May 18, 1627 (282). See also Mendelson and Crawford, *Women*, 182–83; Laura Gowing, *Domestic Dangers: Women, Words, and Sex in Early Modern London* (Oxford: Clarendon Press, 1996), 185–86.
38. In Wolfe, *Life and Letters*: "Lady Falkland to Charles I," May 18, 1627 (285); Conway to Sir Richard Weston, June 9, 1627 (289); "Lady Falkland to Conway," ca. June 26–30, 1627 (291); "Conway to Welstead," July 20, 1627 (295); "Lady Falkland to Conway," August 13, 1627 (297); "Lady Falkland to Conway," ca. August 27–31, 1627 (300); "Conway to Weston," September 8, 1627 (301); "Lady Falkland to Conway," ca. September 21–30, 1627 (301); "Lady Falkland's Petition to the Privy Council," April 1630 (357–58).
39. "Privy Council to Lord Falkland," October 31, 1627, in Wolfe, *Life and Letters*, 304–5.
40. Shepard, *Meanings of Manhood*, 191.
41. "Charles I to Lord Falkland," May 29, 1628, in Wolfe, *Life and Letters*, 313–14; "Chancery Court Decree," May 31, 1628, in Wolfe, *Life and Letters*, 314. Henry protested vigorously. "Lord Falkland to Charles I," June 27, 1628, in Wolfe, *Life and Letters*, 318. This obligation to provide for Elizabeth Cary, along with a continuation of the familial feud over authority, was passed on to the Carys' eldest son, Lucius, after Henry's death. At first, Charles I stepped in to maintain Elizabeth Cary, but eventually the Privy Council implored the new Viscount Falkland to support his mother, as he should. They were seeing, they said, no evidence that he had taken up his responsibility as the male head of household to provide for her. "Privy Council Order of 16 April 1634," and "Privy Council to Lucius, Lord Falkland," December 9, 1636, in Wolfe, *Life and Letters*, 385, 399–401.
42. Jacques du Perron, *The Reply of the Most Illvstriovs Cardinall of Perron, to the Ansvveare of the Most Excellent King of Great Britaine, the First Tome*, trans. Elizabeth Cary (Douai: Martin Bogart, 1630), epistle to the reader and dedication.
43. Cary, *Reply*, 2r–v. Karen Nelson recognizes Cary's translation of Perron as a neglected text of Cary's in "'To Informe Thee Aright': Translating Perron for English Religious Debates," in Wolfe, *Literary Career*, 147–63. As Susan Frye has described, Cary's works of religious controversy serve both to legitimate her writing and claim an important role for women's voices in the public sphere. See *Pens and Needles*, 99.
44. Wolfe, *Life and Letters*, 214. R. W. Serjeantson has attempted to deduce what Elizabeth Cary's arguments would have been in "Elizabeth Cary and the Great Tew Circle," in Wolfe, *Literary Career*, 165–82.
45. "William Laud to Charles I," July 20, 1634, in Wolfe, *Life and Letters*, 386–87; Marie Rowlands, "Recusant Women, 1560–1640," in *Women in English Society*,

1500–1800, ed. Mary Prior (London: Methuen, 1985), 150; Crawford, *Women and Religion,* 60–61. Mendelson and Crawford, *Women,* 163.

46. "Henrietta Maria to Lord Aston," November 17, 1635, in Wolfe, *Life and Letters,* 391–92.

47. "Lady Falkland to Aston," December 19, 1635, in Wolfe, *Life and Letters,* 392–94.

48. "King's Bench Examination of Lady Falkland," May 16, 1636, in Wolfe, *Life and Letters,* 395–96.

49. "Star Chamber Examination of Lady Falkland," May 25, 1636, in Wolfe, *Life and Letters,* 397–98.

50. "King's Bench Examination of Lady Falkland [2nd]," May 28, 1636, in Wolfe, *Life and Letters,* 398–99.

51. With the notable exceptions of Catholic martyrs, such as Margaret Clitherow and Ann Line, women recusants generally suffered lighter punishments than men. Their legal status under coverture meant that women were not held to be responsible for their transgressions in the same way men were. It was not unusual for courts to give Catholic women lighter sentences and fines than Catholic men, even when a group of men and women were presented for participation in the same criminal recusant activities. Scully, *Into the Lion's Den,* chapters 6 and 8; Lisa McClain, *Lest We Be Damned: Practical Innovation and Lived Experience in Protestant England, 1559–1642* (London: Routledge, 2004), 239.

52. Mendelson and Crawford, *Women,* 215–66, esp. 228.

53. Lewalski, *Writing Women,* 190. Both younger sons eventually renounced their Catholicism. Anne, Elizabeth, Lucy, and Mary Cary remained nuns until their deaths. The fifth Cary daughter, Victoria, was married in 1640 to Sir William Uvedale.

54. Marion Wynne-Davies, "'To have her children with her': Elizabeth Cary and Familial Influence," in Wolfe, *Literary Career,* 223–42.

55. McClain, *Lest We Be Damned,* 150–82.

56. Fletcher, *Gender,* 220; Crawford, *Women and Religion,* 50, 58–59; Rowlands, "Recusant Women," 151, 154–56, 160. Gentry and burgesses, according to Rowlands, were unwilling to allow the state such power within the family or to step on the rights of men, husbands, fathers, and masters within their own homes.

57. William Gouge, *Of Domesticall Duties* (London: John Haviland for William Bladen, 1622) fol. 2v.

58. "Lord Falkland to Sir John Coke," December 29, 1626, in Wolfe, *Life and Letters,* 271; "Lord Falkland to Conway," July 5, 1627, in Wolfe, *Life and Letters,* 293–94.

59. Mendelson and Crawford, *Women,* 393.

60. For an in-depth discussion of this idealized image, see Rowlands, "Recusant Women," 175; Dolan, "Reading, Work."

61. Scully, *Lion's Den,* chapter 6; Dolan, "Reading, Work."

62. Rowlands, "Recusant Women," 149, 160–61. Catholic male heads of households often conformed outwardly to protect a family's finances and status; Catholic

women were able to engage in private resistance at home. Cary's life and work challenges this generalization.

63. Hughes, *Gender*; McDowell, *Grub Street*; Wiseman, *Conspiracy*; Gillespie, *Domesticity and Dissent*.
64. Lewalski, *Writing Women*, 187.
65. Mendelson and Crawford, *Women*, 202–3, 225–26, 388; Rowlands, "Recusant Women," 162.

CHAPTER 5

Eleanor Davies and the New Jerusalem

Amanda L. Capern

E leanor Davies was a great believer in historical moments. In her first work—*A Warning to the Dragon and All His Angels* of 1625—she told readers that "The Lord is at the Dore."[1] This immanence of God made her watchful and purposeful, reading the signs in her daily life, counting days, weeks, and years because she believed that Christ would come again. His arrival had been predestined from the beginning of the world: "from the going forth of the Commandement, which is the beginning of the Creation to the building of the New Jerusalem, the second comming of Messiah, the Prince the Sonne of God, it shall be Seaven Weekes or Seaven Moneths."[2] For Davies, time was elastic, but history was absolute. What the biblical prophets (in this case Ezekiel) said would come to pass, really *would* come to pass, but their promises were oracular; they had complete authority but were also elusive. Davies accepted this. She *knew* that she was living in the latter days, but when it came to God's final judgment, "the daye and houre knoweth no man."[3] God could not be known as such and what she called knowledge was a spiritual transformation that took place when "He powreth out his Spirit upon his hand-maidens," like herself.[4] This essay uses *A Warning to the Dragon* and Davies' works of the 1630s and 1640s to examine her theology. Broadly, it will argue that the pan-European Calvinism, which she shared with those Protestants who Patrick Collinson once called "the hotter sort," or Puritans, resulted in a very particular interpretation of history as integral to the further reformation of the British church according to God's apocalyptic plan for the New Jerusalem. It will also argue that her adoption of this theological position was gendered in ways that have helped to obscure her thought.

I

Reformation historiography has recently focused attention not only on the
slow legal process that changed state religion—what Christopher Haigh once
called "England's Reformations"—but also on the doctrinal and ecclesiastical divisions that existed between Protestant and Catholic across and within
the boundaries of England, Scotland, and Ireland. The sometimes sluggish
parish-level response to Protestant doctrinal confession and liturgy reflected
the frequently partial accommodation of the new with the old in people's
religious faith in a reformation process that featured Protestants and Catholics actually sharing some key objectives, most notably the rejection of superstition. Understanding the religious dynamic of the British archipelago has
resulted in a rethinking of periodization and the emergence of rather a syn-
cretic account of reformation and civil war, prompted by Conrad Russell's
vision of the collapse of the Stuart composite monarchy from 1637 and John
Morrill's proposition that the civil wars of the 1640s were "wars of religion."[5]
Eleanor Davies' prophetic ideas throw light on why the two historiographies
of reformation and civil war have elided.

Eleanor Davies was born in 1590, just as the Protestant Reformation,
in England at least, had become more securely achieved at parish level; the
last vestiges of Catholic worship were removed, forcing English Catholics
to resort to occasional conformity to hide their deepening commitment to
post-Tridentine religion.[6] One text that proved vital in collective conversion
to Protestantism was William Perkins' *The Foundation of Christian Religion*,
which provided a scheme of practical piety that went beyond the confessional
faith of *The Thirty-Nine Articles*. According to Christopher Haigh "where the
protestant reformation really succeeded, it made Perkins-style Protestants"
in a culturally dynamic process that was entirely reliant upon practical piety
to secure change in popular worship. The key was assurance of election as
this counteracted the seemingly ineluctable doctrines of the fall and sin.[7]
Eleanor Davies was born just when catechizing in the new Protestant credo
was succeeding more often than it failed. Perhaps even more importantly,
she moved in her early teens from England to Ireland, becoming a member
of the embattled Protestant minority there, first in Ulster, which was filled
with Scottish Presbyterian colonizers, and then in Dublin, from 1609, after
becoming the wife of the attorney-general, Sir John Davies.[8] Eleanor Davies'
main biographer, Esther Cope, has said that it "is tempting to draw a picture
of an isolated existence" and of a woman who "turned inward" in a way that
"laid the foundations for her future prophetic career."[9] While it is impossible
to know for certain, it does seem that Davies was affected by her environment. Her husband was involved in attempted land redistribution in Ireland

and was a strong supporter of rigorous discipline in the Church of Ireland, both strategies that were designed to combat the Catholicism that lay beyond the tiny area of the Pale.[10] As a young woman, Davies attended Sunday services that were vociferously anti-Catholic and informed by the catechizing that emerged from Trinity College in Dublin where James Ussher, the Professor of Theological Controversies, claimed that the Protestant church had a predestined history that would end in the thousand year reign of Christ and the destruction of the Church of Rome.[11] Davies' prophetic rumblings in *A Warning to the Dragon* were, then, shaped by this context.

Esther Cope has argued that Davies wrote "easily and often," but she did not actually begin her writing career with *A Warning to the Dragon* until she was thirty-five years old. It will be argued here that the remarkable productivity commented on by Cope represented the systematic insertion by Davies of her voice into the Reformation politics of England after 1625.[12] Davies claimed post facto to have been suddenly inspired by the prophecies of a young boy with a stridulant voice. Much has been made of this explanation by her posthumous biographers, starting with George Ballard in the eighteenth century and continuing with Mary Hays in the nineteenth century, who called the pamphlet in which this story appeared "sublimely incomprehensible."[13] However, it is enlightening to consider the bigger picture for Davies at the time. She and her husband were living on their newly acquired English estate of Englefield manor in Berkshire after returning from Ireland, and he was desperately trying to secure a public office from the new king just at a time when English ecclesiastical politics were being rocked by Richard Montagu's *A New Gagge for an Olde Goose* (1624).[14] Montagu was accused of introducing Arminian or Pelagian doctrine into the English church, pushing the church seemingly closer to Catholicism just when the new Catholic queen, Henrietta Maria, was hearing Mass in her private chapel. Viewed from the perspective of an Anglo-Irish immigrant, the Protestant Reformation seemed under attack from external and internal forces of evil that opened the floodgates to greater toleration of anti-Christian practices. The plague in London in 1625 was just one further sign of God's anger, prompting Davies to travel with her visionary words to the royal court, which was in quarantine in Oxford, to present *A Warning to the Dragon* to George Abbot, Archbishop of Canterbury. Davies made no attempt to conceal her identity as the author, and she presented it in her maiden name—"Eleanor Audeley." The name was printed backward, symbolizing "a true looking-glasse" that will "open the eyes of the blinde, to bring them that sit in darkness a light to leade them out of the Prison-house."[15] She addressed Charles I directly by appealing to him to behave as his father James I had, who, in his role as Michael, "the great Prince that defend[ed] the Faith," had ratified the Calvinist (and anti-Arminian) confessional doctrine of the Synod of Dort in 1618.[16]

The prophecy of *A Warning to the Dragon* was phrased analogically and was mostly drawn from the Book of Daniel. Davies co-opted Daniel's wisdom, claiming thereby to have received it indirectly from the angel Gabriel, who conferred power from God to spread word of his presence and the "building of the New Jerusalem." After her name at the end of the text she wrote "Reveale O Daniel," a loose anagram and a linguistic device that revealed her own agency as much as the voice of the biblical prophet. Davies also used Luke 21 as an important signal to her readers of her biblical knowledge. This New Testament text was linked with the Book of Daniel, and the connective device enabled her to demonstrate her knowledge of divine purpose with the observation that Daniel's visions brought the same message from God that Christ had brought to "his Servants" in the Temple. The story of the Temple warned the king of the wars and desolation that would follow his failure to act, but as a warning it was also aimed at the English clergy so that they would know from the "signs in sun and moon and stars . . . that the kingdom of God is near." Her reference to Daniel 1:8—"but Daniel resolved that he would not defile himself with the king's rich food, or with the wine which he drank"—could be perceived as provocative, especially as the message was that she, herself, was not at the tabernacle, but at "the bridegroom's feast."[17] The opening gambit and meaning of *A Warning to the Dragon* would have been understood perfectly by Davies' contemporaries. She claimed she had been woken by a dream that shaded into a vision on July 28, 1625. This was directly from Daniel 7:1—"In the first year of Belshazzar king of Babylon, Daniel had a dream and visions of his head as he lay in his bed." Belshazzar was central to Davies' message because she could use the feast he held for one thousand of his lords as an analogy for the reign of Charles I. Indeed, Esther Cope has pointed out that Davies' use of the spelling "Belchaser" at times was deliberate because the anagram of "Be Charles" made her meaning absolutely clear.[18] The writing that appeared on the wall in the story of the feast ("mene, mene, tekel"), placed there by the disembodied hand, signified the numbered days when the seven tribes, or exactly 144,000 saints, would be saved. In the book of life, sealed by Daniel until the end, were "the names of Saints that shall live for ever." "Thus the hidden mystery of this enigmaticall writing is here" she said, "the secret of numbers to teach us to number her dayes." The humbling and defeat of corrupt kings who destroyed Jerusalem would be punished. Babylon, "the mother of harlots," the creation of that Babylonian king, Nebuchadnezzar, would fall.[19] After the lengthy prologue, the text proceeded to paraphrase Daniel's vision of the four beasts from the sea—the lion, the bear, the leopard, and the septi-cephalic beast of ten horns—all of which

Davies identified with the Antichrist and all of which would be destroyed by the everlasting gospel.

Historians have sometimes focused on Davies' insertion of the personal into her political writings, and gender turns this observation into a subtle signal that the reader should read her words as less seriously political than those of her male contemporaries. Yet in *A Warning to the Dragon*, Davies spoke of her vision of Daniel to issue a highly politicized message to Charles I about his reign, admonishing him to take control of his clerical advisors. The fact that the time of judgment was at hand explained why Daniel revealed himself to her—the "handmaid" chosen—the Spirit pouring into her mouth for the sake of "further reformation." Integral to the exegetical message in *A Warning to the Dragon* was also the revisualization of the British reformation process, past, present and, crucially, future. For Davies, Reformation history was at once temporal and sacral: the temporal involving the visible church and the sacral involving the church of Christ lying invisible and within its believers before the second coming of Christ when a union—a marriage even—took place between the Lamb and "the faithful scattered people shod with the everlasting ghospell [*sic*] of peace." "Here is the body of the beast destroyed," Davies added at this very point in her text, so placing Antichrist in British Reformation history as the heretical corruption of the temporal church. The Antichrist was the Church of Rome: "This is Judas the Divell, the King of Babilon and Egypt, the raigne of Antichrist Pope of Rome . . . hated mortally the King of Rome and Italie." The great city in three parts to which she referred was the great schism, and she deployed the parallel to provoke thought about current church politics. Davies' revelation of the role of the temporal church contained, in addition, some very specific references to British Reformation history. The paraphrase of Daniel chapters 8 to 12 was very close to the original, but she strategically inserted sections that laid out the role of the temporal monarchy. James I was the king of the north, or Prince Michael, the archangel saint, or "prince of the covenant," repelling the king of the south who battled with him "with all his Spanish pikes." Of the seven kingdoms spoken of in Revelation, "five are fallen down dead drunke," but one had stood, and this was "the British Islands, the right Inheritance of King James the first." The dragon, or Antichrist, needed to be warned that the last remaining temporal kingdom existed literally now, ahead of the beginning of the sacral kingdom of Christ, "and at that time shall Michael stand up, the great prince that defends the faith, Charles king of Great Britaine, France and Ireland, which standeth for the faithfull children of our nation, the Saints of the most highest." It cannot have been a comfortable message for Charles I to receive, because it warned that the "little Horn" that had the eyes of a man was the king of the East signifying "the end of the matter of these earthly monarchies." Charles I, Davies believed, stood against the Antichrist with the saints, to be counted and numbered along with the rest of them.[20]

II

Eleanor Davies' debut appearance in 1625 with *A Warning to the Dragon* is an important milestone in the development of women's theological writing. Her tactic of locating her subject position in Reformation history was so powerful that she can be regarded as one of the precursors to the later female religious radicals, such as the Philadelphians, who, according to Sarah Apetrei, developed a form of "visionary feminism."[21] Before the civil wars, women's religious activism was usually expressed as inward-looking and often familial. Their religious works, from Katherine Parr's *Prayers and Medytacions* of 1545 onward, had public purchase in the name of private piety, and although the purpose might be the collective public good, they did not seek to lobby public authorities or chastise monarchs on their spiritual duties. Instead, they reflected on the death of a parent, like Rachel Speght's *Mortalities Memorandum* of 1621, or on maternal duties and the salvation of children, like Elizabeth Clinton's *The Countess of Lincolne's Nursery* of 1622 and Dorothy Leigh's *The Mother's Blessing* of 1616. Clinton, for example, linked a woman's assurance of being in a state of grace with her physical nourishment of infants; Leigh similarly was interested in securing for children "the right way to heaven."[22] Theirs was a Puritan *écriture feminine*, and their texts were so highly valued that they were commercial bestsellers.[23] Davies was a contemporary, but she had very different authorial intentions, asserting publicly a doctrinally exact and pure form of Calvinism uncoupled from the altruisms of female domesticity.

Lying at the theological heart of *A Warning to the Dragon* were the narrative consequences of the fall and Christ's atonement for human sin. Through this tale of desolation and rebirth Davies reached out to those godly Calvinists and zealous Puritans whose thirst for further reformation could never quite be quenched. Her work featured the doctrine of double predestination, following the lead of Theodore Beza, but she also systematized further through a federal or covenant theology of the kind that can be found running like a thread from Heinrich Bullinger onward, mitigating the fearful consequences of God's omnipotence.[24] Davies actually intended her prophecy to act as a practical, if urgent, call to piety. Possibly influenced by the catechistical work of William Perkins, all the key doctrines identified with his pastoral theology can be found in *A Warning to the Dragon*. The two Lutheran planks of obedience—*sola fidei* (faith alone) and *sola Scriptura* (scripture/Word alone)—were ever-present in the work. The importance of scripture as a building block of faith was implicit in the work's one-hundred pages of biblical commentary, which deployed not only the books of Luke and Daniel, but also Revelation, the fourth and fifth books of Moses, and some of the Apocrypha. "Scripture will repair the want of method," Davies said. *Sola fidei* was inherent in the statement "there is no access but by faith."[25] The doctrine of the fall was linked closely to the doctrine of sin, tying sin firmly to human fault. *A Warning to the Dragon* featured beliefs in the Trinity, the salvific power of the passion and Christ's atonement, and eschatology.[26] Although the text was one of bleak warnings about last things, it was also a call to conversion. Certainly there were portentous references to sin and the corruption of Rome (Babylon) plus the precisely calculated message, which she left to the end, that: "Last of all, the world is numberd [*sic*]. . . . There is nineteen yeares and a halfe to the day of Judgement." However, in closely linking Father, Son, and Holy Ghost, all three potentially acted within the Abrahamic covenant to bring the sinner hope of salvation.[27]

Diane Watt has argued that Davies "had, for a time, some sympathy with the Calvinist doctrine of absolute predestination, but later in life she developed a strong belief in the ultimate salvation of all mankind."[28] The judgment is based on such tracts as *The General Redemption* of 1647, but Davies' ideas in the 1640s were very much those of 1625, when she also emphasized the role of Christ.[29] *A Warning to the Dragon* argued for a double predestination that brought eternal life to those in a state of grace and eternal death to the damned or, as she called them in her General Epistle, "them that are gone astray."[30] God was all-knowing and all-powerful, so "who can tell if God will turne and repent, and turne away from his fierce anger, that wee goe not into Perdition."[31] However, the hope lay in the Christ-centered nature of her prophetic message, and she locked God's son, himself, into a doubled theological system. She linked Christology to the absoluteness of God's decree: "the Lambe slaine by the eternal Decree purposed from the foundation of the world."[32] Christ's death, then, was necessary, but Calvinist theologians struggled with the problem of how to resolve the universalism of his death with the unavoidable conclusion that not all sinners could be saved. Some theologians adopted a tactical philosophical binary, making a distinction between the all-embracing sufficiency of Christ's death and its effective application only to the elect.[33] Others looked to the doctrine of Christ's descent into hell, to suggest that Christ met with, and was rejected by, the damned. The latter left a small space within which all believers could imagine that universal salvation actually embraced them.[34] Davies opted for the descent to hell: Christ "tasted Death it selfe for us; so many melting trials and torments the innocent Lambe for a brood of Vipers whose damme is Death whose sting is Sinne."[35] Christ's atonement for human sin was vital, though his sacrifice brought effectual salvation for the elect alone, who were "washed . . . in his owne Blood" so that his salvation was also theirs.[36] The fall was the fundamental starting point in this narrative of immutable salvation only for some. To those predestined to eternal damnation Davies repeated biblical warnings that "You are impudent and disobedient Children . . . so are your sinnes hidden from you . . . you will know your transgression . . . sinking your Soules . . . forsaken of all, but the Divell and his Angells . . . not a drop of water remaining, of Light not a sparke."[37] Christ "gave him selfe for our Sinnes" when he cried "with a lowde voice, unable to conceale that passion, My God, My God, why hast thou forsaken mee."[38]

Davies used double predestination as an organizing principle in her 1625 text, but her soteriology constantly coupled salvation of the elect to the double covenant (the first of works and the second of grace) so that it clearly ensured the salvation of the saints (or God's covenanted people) during the last days of final judgment. Her revelation of Christ's atonement for sin stated that Christ had fulfilled the role of the second Adam. The faithful were brought from darkness to light "into the Land of Rest," the second covenant, sealed "with the sprinckling and shedding of His Blood."[39] Her text echoed works such as Robert Rollock's *A Treatise of our Effectual Calling* of 1599, which was driven by the idea of "the written Covenant of God." Indeed, just as Rollock's *Lectures upon the History of the Passion* of 1616 had drawn upon the Gospels, especially the books of John, closely followed by Luke, so too did Davies' work in 1625.[40] Covenant theology urged a further reformation that was militant in its quest for salvation. The armies of the godly or elect were engaged in a war with the devil ahead of building the New Jerusalem. Davies was a millenarian thinker with an utter faith in the proximity of the second coming that would usher in the subordination of the temporal visible church to the invisible church of Christ. The "armies of the ungodly" she described as "those who broke the covenant." The godly had to avoid the temptation to whoredom while the chronology of God's covenant played out. They had to expect wars and fire, with floods issuing from the mouth of "the Serpent . . . to trie them of the holy Covenant." God would "confirme his truth and Covenant," she said, only with the saints who were "the seed of Abraham," or those whose salvation was promised by the spiritual second covenant, which took place after "the Sealing of the first Covenant [The Mosaic covenant of the Law or works], a yoake which our Fathers were not able to beare." The second Abrahamic covenant, "is Spirituall, to put his Lawes in their mindes" when the children of Israel found the burden of the first covenant too heavy to bear.[41]

Eleanor Davies has often been portrayed as a prophet of doom, but she saw herself as a preacher of reform and hope. She uttered her warnings to

Charles I and Archbishop Abbot to spur them into a reforming zeal and told her wider audience that in the sprinkling of Christ's blood both covenants were sealed for an everlasting covenant and "the spirit giveth light to stony hearts."[42] Her very final word in *A Warning to the Dragon* was "And I think that I have also the Spirit of God."[43] In saying this she not only declared her assurance that she was one of God's chosen saints who would survive, but she also sought to reassure others that in her (and themselves) they could detect their own salvation. She possessed, unusually, an unshakeable belief that she had been gifted with a special spiritual authority that heralded the third age in the history of salvation. According to *A Warning to the Dragon*, in this new age the temporal church would be replaced by the age of the Spirit, ending Britain's reformation process by restoring the church to its ancient purity.

III

When Davies took *A Warning to the Dragon* to Archbishop Abbot, she might have been expecting a greater sympathy for its contents.[44] Abbot himself was a Calvinist who believed in double predestination, and Davies was only echoing the very vocal concerns about the dangers of Catholicism that could be found among the Irish and English Puritan clergy. Preaching before Charles I in England in 1624, James Ussher, by then Bishop of Meath and about to become Archbishop of Armagh, had similarly warned that the Church of Rome was reducing the members of the pure church to "strangers from the covenant of promise." While Davies was putting her case to Abbot and the king, Ussher corresponded with like-minded Puritans in England about how "the purity of the reformed religion [which] hath so long been maintained . . . [is now coming] into the hands of the enemy."[45] The mid-1620s context of fear is, therefore, the vital key that explains why Davies began to write when she did, but the other is the lurking presence of the confessional theology of the Church of Ireland, which had embedded double predestination in the Irish Articles of 1615.[46] The Irish Articles stated plainly that: "by the same eternall counsel God hath predestinated some unto life and reprobated some unto death; of both which there is a certain number." Irish Protestantism was supralapsarian; the promise that there was in "Christ the mediator of the second covenant" was considered to be antecedent to the breaking of the covenant of works by Adam. In wording that echoed Irish confessional faith, Davies rendered the covenant of works redundant for the elect because Christ "endured most grievous torments immediately in his soule, and most painful sufferings in his body . . . to be a sacrifice not only for originall guilt, but also for

our actuall transgressions."[47] Davies' Irish Protestant confessional orthodoxy locates her in a pan-European Calvinist reformation that connected
Dublin to Geneva, Amsterdam, and Edinburgh.

Davies and her ideas also fitted in perfectly with the English "Puritan
underground," or that Puritan reforming strand of the English Reformation that revered the martyrs of Foxe's *Actes and Monuments* and paid homage to the idea of the "holy commonwealth." David Como has argued that
it included women like Ann Fenwick, whose preaching ability was highly
praised, and he has found evidence of rousing and militant sermons that
were anti-clericalist and antiformalist circulating in manuscript and occasionally making their way into anonymous publications, such as Fenwick's
The Saints Legacies of 1629. If there was a Puritan underground, there was
also an identifiable theological consensus that connected it to members
of the social and intellectual establishment, such as Samuel Hartlib, an
international scholar who, like the Erastian John Dury, desired European
cooperation for universal reformation. Godly reformers were very keen to
encourage the circulation of ideas in manuscript form to bind the English
godly network to the wider campaign.[48] So Davies was not alone in her
Puritan activism and was not the only woman active either. Specifically at
stake was the doctrine of double predestination, which Davies made a key
intellectual topos in *A Warning to the Dragon*. She had spoken of "light
and darkness" and "eternal bliss." The language was of militancy because
the "transgressors . . . have shed the Blood of Saints and prophets." As far
as Eleanor Davies was concerned it was the Arminian heresy that was to
blame for the idolatry and altar-worship that undermined reformation in
1625, saying "you have made idols and images not by my direction." She
posed the rhetorical question: "them that forsake the covenant . . . what
shall become of these cursed children." The answer came back from Daniel
12:1–2—when the Lord arrived, all would be separated into those who
would enjoy "the Resurrection of Life . . . and those that have done evil
unto the Resurrection of Damnation."[49]

Eleanor Davies' daughter, Lucy Hastings, is understood to have once said
that her mother was "[i]n a woman's body a man's spirit . . . she not only
took but ruled." But modern readings of this early modern gender inver-
sion are a bit problematic.[50] For example, Davies adopted, for rhetorical
purposes, whatever language of authority she thought would most persuade
her audience of the danger posed to the reformation church. Anagrams
were her favorite literary device, though this should not be seen as peculiar
to her; the anagram was commonly used by early modern rhetoricians to
display their intellect and learning.[51] However, Davies' literary construction
was determined by gender. She had a feminine radical imagination. Unlike

educated male Puritans who resorted to displays of classical learning—the "road to Jerusalem . . . [taking a] detour through Athens"[52]—Davies played with language as an educated woman would, not by citing Cicero or Virgil, but by using the Aristotelian and Ramist constructions that she heard in sermons and by using the puzzles and mnemonics used in the intellectual exercises of sermon-recall and catechistical repetition. Her modes of representation reflect the gender of her pedagogy—she spoke of "A and O, *alias, Da:* [Davies] and *Do:* [Douglas] . . . Daughter of *Audleigh* or *Old-field*." It is obvious that she projected her prophetic voice, but discerning her theological voice proves problematic if it is judged against that of her male contemporaries.

Historians of historical theology look for Davies' references to past authority while historians of women look for her demonstrable piety—neither succeeds totally in finding what they are looking for. Instead they discover that she was Alpha and Omega from the revelation made to John (Rev. 1:8) and that she promoted herself as a prophet who could lay out the history and future of the world's time because of the completeness of her personal capture of God's Word. Luke 21, with which she began *A Warning to the Dragon*, spoke of the snare that was set for humankind, so Davies followed the Bible's lead, locating herself centrally in that narrative with the best anagram of her name that she could find, "A Snare O Devil."[53] What has been described as opaque prose exhibiting "syntactical confusion" and egocentric use of nominative anagrams was expected in Puritan displays of learning in women; she was just more biblical than most.[54] Davies did not exactly transcend her feminine self when she adopted the voice of Daniel; she claimed instead that "[it] seemed good unto me, having a perfect understanding given mee in these things, and the dispensation of them, an office, not a trade; to roote out, to pull downe, to build and to plant, by the grace and bounty of Jesus our Lord God." When Davies was in the active service of reformation, it was a duty that she saw as integral to her female identity. She said that it was for this reason that she presented her text to her readers, so that they could be joined to "the first Arke . . . some cleane and purified, others having need of purging." She told the king that he needed to "tread downe the power of his [God's] enemies."[55] She believed that the witnesses upon whom God poured His Spirit to prophesy were both masculine and feminine incarnate embodiments of Christ, not *without* gender as such, but containing *doubled* gender that resolved and unified men and women into oneness. By self-identifying as the "elect lady" she effectively slipped out of the identity of the patronymic "lady" (or woman of the temporal world and aristocracy) and into that of the lady of II John 1, the one in whom truth abided forever.

IV

As far as Eleanor Davies was concerned, the historical moment of 1625 continued with unabated ferocity throughout the 1630s. She responded to the spiritual threat by continuing with her determined repetition of the message of *A Warning to the Dragon* in at least four works in 1633 and two in 1636. She extended her identification of the Antichrist to William Laud, whose "beauty of holiness" campaign, to which Puritan opponents objected, focused on worship at the altar. *Bathe Daughter of Babylondon* cast the city of Bath as the whore of Babylon and London as Babylon itself, mimicking and mocking Archbishop Laud's career trajectory up through the episcopate. She labeled him as the "Beast ascended out of the Bottomlesse pitt" and drew on Revelation 17 to advise Charles I that hers was "the word of God to the King."[56] *Given to the Elector* claimed to be a song to Sion, denouncing Babylon and repeating the biblical story of Belshazzar's feast "in presence of his numerous peers. . . . Whom Devils Legions do possess | a Monarch turn'd a Slave." Again she referred to the writing on the wall because "polluting holy things" led to the numbering of the days.[57] *All the Kings of the Earth Shall Prayse Thee* took the heart out of *A Warning to the Dragon*, returning once again to Daniel's vision during the reign of Belshazzar.[58] During the 1630s Davies trod dangerously, posing as serious a challenge to the English authorities as William Prynne. Sometimes in exile, she resorted to publication in Amsterdam, appealing through her works, sometimes directly, to potential pan-European Calvinist allies. *Given to the Elector* was addressed to the Protestant elector of the Rhineland and *All the Kings of the Earth Shall Prayse Thee* was addressed to Elizabeth of Bohemia, sister of Charles I, begging to "crave Royall patience" before issuing a prophecy that complained about Charles I. Continuous effort was put into silencing her voice, but she still managed to write her final tract of the 1630s—*Spirituall Anthem*—while briefly between incarcerations and living in the cathedral close in Lichfield. There she made quite an impact, walking with female supporters into the cathedral to smear new, purple, wool altar hangings with tar and wheat paste.[59] "Soe howse of God poluted smell and veiw," she said, "Lawe. Bonds. all asunder rent . . . Yee that Beraye [defile] your rayement white, fryers [friars]."[60] Her words landed her in St. Mary of Bethlehem lunatic asylum and gained her the epithet of Sir John Lambe that there was "never soe made a ladie."[61] However, Davies is best understood if not thought of as mad, but as a controversialist theologian who wrote in a feminine style.[62]

In 1640 the church authorities had reason to fear the reputation Eleanor Davies had acquired among ordinary people as a "cunning woman."[63] Once church discipline began to lose its grip, crowd action increased, the symbolic destruction of Archbishop Laud's reformation became rife, and Charles' kingdoms began to move from troubled Reformation politics to war. For example, a woman called Cicely Mytton marched straight into her local church and smashed the stained glass windows.[64] The extent of the iconoclasm has recently been documented by John Walter, whose argument that it should be understood as the theological literacy, even piety, of ordinary people could equally be applied to an aristocratic woman, such as Eleanor Davies, who could feel just as marginalized by formal politics.[65] In September 1640, Davies was released and took lodgings in Whitehall, where, she later claimed, she waited "to be a beholder of the Prophetical Tragedy."[66] She detected no historical break between reformation and unfolding civil war. The numerical feasting and fasting of the unfolding Israelite reformation was to be enumerated in multiples of seven—the seventeenth day and seventh month and seventh year to the seventh jubilee and so on ("Times mistery unknown that treasure").[67] The escalation of conflict did not take her by surprise; indeed, she associated the Scots with the Chaldeans of the Bible, and she thought the Irish rebellion of 1641 was utterly predictable. "[F]eere Ireland," she said, "broken in peeces . . . divided between two Religions . . . to wallow in the mire, of Heathenisme covetousnes and Idolatry."[68] She viewed the thirty years war on the continent similarly. Convinced of her special understanding of events, she reminded her readers over and again of her original prophecies of 1625. When she thought the original prophecy was vindicated, she reprinted old work with new marginalia and topical commentary. For example, *Given to the Elector* of 1633 was reprinted once in 1643 as *Amend, Amend* and under its original title in 1648. Indeed, her reputation and authority grew dramatically during the time of revolutionary possibility.[69] George Thomason, the energetic civil war book collector, began buying her printed works systematically, labeling them with the name Davies to assert and confirm the authorship of "The Lady Eleanor."[70] He collected eight out of the twenty-four of her works published between 1640 and 1645.[71] The first work to catch his eye was *The Lady Eleanor Her Appeale* of 1641. Reprinted twice in 1641, it gave her version of events: "God able to change all, and them reforme."[72]

The Lady Eleanor Her Appeale was directly addressed to the House of Commons, in a sense pledging allegiance to their reforming politics from the outset. In it Davies argued that Babylon was falling and "like this dreame the World gone in a moment." It was "high time to make some preparation," she said, and reminded the members of Parliament that God, himself, had divided (and numbered) the kingdom while, under Prince Michael's (Charles I's) nose, Daniel's prophecy had been "shut up prohibited." Her covenant theology became a reformation call of absolute immediacy—the saints were the covenanted people, "His Elect, From Adam unto Abraham." The composite kingdom faced chaos, but she was in no doubt that out of the chaos the real reformation would take place. In "Great Brittaines foure Crownes or Kingdomes," England was "The Reformations Leader."[73] Many of Davies' works between 1641 and 1645 took up and developed the theme of Britain's struggle for reformation within what was a widely shared theological paradigm of double predestination and the double covenant. Against the backdrop of royalist victories in 1643 and 1644, she spoke of the four crowns matching the four beasts: the lion of England (and France) stood with and against "a Lyon rampant," identified as Scotland, and "the Irish Instrument . . . also out of Tune." The king, Belshazzar was "the last of those C[h]aldeans of great Babylon." "O King of great Britaine!" was her imperative cry, listen and understand Daniel's prophecy (given in 1625) because there are now "devided Kingdoms rent in pieces."[74] This anxious tract about a divided kingdom was collected by Thomason on September 23, 1644, just after the bloodshed of the first Battle of Newbury. Davies spoke much of the "king at armes," the short-horned beast that expressed the "Character of tirrants [tyrants]" and "that cursed womans spirit," or the supernatural power of Henrietta Maria to prevent peace, with her "Charmes and Spells like Satans." With the war going badly for Parliament, Davies raged "Woe to the House of God, and the House of Parliament both" and claimed that the seventeenth century was "the revealed time of the Resurrection," the reformation being spelled out by "the writs of Parliament" ahead of the second coming of the Lord and the day of judgment.[75]

It is telling that none of Davies' works in the 1640s concerned themselves with the political liberty or legal freedoms of Parliament, instead focusing on her two key political issues of the warmongering of Charles I and Henrietta Maria and of Parliament's reformation of the temporal church. In *Samsons Fall* of 1642, she blamed Charles I for falling prey to a woman, claiming that God had given a sign that Samson had "become as another man." The blindness of love had transformed Charles I from "a Saviour or Defender" to "Samson the prisoner" and "our British Union, fast knit and bound, soon dissolved after." The "Irish flourishing plantation . . . in a night all undone," she said, so blaming Charles I for the Irish rebellion.[76] She firmly located herself outside the royalist circles to which she had once belonged. *Samsons Legacie* of 1643 matched the fears held by parliamentarian propagandists that Charles I was swayed by "evil counsel," including a "popish and malignant party" ruled by Henrietta Maria.[77] In *Samsons Legacie* she argued that Delilah (Henrietta Maria) was dangerous because "*She prest him* [Samson] Daily, vext his Soule, his Conscience to the *Death*." The supernatural influence of the moon on the sun "separated Himself from his Head-Kingdoms Parliament Assembled," she said, in a tract that preempted a pamphlet by an anonymous propagandist of 1644 called *The Great Eclipse of the Sun*. Davies argued that "looking thereby more like the sons of Divells," the long hair of the Cavaliers was a providential sign or "plague token" (a reference back to 1625 again) of Samson, whose fall led to his losing the Spirit of the Lord. She related Charles' demise back to his crowning Archbishop Laud "with that high place of Government,"[78] which undid the reformation of that "godly Queen Elizabeth."

In this way, Eleanor Davies transformed from critic-cum-advisor of the king to rampant antimonarchist by 1644, delivering a blistering attack upon the king in that year in *Apocaplyps* by saying that "great brittains revealed forewarning" was that Israel was not an actual kingdom, but instead belonged to Christ. The king, Belshazzar, led "his riotous lords" on "profane feasting days" and the beast "must be killed."[79] The language she used for England's Reformation changed too, becoming more belligerent. The Reformation sometimes became "this great Revolution ushering the day of Judgement, his coming in the clouds." The monarch who had had access to Jacob's ladder stretching to heaven was James I, because Charles I had "reared altars to Baal." In another tract aimed at the House of Commons "to set their House in Order" she spoke of the account that was weighing up against the tyrant, no matter how much he might have been misled by "sinister counsel."[80] *Samsons Legacie* similarly railed against monarchical tyranny: the "sonns of god [who] became Tyrants" with armies would face the fight put up by David (Psalm 90) before the confirmation of the covenant with the saints. Angrily she denounced the Cavaliers who labeled the saints as "Puritans: and now, Round-heads," while "Papists, the Queenes Armie . . . prophaine[d] Protestants, before the day of Judgement."[81] In *Samsons Fall* she issued a rather seditious prophecy, referring to Charles I as the lion in the Book of Revelation and saying: "And there was no king."[82] She became more, rather than less, radical in her commentary on temporal monarchy as the civil war progressed and the kingdom of Christ became more real. As the original prophecy of nineteen and a half years ran out, and William Laud was executed, with perfect timing, in 1645, she came to argue that "*Time* [was] *made knowne of HIS comming*, with that shift . . . *Cut off* (to wit) his Head."[83] *The Revelation Interpreted* of 1646 spoke of the adored image of Caesar, but meant by this "that Monarchies period" after the disruption of "Brittaines unhappie faction" had given way to the reign of Christ. This, she calculated, would commence in 1700.[84] In other words, when the original prophecy expired, she offered a vision of transformation through to the century's end.

V

Davies' active engagement in reformation during the civil wars worked in two ways. First, she turned her prophetic gaze toward the work of the Westminster

Assembly, and second, she paid close attention to the Paul's Cross sermons. In tracts written between 1644 and 1645 she told the members of the Westminster Assembly that they never faced darker times and that schism was allowing the return of dangerous doctrines such as transubstantiation.[85] "Reverend Men of God and Judges," she said, "there is nothing so secret, That shall not be discovered. . . . The halfe of seven until which Sabaticall Number fulfilled, be bidden to rest, etc. viz. the 1700 yeare."[86] Charles had brought down the temporal church, but she praised a Paul's Cross preacher for his "solemn Thanksgiving" for James I. Like the Paul's Cross ministers she interpreted contemporary events providentially, as mercies or judgments, for example, speaking of "deliverance" in *The Day of Judgements Modell*, written after the king's surrender to the Scots in May 1646. "The great and dreadful day in the month of May," she said, before drawing on her belief in double predestination to argue (as she did consistently over several tracts) that the number of the saved would be 144,000. As with her chronologies, this number was absolute—in the sense of being a biblical truth—but it was not fixed in human lived experience and was, therefore, unknowable because human calculations were false per se. In other works Davies made periodic references to Edward VI and Elizabeth I, thinking them instrumental in paving the way for the reign of Christ.[87] The mercies of God, she claimed in one tract, were "mercys Englished," they were on "Brittains Mapp."[88] She believed that if the confession of faith and directory of public worship that the Westminster Assembly arrived at came close to God's law, the ministers would all be saved. She told them this directly.

In *The Star to the Wise*, which was published the year that the Westminster Assembly was established, she made another of her direct calls to the members of the House of Commons in the cause of "further reformation." She designated Parliament, the godly ministers, and herself as being among those who would rise and shine with the aid of "Parliaments signification." Reformation would prevent them from sinking into the darkness of the damned. Citing Revelation 11, she pointed out that the "Churches Intelligence aforehand of that time" was their reassurance of election and that their luck, in this regard, dated back to "the Word of the Lord" revealed to her back in 1625.[89] Davies accorded considerable agency to the reformers at Westminster, but, crucially, it was equal only to her own. She pointed out the symbolism of the assembly's location, both because "Henry sevenths Chappell" was where his "sons Royall Issue so soon re-edified or reformed the Church," but also because the number seven had considerable significance in her many calculations of biblical time. "The Lord of Sabbath" held "the seven stars in his right hand" and "That Book sealed with seven seals" indicated the journey of the saints from the "first Adam" to the "second Adam."[90] Here, again, covenant theology was enormously important to Davies' understanding of events, because all of history and time worked this way to define the relationship of God and His creatures. The concept of the two Adams held the idea together, yet again: sin entered the world by the first Adam, and the second Adam—Christ—died to expurgate it. "Wherefore, as by one man sin entred into the world, and death by sin. . . . That as in Adam all dyed, so in Christ are all made alive." In this work, *The Mystery of General Redemption*, she grappled, as she had in 1625, with the problem of how Christ might die for all in a system in which only some would be saved. She came up with the same answer as she had two decades earlier—Christ's descent into hell. "Saviours soul not left in Hell, applied, nor his body in the earth to see corruption. . . . But every one in his order . . . and he one able to distinguish between the general and the special." In other words, "the mystery of general redemption" was that, in addition to the general redemption, there was also special provision for the saved. The logic was the same as the disrupted chronologies of God's special providence, which could remove some events out of fixed linear time, to operate in some luminal space where God's power, in a sense, was at its most visible. Christ had "the Keys of Death and Hell." "So with his secret Providence proceeding," she said, "the common Salvation hidden."[91]

Davies' daughter, Lucy, once claimed that her mother was "learned above her sex," and there is quite a bit of evidence to support the claim. In her elaboration of the doctrine of Christ's descent into hell, Davies demonstrated a theological understanding that went beyond that of most seventeenth-century Calvinist lay people. Occasionally she dropped some Latin into her texts. A favorite was *secula seculorum* to express the concept of eternity. Eternity, itself, was conceptually rooted in a set chronology, but mysterious and "in all ages." Time was like the Gordian knot; if only one could untie it, all of God's implied power would become comprehensible.[92] Davies delved into the meaning of Easter and the resurrection, so that Christ's descent could be aligned to Christ's ascent in the theological schema upon which salvation depended. This is noticeable in a whole sequence of linked works between 1645 and 1646, when she began to prepare herself fully for the extended time of judgment, after the first signifier of the nineteen and a half years had passed. One of the first, *The Brides Preparation*, used Revelation 21 for a vision of "the bride the Lambes wife" who watched on "as the second death appointed" took place, unbelievers being consigned to "add or diminish from the words of this book," or the sealed book "shewing the Lords second comming."[93] Four works—*For the Blessed Feast of Easter, Je le Tien: The General Restitution, Ezekiel the Prophet* and *Ezekiel Cap. 2*—concerned themselves with glorious visions of the life-death-rebirth model of Christ that was critical to Davies' Abrahamic Christianity and that allowed the liminal event of Christ's descent into hell to take place before his ascension to heaven and return to earth in the white clouds. "Behold hee commeth," she wrote, in *For the Blessed Feast of Easter*: "I am Alpha and Omega. . . . I am the first and the last King; I have the keys of Hell and Death." Again, she made reference to the prophecy of the seven stars.[94] The prophet Ezekiel appeared with frequency in her works because he represented "resurrection's voice,"[95] and she regularly referenced Whitsuntide or Whit Sunday, the seventh Sunday after Easter, because the chronological elasticity of the mystical number seven also helped with the tale of Christ's resurrection and promise of grace.[96] *Je le Tien* was, arguably, the most learned work in the sequence, elaborating the notion of Christ's possession of the keys of death and hell to disprove the twinned ideas "that out of Hell is no redemption. . . . As by this attainder of Adams house suppos'd irrevocable."[97] On the eve of the king's downfall, then, Davies' message was that the seed of Abraham would be redeemed by Christ, and she identified the saved with those who would triumph—or the saints—during the preordained last days of the English Reformation.

VI

Eleanor Davies' reputation has not survived well. Recent studies of religious radicalism in the 1640s fail to take her ideas into account, looking instead to the tracts of Gerrard Winstanley and the Diggers or the performative gestures of the apprentice—men and plebeian women who destroyed images, burnt altar rails, and used the "licensed disorder" of Plough Monday to seek popular justice for 1630s church reform.[98] Yet in the 1630s Davies had beaten the crowd to the desecration of sacral spaces. Contemporary propaganda about her as mad "she-prophet" colored later biographies, and they, in turn, have informed modern interpretations of Davies as "eccentric prophetess" given to "impolitic pronouncements." Basically, Davies is too aristocratic for accounts of popular radicalism, and she was too uninterested in female education and sexual equality for her work to make it into feminist historiography of the female "republic of letters."[99] Contextualizing Davies requires exploration of who she thought she was and what she thought she was doing. Although there was a continuation of her systematic theology from 1625 to the late 1640s—indeed, double predestination and covenant theology ran like structural cement through her elaborate and rolling record of reformation events—her prophetic voice shifted from Daniel to Elijah the Tishbite as she stopped warning Prince Michael and began a more personal fight with Baal. She spoke providentially of the war between Gog and Magog as "Mercy and Judgements going together, in these last days reveal'd."[100] She used Elijah's tales of anti-messianic forces fighting Jerusalem to give assurance that the New Jerusalem of the saints would one day be victorious. Importantly, she formed the Christian republican and deeply radical conclusion that Charles I, Henrietta Maria, and William Laud would all have to go. In *Great Brittains Visitation* of 1645, she described how her original prophecy had ended with Laud's "sable hearse," before "the quaking Earth Mother" went into "a consumption" and "the Sunn" (Charles I) went "as black as Sack cloth of haire" and "the Moone" (Henrietta Maria) "overwatched with her red face looking like blood."[101]

In 1649 Davies wrote at least two dozen pamphlets in the wake of the regicide. *The New Jerusalem at Hand* declared that there would be no "Charls the second" and that temporal monarchy would be overthrown by the investiture of Saul. Her Calvinist perspective merged reformation and the civil war into a single process, and she believed herself a witness to knowledge of "a Reformation set before the End," ushering in "a new Heaven and a new Earth."[102] Within this reformation she asserted not only female power but also her own power as an individual woman. In the early 1640s she had equated her own role with the biblical woman whose washing of the body of the Chaldean (Scottish) king (Charles I) would lead to the complete recovery of the kingdom, and in *The Star to the Wise* she had conjured up the "Celestiall Woman" who would show "the time of the Churches great deliverance."[103] By 1645 she spoke of "the woman who openeth her mouth in wisdom; and the doctrine of mercy is under her tongue"; by 1647 she linked woman to the two Adams of the double covenant: "such a numerous generation promised Abraham. . . . Woman, behold thy son, figur'd in Adam and the Serpent both."[104] By then she sometimes ended works with Amen, suggesting that she saw herself not just as a prophet, but as a preacher, and this is, perhaps, confirmed by her actions in 1650. In that year she stood in the barn on her estate at Pirton and told Gerrard Winstanley and the Diggers that she was "the prophetess Melchisedeck," and so elevating herself to the high priesthood and implying the significance of her role in the invisible church of the righteous. She preached to them as if she was second only to Christ.[105] Therefore, although this essay has maintained from the beginning that Davies was an important Calvinist covenant theologian, it also seems possible to assert at the end that she was a highly politicized woman who radically imagined a feminine spiritual presence— even transformative power—in the English Reformation as it turned into the millennial world of war.

Notes

1. Eleanor Davies, *A Warning to the Dragon and All His Angels* (London: B. Alsop, 1625), 85. *Early English Books Online* was used to access the works of Eleanor Davies for this essay unless otherwise indicated. For recent biographical treatment of Eleanor Davies, see Esther S. Cope, *Handmaid of the Holy Spirit: Dame Eleanor Davies, Never Soe Made a Ladie* (Ann Arbor: University of Michigan Press, 1992) and Diane Watt, "Davies, [*née* Touchet] . . . Lady Eleanor (1590–1652)," *Oxford Dictionary of National Biography* (2004–10): doi.org/10.1093/ref:odnb/7233. For other work on Eleanor Davies, see Esther Cope, "Dame Eleanor Davies Never Soe Made a Ladie," *Huntington Library Quarterly*, 50.2 (1987):133–44; Esther Cope, "Eleanor Davies and the Prophetic Office," in *Women, Writing and the Reproduction of Culture in Tudor and Stuart Britain*, ed. Mary E. Burke, Jane Donawerth, Linda L. Cove, and Karen Nelson (Syracuse: Syracuse University Press, 2000), 207–19; *Prophetic Writings of Lady Eleanor Davies*, ed. Esther Cope (New York and Oxford: Oxford University Press, 1995). Davies' most modern editor is Theresa Feroli—*Eleanor Davies, Writings 1641–1646* and *Eleanor Davies, Writings 1647–1652* (Aldershot, UK: Ashgate, 2011).
2. Davies, *A Warning to the Dragon*, 42.
3. Davies, *A Warning to the Dragon*, 90.
4. Davies, *A Warning to the Dragon*, 84. For human adjustments of historical chronologies see Penelope Corfield, *Time and the Shape of History* (New Haven and London: Yale University Press, 2007), 193. For the centrality of biblicism in society, see Naomi Tadmor, *The Social Universe of the English Bible: Scripture, Society and Culture in Early Modern England* (Cambridge: Cambridge University Press, 2010).
5. Christopher Haigh, *English Reformations: Religion, Politics, and Society under the Tudors* (Oxford: Oxford University Press, 1993); Alexandra Walsham, "The Reformation and 'the disenchantment of the world' reassessed," *The Historical Journal*, 51.2 (2008): 497–528; Conrad Russell, *The Fall of the British Monarchies 1637–1642* (Oxford: Oxford University Press, 1991); J. S. Morrill, "The Religious Context of the English Civil War," *Transactions of the Royal Historical Society*, fifth series, 34 (1984). In many ways, this essay pays homage to the work of John Morrill, whose advice over many years has deeply informed my thinking. See also Peter Marshall, *Reformation England 1480–1642* (London: Bloomsbury Academic, 2003) and Nicholas Tyacke, *England's Long Reformation 1500–1800* (London: Routledge, 1997).
6. Alexandra Walsham, *Church Papists: Catholicism, Conformity and Confessional Polemic in Early Modern England* (Woodbridge: Boydell & Brewer, 1993); Michael Questier, *Conversion, Politics and Religion in England 1580–1625* (Cambridge: Cambridge University Press, 1996).
7. Haigh, *English Reformations*, 287, 291.
8. Watt, "Davies," doi.org/10.1093/ref:odnb/7233.
9. Cope, *Handmaid of the Holy Spirit*, 15.
10. Sean Kelsey, "Davies, Sir John," *Oxford Dictionary of National Biography* (2004–10): doi.org/10.1093/ref:odnb/7245.

11. James Ussher's first published articulation of this idea was in *Gravissimae Quaestionis de Christianarum Ecclesiarum* of 1613.
12. Cope, *Handmaid of the Holy Spirit*, 11, 40.
13. George Ballard, *Memoirs of Several Ladies of Great Britain* (London: W. Jackson, 1752), 272–3; Mary Hays, *Female Biography* (London: Richard Phillips, 1803), 31. The Scottish boy prophet was identified by Davies as George Carr in *The Lady Eleanor Her Appeale* (1646). Hays followed Ballard closely, while rendering his relatively sympathetic account of Davies into something more colorful.
14. The full title of Richard Montagu's work was *A Gag for the New Gospell? No: A New Gagge for an Olde Goose.*
15. Davies, *A Warning to the Dragon*, "General Epistle," Sig. v–vi, 1. Eleanor Davies' father was Baron Audeley and first Earl of Castlehaven.
16. Davies, *A Warning to the Dragon*, 50.
17. Davies, *A Warning to the Dragon*, 4.
18. Cope, *Handmaid of the Holy Spirit*, 110.
19. Davies, *A Warning to the Dragon*, 1–15.
20. Davies, *A Warning to the Dragon*, 14, 18, 32, 36, 74–76, 81, 84. Esther Cope argues for a higher degree of personalization of the biblical imagery, suggesting that Eleanor Davies drew parallels between the "Prince Michael" and herself; see Cope, *Handmaid of the Holy Spirit*, 41, 136.
21. Sarah Apetrei, *Women, Feminism and Religion in Early Enlightenment England* (Cambridge: Cambridge University Press, 2010), 207, 233–42.
22. Patricia Crawford, "The Construction and Experience of Maternity," in *Women as Mothers in Pre-Industrial England*, ed. Valerie Fildes (London: Routledge, 1990); Amanda L. Capern, *The Historical Study of Women: England, 1500–1800* (Basingstoke, UK: Palgrave Macmillan, 2010), 28, 214–18, 220 ff.
23. Kimberly Ann Coles, *Religion, Reform and Women's Writing in Early Modern England* (Cambridge: Cambridge University Press, 2008).
24. Richard A. Muller, "Calvin and the 'Calvinists': Assessing Continuities and Discontinuities between the Reformation and Orthodoxy," *Calvin Theological Journal*, 30 (1995): 345–75 and 31 (1996): 125–60; *After Calvin: Studies in the Development of a Theological Tradition* (Oxford: Oxford University Press, 2003).
25. Davies, *A Warning to the Dragon*, "General Epistle," Sig. iv.
26. Haigh, *English Reformations*, 287, 291.
27. Davies, A Warning to the Dragon, 4–5.
28. Watt, "Davies," doi.org/10.1093/ref:odnb/7233.
29. Davies was not alone in her theological career trajectory—Richard Baxter, for example, also veered toward Arminianism in the 1640s.
30. Davies, *A Warning to the Dragon*, "General Epistle," passim.
31. Davies, *A Warning to the Dragon*, 84.
32. Davies, *A Warning to the Dragon*, 2.
33. Alan Ford, *James Ussher: Theology, History and Politics in Early-Modern Ireland and England* (Oxford: Oxford University Press, 2007), 108–9.
34. I am grateful to my colleague Dr. David Bagchi for very interesting discussions about the rather arcane doctrine of Christ's descent into hell or the harrowing of hell.

35. Davies, *A Warning to the Dragon*, "General Epistle," Sig. iii–iv.
36. *The Interpreter's Dictionary of the Bible: An Illustrated Encyclopedia*, vol. 1 (Nashville, TN: Abingdon, Press, 1962), 309–16.
37. Davies, *A Warning to the Dragon*, 17–18.
38. Davies, *A Warning to the Dragon*, "General Epistle," Sig. A3, 69.
39. Davies, *A Warning to the Dragon*, "General Epistle," Sig. A3v, 4, 18.
40. Robert Rollock, *Select Works of Robert Rollock* (Edinburgh: The Wodrow Society, 1844).
41. Davies, *A Warning to the Dragon*, 3–4.
42. Davies, *A Warning to the Dragon*, 3.
43. Davies, *A Warning to the Dragon*, 100.
44. Cope, *Handmaid of the Holy Spirit*, 41.
45. "A Sermon Preached before the King's Majesty 20th June 1624 on the Universality of the Church of Christ," in *The Life and Whole Works of the Most Reverend James Ussher*, vol. ii, ed. C. R. Elrington (Dublin: Trinity College Dublin, 1847–1864), 477, and vol. xvi, "Samuel Ward to James Ussher," September 25, 1622, 177–78.
46. Ford, *James Ussher*, especially chapters 2–5.
47. *The Irish Articles* (Dublin, 1615) in *The Life and Whole Works of the Most Reverend James Ussher*, vol. i, ed. C. R. Elrington (Dublin: Hodges and Smith, 1847–1864), citing 35–36, 38, 47. *Gravissimae Quaestionis de Christianarum Ecclesiarum . . . Successione et Statu Historica Explicatio* (Dublin, 1613) is in volume ii.
48. David Como, "Women, Prophecy and Authority in Early Stuart Puritanism," *Huntington Library Quarterly*, 61.2 (1998): 210 [203–22]; Peter Lake and David Como, "Orthodoxy and Its Discontents: Dispute Settlement and the Production of 'Consensus' in the London (Puritan) Underground," *Journal of British Studies*, 39.1 (2000): 34–70. See also *Samuel Hartlib & Universal Reformation: Studies in Intellectual Cultural Communication*, ed. Mark Greengrass, Michael Leslie, and Timothy Raylor (Cambridge: Cambridge University Press, 1994).
49. Davies, *A Warning to the Dragon*, 7, 32, 78, 80, 84.
50. Theresa Feroli, *Political Speaking Justified: Women Prophets and the English Revolution* (Newark, DE: University of Delaware Press, 2006), 75, and *Eleanor Davies: Printed Writings*, ed. Theresa Feroli (Aldershot, UK: Ashgate, 2000), x; Mack, *Visionary Women*, passim; Ann Hughes, *Gender and the English Revolution* (New York: Routledge, 2012), 76.
51. Cf. Cope, *Handmaid of the Holy Spirit*, 12.
52. Nicholas McDowell, *The English Radical Imagination: Culture, Religion and Revolution, 1630–1660* (Oxford: Oxford University Press, 2003), 39, and citing John Morgan, *Godly Learning: Puritan Attitudes towards Reason, Learning and Education, 1560–1640* (Cambridge: Cambridge University Press, 1986), 78.
53. Davies, *A Warning to the Dragon*, frontispiece, Sig. A1.
54. Mack, *Visionary Women*, 23, 32. Mack has argued that some of Davies' readers thought her "gifted but insane." See also, "Women as Prophets during the English Civil War," *Feminist Studies*, 8.1 (1982): 19–45.
55. Davies, *A Warning to the Dragon*, "General Epistle," Sig. iv–v, Sig. x.

56. Eleanor Davies, *To the Kings Most Excellent Majestie* (1645). The 1633 petition was reprinted in 1645 with an attached prophecy identifying William Laud as "Lambeth" turned into anagram as "Bethlam," to reference Laud's fate in 1645 with her own punishment by incarceration in Bethlam in 1636.
57. Eleanor Davies, *Given to the Elector* (Amsterdam, 1633; rep. 1648), 4, 8–9.
58. Eleanor Davies, *All the Kings of the Earth Shall Prayse Thee* (Amsterdam, 1633), Sig. B3v.
59. Cope, *Handmaid of the Holy Spirit*, 84.
60. See *Writings of Lady Eleanor Davies*, 73.
61. Cope, *Handmaid of the Holy Spirit*, 60–63, 86.
62. The equivalent for natural philosophy would be Margaret Cavendish.
63. Ballard, *Memoirs of Several Ladies of Great Britain*, 277, citing Peter Heylin, *Cyprianus Anglicus* (1668).
64. Hughes, *Gender and the English Revolution*, 73, citing *Civil War in Staffordshire*, ed. I. Carr and I. J. Atherton, 13.
65. John Walter, "Abolishing Superstition with Sedition? The Politics of Popular Iconoclasm in England 1640–1642," *Past & Present*, 183 (2004): 79–123.
66. Davies, *Given to the Elector*, 10.
67. Eleanor Davies, *The Lady Eleanor Her Appeale to the High Court of Parliament* (1641), Sig. A3v.
68. Davies, *The Lady Eleanor Her Appeale to the High Court of Parliament*, 17.
69. Alexandra Walsham, *Providence in Early Modern England* (Oxford: Oxford University Press, 1999), 220.
70. See Eleanor Davies, *The Star to the Wise. 1643. To the High Court of Parliament, the Honorable House of Commons* (London, 1643), annotation to frontispiece, dated November 25.
71. Thomason under-collected Quaker tracts compared with other religious and political works, and interestingly, he did cut down the number of works he collected by Eleanor Davies in the final few years of her writing career, between 1650 and 1652.
72. Davies, *The Lady Eleanor Her Appeale to the High Court of Parliament*, 8.
73. Davies, *The Lady Eleanor Her Appeale to the High Court of Parliament*, 8, 13–17.
74. Eleanor Davies, *From the Lady Eleanor, Her Blessing to Her Beloved Daughter* (1644), 4–5, 7, 10, 12.
75. Davies, *From the Lady Eleanor, Her Blessing*, 14–20.
76. Eleanor Davies, *Samsons Fall* (1642; 1649), frontispiece, 7–10, 12–13, 16; *Samsons Legacie* (1643), 5, 9.
77. See, for example, Anon., *Strange and Terrible News from Holland* (1642), and Anon., *The Queens Proceedings in Yorkshire* (1643).
78. Davies, *Samsons Legacie*, 6–7, 12–13.
79. Eleanor Davies, *Apocalyps, chapter 11* (1648), 4–5.
80. Eleanor Davies, *A Sign Given Them Being Entred into the Day of Judgement* (1644); reprinted 1649), 4–5, 8–9, 11.
81. Davies, *Samson Legacie*, 3, 6–8, 12–16, 19–20.
82. Eleanor Davies, *Samsons Fall* (1642; 1649), 12–13, 16; *Samsons Legacie*, 5, 9.

83. Eleanor Davies, *As Not Unknowne* (1645; reprint of 1633 with annotation), broadside, 1 sheet.

84. Eleanor Davies, *The Revelation Interpreted* (1644), 3.

85. Eleanor Davies, *Of Errors Joynd with Gods Word* (1645), passim.

86. Eleanor Davies, *I am the First and Last* (1644), Sig. A2, 6.

87. Davies, *A Sign*, passim.

88. Eleanor Davies, *Great Brittains Visitation* (1645), 32; [Eleanor Davies], *The Mystery of the General Redemption* (1647), 8.

89. Davies, *The Star to the Wise*, 16–18.

90. Davies, *The Star to the Wise*, 13.

91. Davies, *The Mystery of the General Redemption*, 4–5, 15.

92. Davies, *The Mystery of the General Redemption*, 8.

93. Eleanor Davies, *The Brides Preparation* (1645), 8.

94. Eleanor Davies, *For the Blessed Feast of Easter* (1646), 5.

95. Eleanor Davies, *Ezekiel Cap. 2* (1646), 3.

96. Eleanor Davies, *For Whitsontyds Last Feast: The Present, 1645* (1645), passim.

97. Eleanor Davies, *Je le Tien, the General Restitution* (1646), 4–5, 28, 42, 44.

98. Walter, "Abolishing Superstition with Sedition?" 79–123.

99. Patricia Crawford, *Women and Religion in England 1500–1720* (London and New York: Routledge, 1993), 5, 107; Hughes, *Gender and the English Revolution*, 76, 117; *The Cambridge Companion to Writing of the English Revolution*, ed. N. H. Keeble (Cambridge: Cambridge University Press, 2001); Hilary Hinds, *God's Englishwomen: Seventeenth-Century Radical Sectarian Writing and Feminist Criticism* (Manchester: Manchester University Press, 1996); Marcus Nevitt, *Women and the Pamphlet Culture of Revolutionary England, 1640–1660* (Aldershot, UK: Ashgate, 2006); Diane Purkiss, *Literature, Gender and Politics during the English Civil War* (Cambridge: Cambridge University Press, 2005), 214–15, citing *Signes and Wonders from Heaven, with a True Relation of a Monster Borne in Ratcliffe Highway* (London: 1645); Carol Pal, *Republic of Women: Rethinking the Republic of Letters in the Seventeenth Century* (Cambridge: Cambridge University Press, 2012), 201.

100. Eleanor Davies, *The Restitution of Reprobates* (1644), 4–5; *The Interpreter's Dictionary of the Bible: An Illustrated Encyclopedia*, vol. 2, 88–90.

101. Davies, *Great Brittains Visitation*, 23.

102. Davies, *For the Blessed Feast of Easter*, 12.

103. Davies, *The Lady Eleanor Her Appeale*, passim; *The Star to the Wise*, passim.

104. Davies, *A Prayer or Petition for Peace*, passim; *The Mystery of the General Redemption*, 17–18.

105. "Letter to Lady Eleanor Douglas," December 4, 1650, in *The Complete Works of Gerrard Winstanley*, vol. ii, ed. Thomas N. Corns, Ann Hughes, and David Lowenstein (Oxford: Oxford University Press, 2009), 422–29. I am grateful to Professor Colin Davis for alerting me to the importance of Eleanor Davies' connection with Winstanley.

CHAPTER 6

The Failure of Godly Womanhood: Religious and Gender Identity in the Life of Lady Elizabeth Delaval

Sharon L. Arnoult

For most women in early modern Europe, religious identity was bound up with other identities, particularly with their identity as women. Indeed, in some ways the two were so intertwined as to be almost inseparable: religion was the ultimate foundation and justification for the beliefs, duties, and expectations early modern society had about and for women and that women had for themselves. As Sara Mendelson and Patricia Crawford have pointed out, "During the sixteenth and seventeenth centuries, the religious establishment was perhaps the most powerful medium through which theories about human nature and society were disseminated to the general population."[1] Nowhere were those theories clearer than in the realm of gender. Religion defined the parameters of femininity. The weaker vessel was the daughter of Eve, inclined to sin and vanity, but this inclination could be countered and transcended by the female inclination to piety born of weakness and dependency. Such piety, properly guided by prayer, wise counsel, and a woman's own self-discipline, could produce the opposite of the daughter of Eve: the godly woman. Significantly, this acquisition of godliness was directly related to a woman's proper fulfillment of gender prescriptions: "Theology defined the good daughter, wife, mother, and widow in terms of her conformity to her role, and laid special stress on the importance of 'relative duties' in women's striving for salvation."[2] Moreover, although women were born female and baptized Christians as infants, developing their identities through these prescribed roles needed action on their part. Education by family and society provided the template of what a godly woman was and how it could be attained, but women's agency was also required in the inculcation and development of their religious and gender self-conceptions and aspirations. In short, women literally realized their religious identity through their gender identity, and vice versa. Thus, in an era in which gender prescriptions and religious piety were taken very seriously, what did it mean for a woman to pursue "godliness"? How specifically was the pursuit of godliness defined for a woman? What roles were acceptable for a woman to take, both in her own spiritual growth and in her attempts to religiously influence others? And lastly, crucially, how could—or couldn't—a woman reconcile the demands of godliness with her own sense of self?

This chapter seeks to answer these questions at least in part by examining the autobiographical meditations of Lady Elizabeth Delaval. These meditations illuminate the dense interconnections between religious and gender identity for an elite woman in late early modern England, demonstrating how it shaped her expectations and interpretations of both herself and other women. However, these meditations also reveal a sense of self that was deeply embedded in a need for earthly happiness and personal fulfillment that struggled, and mostly failed, to align itself to the existing religious gender ideals, suggesting the stirring of a new, more modern sense of self as an entitled individual. Elizabeth Delaval's meditations demonstrate how deeply and profoundly her examination and evaluation of herself as a woman were conditioned by her desire to live up to the imperatives of her religious identity. They also affected how she viewed and judged other women as well, suggesting a wider circle of influence and exchange for women's spiritual writing.

Most of Elizabeth Delaval's life story comes from the autobiographical meditations that she began in her teens and later revised. The composition of a diary or memoir for spiritual purposes—to provide a forum for self-scrutiny and occasion for reflection on God's mercies as well as one's own sins—was a popular practice amongst those early modern Englishwomen with the time, literacy, and religious inclination to pursue it, which means it was almost always a pursuit of upper-class Englishwomen.[3] There were conventions to this genre, shaped by the numerous guides to the practice that flourished at this time as part of the effort to define the proper paths for female godliness. Elizabeth's work reflects these conventions although, as Margaret Ezell notes, Elizabeth fashioned her life story as much (or more) to the conventions of the romance novels she devoured as a girl.[4]

Elizabeth was the daughter of James Livingston of Kinnaird, whose loyalty to the Stuarts caused him to be made Viscount Newburgh in 1647, and later Earl of Newburgh, Viscount of Kinnaird, and Lord Livingston of Flacraig at the Restoration. Newburgh married Elizabeth's mother Katherine, the widow of George Stuart, seigneur d'Aubigny, sometime in 1648, and Elizabeth was born either that year or the next. Elizabeth's time with her biological mother was brief, for the infant was left behind with her paternal aunt when her Royalist parents fled to The Hague in 1649, where Elizabeth's mother died the following year, 1650.[5]

Left in her aunt's care "in my cradle," as Elizabeth often recalled, she continued to live with her father's sister, Dorothy Lady Stanhope, until 1662, when Elizabeth departed to become a maid of the privy chamber to Queen Catherine of Braganza. The court was a heady environment for the young woman; Elizabeth ran up debts and found it difficult to remain focused on piety with so many diversions. She engaged in a flirtation with an unacceptable man, a violation of a godly daughter's filial duty, prompting a resolve "never more to hear a young man talke of love to me . . . unlesse he is aproved on by my parent's [sic] and is also at liberty to dispose of himselfe."[6] She then fell deeply in love with a young man who was eminently suitable: the son of the Earl of Anglesey, just four years older than Elizabeth and as madly in love with Elizabeth as she was with him. Initially Elizabeth's father approved, as did the young man's parents, but Elizabeth's aunt was cold to the match, and so things were left unresolved as Lady Stanhope took Elizabeth home with her. Lady Stanhope had promised Elizabeth to Lord Roos, the future Earl of Rutland, once he was able to extricate himself from his first marriage, a long and complicated process during which Lady Stanhope had to keep Elizabeth free. Elizabeth's position at court meant her aunt could not keep her away indefinitely, and when she returned, young Lord Annesley pleaded with her to elope with him. But Elizabeth would not commit such a violation of daughterly duty. Meanwhile, fearing exactly such an elopement, Lord Roos prevailed upon his mother to make a "better offer" of one of her daughters to Lord Annesley's parents; considering the continued obstruction of Elizabeth's aunt, the Earl and his wife agreed, but decided not to speak to their son about it until Elizabeth had been off in the country with her aunt for a while. En route to her aunt's estate, Elizabeth stayed with her cousin and her cousin's husband, who persuaded her to agree to elope with her beloved, pointing out that her father and his parents had no objections to the match, only her aunt. Elizabeth wrote a letter to Lord Annesley informing him of this, but the letter ended up in the Earl's hands, who was enraged and went so far as to threaten to disinherit his eldest son "if he presumed to disobey his will."[7] The young man complied with his father and asked Elizabeth to release him from his promises to her. Elizabeth did so, later writing "I am still sometimes amaized when I consider how imediately affter I left him Lord Annesley proved falce."[8]

Shortly thereafter Elizabeth's father arranged her marriage to Robert Delaval, "a man I did not love."[9] Elizabeth refused at first, but eventually gave in.

She and Delaval were married in 1670 and, perhaps predictably, it was not a happy union. Their marriage produced no children, and in 1681 Elizabeth left her husband, who died the following year. In 1686, Elizabeth Delaval married a much younger man; she became a Jacobite agent following the Glorious Revolution, relocating to France in 1689, where she died in 1717.[10] Her meditations and prayers were composed between 1662 and 1672. She later revised them, perhaps in anticipation of publication, and at that time added autobiographical material and notes, but these do not address the later events of her life.[11] Consequently, her reflections are those of a young woman. Like many early modern Englishwomen, Elizabeth Delaval looked to her religion to provide solace and give meaning to the vicissitudes, both blows and blessings, of her life, while struggling to grapple with the demands and ideals set out for her, both as a Christian and as a woman.

Prescriptive literature in early modern England was quite clear on what constituted proper female behavior, which Suzanne W. Hull, writing about the didactic works aimed at early modern Englishwomen, summed up as "chaste, silent and obedient."[12] Of these, the most important was obedience; to some extent chastity and silence themselves were the products of obedience, as women reined in their sexuality and held their tongues in obedience to the commands of both God and male authority figures, fathers and, in particular, husbands. Beyond obedience was the religious requirement that women be subordinate to men, and wives especially be subject to their husbands in all things, following the instructions of Paul. These same texts were emphasized in the Church of England's homily on marriage, which would have conveyed the necessity of wifely obedience to every Englishwoman. These texts were also cited by William Gouge in his section on "Particular Duties of Wives" in his popular and influential *Of Domestical Duties* (1622). Gouge's overwhelming mandate for women was subjection. For Gouge, this subjection included the wife's recognition of her husband's superiority and her reverence to him on that account, but he stressed that "The principle part of that submission which . . . is required of a wife, consisteth in obedience."[13]

Like many early modern women, Elizabeth struggled with obedience, noting in herself "a perversenesse in my nature hateing all maner of subjection" and even in the matter of her marriage could not even bring herself to win over her aunt "by kind submissive way's" even though her young man "begged it off me upon his knee's."[14] She therefore laid the blame for her failure to gain happiness as a woman—marriage to a man she loved—on her religious failure to submit and be obedient. Even when she did obey, she noted that it was often "with unwillingnesse."[15] Lack of submission and obedience to her father, aunt, and teachers was one with her inability to submit to and obey God, and these were two of the sins Elizabeth struggled with and repented of the most. She located the source of these two sins in her pride and vanity, especially her ambition and desire for praise and validation from those around her: "Gredily have I thirsted after honours and greatnesse in this world . . . though I have often smarted for my eager pursuite of vaine prayse, yet still do I dayly pursu thoses pathes that lead to destruction."[16] Life at court did not help: "I was no sooner a courtier than I begun to be unhapy, earnestly longing for the queen my misstreses favour. I secretly envy'd those that I thought had a greater share of it then my selfe. . . . Woe is me, my God; how did I in the court trifle away my precious time in labouring to be highly estimed."[17]

Clearly Elizabeth needed to achieve and be recognized for her achievements; her difficulty was that female godliness as defined by her era eschewed any such worldly recognition. Indeed, a truly godly woman would not only have not desired praise from others but also would have not believed herself worthy of it. Elizabeth found herself all too often in the opposite situation:

> prayse is what I have ardently desier'd and lok'd upon as a great good, and when I gain'd it, the delight was so great that I wou'd not entertaine one mortifying thought.
>
> At other times when I have met with reproves (though just ones) instead of being humbled and thankfull for haveing my eyes open'd, I (alass) grow impatient, disturbed, and ambitious to regaine what I have lost in the good opinion of any one, so much guilty am I of this worst sort of pride . . . to have a secret discontent when ever I find my selfe not extreamly valued in the world.[18]

As a result, often Elizabeth's response to reproof was to speak a "mulltitude of rash word's in defence of these my beloved crimes."[19] She vowed to conform to the mandated behavior for a godly woman, to "strive for such humility as may make me patiently suffer a reproach" and otherwise not to speak in anger but "stifle that passion in the birth by keeping silence till I have so far overcome it."[20] But she often failed at this.

By her own confession, when her aunt removed her from court after the marriage to Lord Annesley was proposed, "the rage of anger I am in" caused her to try to make her aunt's life miserable; not only did she "neglect the paying my aunt those dayly duty's that I ow her," but "Out of pure cross-nesse I do not faile to contradict her opinion's dayly" and "make choyse of such devertions as I know to be least agreable to her."[21] Similarly, when her father and aunt pressured Elizabeth to marry Robert Delaval, she "absolutely refused to consent to it" until they agreed to pay her debts: "We had a long and firce argument upon this subject . . . so apt is the fier that is in great youth sudenly to be kindled that the opinion I had that I was ill used by being prest to mary a man I did not love, and to mary also with a weight of debt's upon me, easely lead me into the great fault of speakeing pationate word's to my aunt, my naturall temper being much too violent when ever I thought my selfe injured," of which she heartily repented.[22] Nor was she able to hold her tongue with her new husband. Elizabeth blamed herself when Robert Delaval broke the vows of temperance he had made to her. Instead of following the godly woman's tactic of "grieving truly at what ever Mr. DeLaval did amiss which was offensive" and speaking mildly to him, "on the contrary I have by another sort of behaveour, with proud ill natured words, to often tempted him to fall into the fury of a mad and sinfull passion, and thus have been accessary to his iniquities and miserably increased my own."[23] As with obedient daughterhood, Elizabeth was, in the words of Anthony Fletcher, "simply unable to be the subservient wife."[24]

These were the gravest of Elizabeth's sins, although she cataloged many others, berating herself for sloth, gluttony, and gossip, sins to which women were thought particularly prone. Elizabeth sought in her meditations and prayers to recognize and repent of her faults so that she could amend them. She tried valiantly to conform to the ideals of religious and gender identities, which she never questioned, no matter how difficult and demanding her struggle for godly womanhood was. But time and again she was undone by a sense of self that felt entitled to happiness and fulfillment in this world.

Many women beside Elizabeth Delaval had these same struggles and turned to writing to help them articulate and explore what might be called their spiritual gender issues. Writing down meditations on behavior for the purpose of religious improvement was not solely a female practice, but the composition of such spiritual diaries, meditations, and prayers was one of the few outlets for feminine expression, especially religious expression. Theology was a male preserve, off limits for women who were barred from the necessary university educations. Nor, of course, could women preach or be ordained clergy in the English church. But the composition of prayers and meditations was a way for women to express their religious thoughts through their own personal experience; moreover, to the extent that these prayers and mediations were intended to be circulated among others—as some of them clearly were—this was a way for women to not only express themselves but also to influence others, as Dorothy, Lady Pakington, wrote, "to be some advantage to others . . . some improvement to their spiritual and eternal state."[25]

Although in these books of prayers and meditations women both expressed and promoted the accepted standards of female godliness, this potential for wider influence complicates the straightforwardly proper and private conception of women's meditations and prayers. As Effie Botonaki has pointed out, these compositions allowed women to take on other, usually male, roles while remaining within the boundaries of what was acceptable for women, those of confessor (if only of herself) and spiritual guide chief among them.[26] Moreover, there was a fundamental conflict between this wider influence, and the recognition it might engender, and the prevailing model of godly womanhood, which was, above all, one of self-abnegation. This is especially true considering that women published books of prayers and meditations; indeed, this was almost the only genre in which they could publish without any risk to their modesty. For all that Elizabeth Delaval struggled with her sinful desire for attention and recognition by the world, it is clear that she most likely revised and added to her meditations and prayers in preparation for publication.

Any woman who intruded on the public sphere by publishing risked her modesty, but a writer could offset this transgression by placing her work within what her society considered to be her greatest calling: motherhood. Thus, of women's published meditations and prayers, a widespread form was the popular genre of "mother's blessings" books, such as Dorothy Leigh's *The Mother's Blessing* (1616), in which edifying religious and maternal advice combined to present a model of ideal godly motherhood for general emulation.[27] The godly mother was the ultimate fulfillment of both a woman's religious and her gender identities, and this ideal was widely disseminated in early modern England. It dominated the books that offered advice to women on conduct, education, and domestic management, such as Hannah Woolley's *The Gentlewoman's Companion, or A Guide to the Female Sex Containing Directions of Behaviour in All Places, Companies, Relations and Conditions, from Their Childhood down to Old Age* (1673).

One of the most important duties of a godly mother was the religious nurturing and training of her children, especially daughters, and in this process a woman's own behavior as a role model was paramount. As Hannah Woolley exhorted:

> be ye Mother-patterns of Virtue to your Daughters: Let your living actions be lines of their direction. . . . Look then to your own actions, these must inform them; look to your own examples, these must conform them. . . . There is no instruction more moving, than the example of your living. By that line of yours they are to conform their own. Take heed lest the damp of your own life extinguish the light of your Childrens.[28]

The ideal of the godly mother figures prominently in Elizabeth's memoir, despite the fact that not only did she herself never have children, but circumstances had also robbed her of her own mother while an infant. As a result, Delaval's memoirs reveal that she spent a good deal of her youth searching for a mother substitute, a quest in which she sublimated her need for attention and approval into godly motherhood's ideals, particularly the one where a godly mother was not only pious but also attentive, loving, and self-sacrificing in regards to her children. Although in her personal religious struggles Elizabeth was aware of the conflict between her godly aspirations and her need for self-fulfillment and validation, she was less cognizant that while she clearly measured prospective "mothers" against the prevailing ideal, her evaluation of their godliness was related to the attention and affection these women did or did not give her.

Among the women Elizabeth considered as potential mother substitutes was her paternal grandmother, Lady Gorge. Elizabeth usually spent "four or five months" a year with her grandmother, and the relationship between them was a warm one. After Lady Gorge's death in 1665, Elizabeth remembered her with the usual praise for a godly mother: "She was a pious and tender parent. Her life was an example of good work's and constant regular devotion's. . . . She also spent much time in giveing me dayly instructions as I grew up, all that part of the yeare which I was so hapy as to pass with her."[29] Thus Elizabeth linked her grandmother's piety with the "dayly" attention she gave her granddaughter. Yet Elizabeth made it clear that the woman she primarily regarded as her mother was her father's sister, Dorothy, Lady Stanhope, in whose care Elizabeth had been raised and with whom Elizabeth resided most of the time. Elizabeth wrote that her aunt "was (even before I cou'd speak) so kind a parent as to suply the place of a mother to me."[30] Elizabeth continued to be attached to her aunt, despite the often bitter blame Elizabeth bore her aunt in the matter of Elizabeth's failed romance. Elizabeth often reminded herself of her aunt's great kindnesses, and as we have seen, she was always reminding herself to show her aunt the obedience and consideration a daughter should show a mother, to behave as a child should behave toward a parent, as Hannah Woolley had enjoined it, "with reverence, respect, humility, and observance."[31] But as we have also seen, the relationship between Elizabeth and her aunt was difficult, and those difficulties were rooted in Elizabeth's childhood. Lady Stanhope did not seem to reciprocate Elizabeth's familial sentiments; at the very least, she was unable to give Elizabeth the attention that she craved. During the entire time she lived with Lady Stanhope, Elizabeth recorded that, except for dinner, she was with her aunt "scare halph an houer . . . in the whole 24."[32] When they were together, the aunt was diffident; Elizabeth recalled that Lady Stanhope

> had allway's treated me as an only child but with this difirence, that there was allway's so much of respect mingled with her love to me that a stranger who had seen us together wou'd have geused I have been some great princes child that she toke care of, rather than the daughter of her own brother.[33]

Both Elizabeth's sense of filial duty toward her aunt and her guilt about her need for attention precluded her directly criticizing her aunt on those grounds. Instead, Elizabeth drew on the ideals of godly motherhood to record a portrait of her aunt that could be described as "the anti-godly mother."

Hannah Woolley had instructed mothers to keep a close watch over their children: "As you are a kind Mother to them, be a careful Monitor about them."[34] Lady Stanhope neglected Elizabeth, and Elizabeth makes it clear that, as a result, she formed a close relationship with a servant woman, Mrs. Carter, who became the surrogate mother to Elizabeth that her aunt was not. Mrs. Carter flattered the lonely child and indulged her, sneaking her forbidden foods, sympathizing with her complaints, and spending time alone with her. She puffed up Elizabeth's ego by predicting her "growing beauty in some lettle time wou'd certenly make a conquest of many heart's." Elizabeth adored the woman, recalling that "when tis like enough she did not care to thro away her time upon a child who wou'd most willingly have been allway's at her elbow," Mrs. Carter devised a system whereby she and Elizabeth could leave little notes for each other. Smitten with the only adult woman other than her nonresident grandmother who was willing to give Elizabeth the affection and attention she craved, Elizabeth saw Mrs. Carter as a godly woman as well: "When ever I red any discription of a whorthy good friend," Elizabeth recalled, "I presently aply'd it to her in my thought's, and as I grew up my love to her still more and more increas'd."[35] Love engendered belief in her substitute mother's godliness, and that belief, in turn, intensified further the young Elizabeth's adoration of Mrs. Carter. More than anything else, Elizabeth treasured the "private walks" that she and Mrs. Carter took, during which the servant woman would fill Elizabeth's head with tales of fairies and wishing caps. As Elizabeth later ruefully noted, that should have been a sign to her that Mrs. Carter was not to be a godly mother figure at all, since "so eagerly bent was I upon these thing's that I thought it altogether needlesse to pray or to read the holy scriptures."[36]

Elizabeth's aunt condoned all of this. Since Lady Stanhope did not provide the careful monitoring a godly mother should, "she trusted me allway's with Mris. Carter when ever she pleas'd."[37] It was Elizabeth's governess who broke the servant woman's spell over the young girl by revealing to Elizabeth that her beloved friend had been using her and betraying her. Mrs. Carter had been pumping Elizabeth to tell her anything she heard anyone say about Mrs. Carter, and the servant woman would then confront the person, naming Elizabeth as her source. The governess explained that Elizabeth was now "hated in the family and shun'd by every one when they had a mind to speake freely;" even worse, from Elizabeth's point of view, was the fact that Mrs. Carter had repeated things "which I thought she wou'd sooner have died then have reveal'd to any body."[38]

Elizabeth ended her relationship with Mrs. Carter, "much grived and ashamed" at how she had been betrayed, and the servant woman eventually left Lady Stanhope's employment, to Elizabeth's great relief. Yet even before Mrs. Carter left, Elizabeth had found a much more suitable replacement— Mrs. Corny. Mrs. Corny was "a gentellwoman of great wisdom and true piety . . . daughter to a whorthy good devine" who had come to live with Lady Stanhope. Elizabeth "grew in a lettle while to like her extreamly and at length open'd my heart to her," telling her the whole story of Mrs. Carter and "all the perplexing thought's I had which till then I had kept wholly to my selfe."[39] Elizabeth had finally found the proper, godly surrogate mother she had been seeking. Mrs. Corny listened to Elizabeth "with great patience and did not despise me," but rather she "mildly instruct'd me day after day in all nesesary truth's, which before I wou'd never listen too."[40] For all that Mrs. Corny, by Elizabeth's account, fulfilled exactly the sort of role model that Hannah Woolley approved, it was the fact that Elizabeth genuinely liked her that made her effective. Calling Mrs. Corny "a blessing sent me by God," Elizabeth wrote:

> Ever since I begun to delight in her company (prays'd be God almighty that I did so), she has made it her constant care to draw me from the vanity's of this world and to plant in my heart the love of God, with an earnest desier of obtaineing heavenly wisdom.[41]

Mrs. Corny, then, met all the requirements. Unlike Mrs. Carter, she was of proper social rank—a gentlewoman. Unlike Elizabeth's beloved and godly grandmother, Mrs. Corny was readily available where Elizabeth spent most of the year. Unlike her governess, Elizabeth found Mrs. Corny to be an appealing person, someone she liked. Most tellingly however, unlike Elizabeth's aunt, Mrs. Corny spent time with Elizabeth, giving her attention, and guiding her in piety and Christian devotion, instead of ignoring the girl and gossiping with servants. Yet even after Elizabeth found Mrs. Corny, Lady Stanhope's continued neglect remained a source of resentment.

When Elizabeth returned home after her first sojourn at court, she was upset to find her aunt much taken with a new servant woman, upon whom Lady Stanhope lavished the time and affection she denied her niece. Once again, Elizabeth cloaked her criticism in the tropes of godly female ideals. Hannah Woolley had cautioned against such behavior with servants:

> Be courteous to all the Servants . . . but not over-familiar with any of them, lest they grow rude and sawcy with you; and indeed too much familiarity is not good with any, for contempt is commonly the product thereof.[42]

Elizabeth perhaps somewhat pointedly prayed that God would pardon her aunt's

> excesse of love to a creature in this world. . . . For (alass) she dayly trifled away most of her precious time in Mris. Potters company, which might have been spent in praiseing or in praying to thee, or elce in reading the work's of holy men, by which she might have improved her selfe in the knowledge of thy blessed will.[43]

Not only was Elizabeth clearly feeling jealousy of the one "who posseses that love which I covet," but the one her aunt preferred was a lowborn servant, which offended Elizabeth's sense of class and doubled her mortification:

> How much is my heart now opress'd with grife to find my aunt dote upon a creature with the most tender affection in the world, who is so meanly born that I am asham'd to tell my selfe I envy her.
>
> And yet it is but to true, for whilest she is put into my aunt's bosome, I am treated with a cold respect and selldome have any share of her famillar kindnesse. . . . I will put it out of my thought's that she is daughter to a coachman and that the greatest honour her mother has to brag of is her having been my brother Richmond's nurse.[44]

Although she condemned her aunt's lack of godliness, Elizabeth took "her lack of kindnesse to me and the increase of it to her servant" as a punishment for the many sins Elizabeth had acquired at court.[45] Moreover, remembering how often she had disobeyed or spoken rashly to her aunt, Elizabeth wrote, "Curiosety in inquiering after the faults of our parent's commonly procedes from an evill princeple, from an inclenation in us to have an excuse ready for not paying them due reverence."[46]

Elizabeth's interpretation of her fraught relationship with her aunt was directly linked to the struggle that was at the core of Elizabeth's religious identity: the struggle between a craving for external validation and attention and a guilt-inducing religious ideal that denounced such desires. When Elizabeth returned home after her first stay at court, her desire "to gaine the uncerten vaine glory my heart has thirsted after" led her to spend seven weeks working very hard to stage a "refined pastorall" with servants and locals.[47] She noted it was a great success and did, indeed, earn her praise "to the height of my expectation. . . . I for my part was transported with delight that I had so well gone through the hard tasque that I had set my selfe."[48] Yet in her meditations, she repented of "haveing flung away so much time in vanity," as well as the expense to her aunt. Elizabeth's religious identity did not allow a woman that means to self-fulfillment. The only acceptable path of achievement her spiritual gender identity permitted was the mastering of self-abnegation through submission, obedience, and docility, the hallmarks of the godly woman. Like many women of her era, Elizabeth struggled and, more often than not, failed at this. Despite her best efforts, Elizabeth was never able really to let go of her anger and bitterness at being denied earthly happiness, no matter how often she tried to focus her sights on heaven. Elizabeth continued to have a sense of the injustices toward her, which resulted in a violation and starvation of some essential part of herself. Elizabeth's reflections and prayers did offer her comfort: despite her frustrations, she was assured that she was on the path to salvation, and God would have mercy on her in her weakness as a sinner and a woman. But it is worth noting that she seems to have ultimately abandoned the path of wifely submission, at least where Robert Delaval was concerned, and later she married a man to her own liking. In her meditations, Elizabeth never questioned the ideals of godly womanhood or the standards of godly motherhood, by which she judged the older women in her life, but in her failures and frustrations, and her eventual action to make a happier life for herself, we can see a nascent new sense of a more individual and entitled self, an emerging modern sense of self that would eventually remix and reformulate religious and gender identities.

Notes

1. Sara Mendelson and Patricia Crawford, *Women in Early Modern England, 1550–1720* (Oxford: Clarendon Press, 1998), 31.
2. Mendelson and Crawford, *Women in Early Modern England*, 30.
3. Mendelson and Crawford, *Women in Early Modern England*, 226–27; Sara Heller Mendelson, "Stuart women's diaries and occasional memoirs," in *Women in English Society 1500–1800*, ed. Mary Prior (New York: Methuen, 1985), 185 [181–210]; Anthony Fletcher, *Gender, Sex and Subordination in England, 1500–1800* (New Haven: Yale University Press, 1995), 354–55; Patricia Crawford, *Women and Religion in England, 1500–1720* (London: Routledge, 1993), 79, 82–83; Effie Botonaki, "Seventeenth-Century Englishwomen's Spiritual Diaries: Self-Examination, Covenanting, and Account Keeping," *The Sixteenth Century Journal* 30.1 (1999): 3–21.
4. Margaret J. M. Ezell, "Delaval, Lady Elizabeth," *Oxford Dictionary of National Biography* (2004–10) (hereafter ODNB), doi.org/10.1093/ref:odnb/68215. On the prayer guides written for the public, see Cynthia Garrett, "The Rhetoric of Supplication: Prayer Theory in Seventeenth-Century England," *Renaissance Quarterly*, 46.2, (1993): 328–57.
5. Ezell, "Delaval, Lady Elizabeth"; Rosalind K. Marshall, "Livingston, James, of Kinnaird, first Earl of Newburgh," ODNB, doi.org/10.1093/ref:odnb/16807; Ann Hughes, "Stuart [nee Howard], Katherine, Lady Aubigny," ODNB, doi.org/10.1093/ref:odnb/66716; Douglas G. Greene, "Introduction," *The Meditations*

of Lady Elizabeth Delaval Written between 1662 and 1671, ed. Douglas G. Greene (Gateshead, UK; Surtees Society, 1978), 1. Ezell gives Elizabeth's birth year as 1648, while Greene maintains it was 1649.

6. Elizabeth Delaval, *Meditations*, 155. Hereafter *Meditations* will refer to Delaval's own writings, and "Greene" to those of her editor. Throughout her *Meditations*, Elizabeth Delaval demonstrates very idiosyncratic orthography as here. Consequently, each subsequent instance will not be noted.

7. Delaval, *Meditations*, 170.

8. Delaval, *Meditations*, 173.

9. Delaval, *Meditations*, 69.

10. Ezell, *ODNB*; Greene, 12–17.

11. Ezell dates the entries between 1663–1672 and Greene, between 1662–1671.

12. Suzanne W. Hull, *Chaste, Silent & Obedient: English Books for Women, 1475–1640* (San Marino, CA: Huntington Library, 1982).

13. William Gouge, *Of Domesticall Duties* (1622), 286.

14. Delaval, *Meditations*, 54, 112.

15. Delaval, *Meditations*, 54.

16. Delaval, *Meditations*, 137, 56.

17. Delaval, *Meditations*, 88, 63.

18. Delaval, *Meditations*, 103–4.

19. Delaval, *Meditations*, 52.

20. Delaval, *Meditations*, 38, 47.

21. Delaval, *Meditations*, 112–13.

22. Delaval, *Meditations*, 68, 69.

23. Delaval, *Meditations*, 210.

24. Fletcher, *Gender, Sex and Subordination*, 360.

25. Lady Dorothy Pakington, "Private Prayers," the tenth prayer, "For Resignation," Bodl. MS Add. B. 58., unpaginated.

26. Botonaki, "Spiritual Diaries," 3–21.

27. Patricia Crawford noted that five women published books of motherly advice in the seventeenth century prior to the civil wars. While the Countess of Lincoln's was primarily aimed at promoting breastfeeding, the other four, all by gentlewomen, mixed religious and maternal advice in a classic "mother's blessing" style. Crawford, "Women's published writings 1600–1700," in *Women in English Society 1500–1800*, ed. Mary Prior (New York: Methuen, 1985), 222 [211–31]. After the Civil War, these works, which continued in publication, were joined by Susanna Bell's *The Legacy of a Dying Mother* (1673). None of these had the enduring success, however, of Dorothy Leigh's *The Mother's Blessing*, first published in 1616, which eventually reached nineteen editions before 1640 and was republished after that in at least four more editions, the latest in 1674. See Catherine Gray, "Feeding on the Seed of the Woman: Dorothy Leigh and the Figure of Maternal Dissent," *English Literary History* 68.3 (2001): 563, 585 n4 [563–92]. Gray argues that Leigh's book had a political aspect as well, mounting an oblique attack on "royal, patriarchal" ideology.

28. Hannah Woolley, *The Gentlewoman's Companion, or A Guide to the Female Sex Containing Directions of Behaviour in All Places, Companies, Relations and*

Conditions, from Their Childhood down to Old Age (London: 1673), 3. Hereafter *GC*. Although the publication date for this work is usually given as 1675, the edition in Early English Books Online is dated 1673. Most writers of prescriptive literature in this time period, of course, were men, most notably William Gouge who has already been mentioned, but Bathsua Makin was also writing about women's education and training contemporary to Woolley. Makin's work, *An Essay to Revive the Antient Education of Gentlewomen,* was published in 1673, the same year as Woolley's *Gentlewoman's Companion.*

29. Delaval, *Meditations,* 68.
30. Delaval, *Meditations,* 30. Elizabeth notes that her aunt was the person "who I loke upon as a parent, since she toke me out of my cradell and has ever since provided for me like one, and therefore may justly chalenge that tytle from me; though not wholy so by nature, yet by adoption I may recon my selfe to be her child" (*Meditations,* 111–12).
31. Woolley, *GC,* 22.
32. Delaval, *Meditations,* 31.
33. Delaval, *Meditations,* 124.
34. Woolley, *GC,* 3.
35. Delaval, *Meditations,* 29–30.
36. Delaval, *Meditations,* 31.
37. Delaval, *Meditations,* 30.
38. Delaval, *Meditations,* 33.
39. Delaval, *Meditations,* 34. Elizabeth noted that "My aunt parted with Mris. Carten [*sic*] not without regret, but I rejoyced at her going; for how cou'd I posibly have seen her dayly and not at one time or other have show'd a sharp resentment for haveing been so long deluded by her" (35).
40. Delaval, *Meditations,* 34.
41. Delaval, *Meditations,* 34.
42. Woolley, *GC,* 27–28.
43. Delaval, *Meditations,* 64.
44. Delaval, *Meditations,* 37–38.
45. Delaval, *Meditations,* 63–64.
46. Delaval, *Meditations,* 113.
47. Delaval, *Meditations,* 43.
48. Delaval, *Meditations,* 40.

CHAPTER 7

Haunting History: Women, Catholicism, and the Writing of National History in Sophia Lee's *The Recess*

Kaley A. Kramer

Sophia Lee's *The Recess; Or, A Tale of Other Times* (1783–1785) articulates the fascination that Protestant Britain had with Catholicism late into the eighteenth century. Set during the reign of Elizabeth I, the narrative is located at the fault line between Britain's Protestant future and its Catholic past. Written during the first heyday of British historiography that established the very notion of a "national history"—David Hume, Oliver Goldsmith, and Catherine Macaulay all wrote "The History of England" between 1754 and 1771—*The Recess* excavates the "remainders" and "unsubsumed elements" of these histories.[1] The titular "recess" is a physical reminder of England's Catholic past—a past that the Henrician Reformation aggressively sought to erase. The "site of vanished cultural territory" is the ruined abbey in Lee's novel, a physical artifact that figures the "real" space of history.[2] More importantly, the recess in which Lee's narrators, Matilda and Ellinor (the fictional twin daughters of Mary, Queen of Scots) take shelter is also a metaphor for the crisis of representation in the wake of the Reformation for both Protestant and Catholic historians. Lee's choice of an abbey for her setting brings together the particular nexus between historiography and hagiography: in this specific place both secular and sacred histories can be traced.

For the Protestant reader, narratives about the lives of the saints are tainted with superstition and incredulity. *The Recess* offers the reader a space in which the cultural traces of hagiography (if not strictly hagiographic subject matter) productively complicate the inexorable, progressive, and ontological certainties of histories like Hume's. A "hagiographic document," as Père Hippolyte Delehaye defines it in *The Legends of the Saints: An Introduction to Hagiography* (1927), must be "of a religious character and should aim at edification": "the term may only be applied therefore to writings inspired by devotion to the saints and intended to promote it."[3] This speaks less to the content or form of hagiography and more to its agenda and use. In Delehaye's analysis, the didactic purpose of hagiography must be the "first question" and where this is not a concern (in texts that do not seem to be "inculcating some [moral] truth"), a tale or parable, "fortif[ied] . . . by the authority of a martyr or an ascetic . . . offered an element of interest [to the reader] that was not to be despised."[4] Hagiography, which is not Holy Scripture, occupied a different place in relation to "truth": readers were not required to *believe* in hagiographies—but the connection with scripture obliged readers to acknowledge a deeper "truth" reflected and refracted in saints' lives.[5] In terms of form, Delehaye implies that the hagiography is unbounded, able to "assume any literary form suitable to the glorification of the saints, from an official record . . . to a poetical composition of the most exuberant character wholly detached from reality."[6] The ambiguity of hagiography as a category enabled its dissemination, allowed it to pass from surface to depth, from the universal exegetical system to "one embattled and increasingly defensive denomination of Christianity among others."[7] Without a clear subject and stripped of its symbolic conventions and motifs, "annunciation, vocation, trial, martyrdom, iconoclasm, reliquary encryption," hagiography nonetheless remains detectable as an approach, a method in eighteenth-century literature: a way of *telling* if not necessarily apparent in the story that is told.[8] In this transformation, it partakes of the characteristics of the Gothic and carries a similar threat of persistence and presence. Like the Gothic, it does not *appear* in "novel" forms or narratives, it is revealed as a part of the foundation of narrative and history.

"The point," claims Delehaye, "to be emphasized from the first is the distinction between hagiography and history": "the work of a hagiographer may be historical, but it is not necessarily so."[9] *The Recess* can be taken as an example of the opposite influence: the work of a historiography may also be hagiographic, where secular history demands a transcendence of fact and the fluidity of speculation and probability. Lee's text demonstrates a sophisticated awareness of the goals of historiography, particularly the Enlightenment-driven emphasis on positivistic methods and frameworks. In an age of reason, skepticism, and Protestant common sense, Lee's fictional editor submits a manuscript dredged up from the age of romance that demands faith in truths that are beyond history's purview: those "partialities and prejudices" that determine the "best and worst actions of princes."[10] *The Recess* is both reliant on history and insulated from history: it exists in a miraculous, quasi-super-natural state, preserved sufficiently from the "depredations of time" to remain accessible to a select readership of refined sensibilities (5). Matilda's narrative reinforces this editorial advice to value the truth of human character over the accuracy of historical detail: her story of suffering allows the sympathetic reader "to be juster to his God and himself, by unavoidable comparison" with his milder, more quotidian miseries (5). Yet in order for her narrative to func-tion in this way, the reader must invest some faith in the events and characters related. Matilda's story opens up a discursive space that cannot be fully satis-fied by writings like Hume's, and it is in this gap that the hagiographic mode of *The Recess* provides a supplement to the progressive march of history.

When the first volume of *The Recess* appeared to critical praise in 1783, England's Catholic past had recently reemerged in a spectacular political showdown between enlightened government ministers who pushed through the 1778 Catholic Relief Act and anti-popery factions who violently pro-tested even the limited extension of freedoms in 1780. In spite of a century of Protestant cultural ascendency and national narratives that insisted on its annihilation, English Catholicism survived. However, both its persistent presence in the bright future of the Protestant nation and the harsh treatment its adherents received through legal restrictions were sources of embarrass-ment. Like Lee's "manuscript," Catholicism had survived the reformations in England. By countering the certainty of positivistic historiography through a narrative that not only preserves absences but also cannot be fully assimi-lated, *The Recess* recognizes the necessary persistence of representational modes that are not simply subsumed and replaced. The recess, "an apart-ment" that "could not be called a cave," is the narrators' childhood home, later their sanctuary and prison (7). As a space, it is both full and empty: it houses a Catholic priest without a congregation, a mother whose children are not her own, and children whose infamous parents (the Duke of Nor-folk and Mary Stuart) exist for them only as full-length portraits. Whenever they leave the recess, Matilda and Ellinor are miraculous: they appear out of nowhere, with no connections, no backgrounds, no context, and (initially) vanish from the world just as quickly. Their spectrality invites speculation and the threat of the supernatural as alternatives to the known and certain trajectory of history. In their own struggles, Matilda and Ellinor call up the specters of those remainders of history, women and Catholics, whose refusal to be assimilated or annihilated places them outside of the epistemological framework of history. *The Recess* not only explores the relationship between history and its alternatives but also challenges the necessary dismissal of other narratives that support the plausibility of history itself. The historical setting of the novel is the key to this reading, as it calls up the immediate aftermath of the reformations and explores narratives/subjects that interrupt the necessary transition of Catholic England into Protestant Britain.

The development of historiography in the late eighteenth century emerged in tandem with the growth of a new nation. The Glorious Revolution of 1688 confirmed the Protestant future of England, a future that was extended to cover Scotland in 1707 and Ireland in 1801. That these gestures of inclusion were more political fiats than recognition of any existing common identity became immediately evident at both ends of the century. The Jacobite risings in the first half of the century kept the fear of Catholic invasion via Scotland alive as a direct threat until the death of the Young Pretender (Bonnie Prince Charlie) in 1766; the union with Ireland followed the Irish Rebellion of 1798 and quelled fears of invasion from that quarter during the Napoleonic Wars. Bookended by these anxious times and hedged about by threats from abroad, historiography began to formulate a national myth of origin to stabilize a disparate and often antagonistic set of identities. Competing accounts of the nation relied on rational methods of historical analysis; replacing Catholicism with Protestantism undergirded this process. But history as a discipline reflected the "culture of sensibility" that dominated the eighteenth century.[11] The classical tradition of history-as-events, focusing on the public actions of public men, was limited in a way that no longer satisfied readers and consumers who increasingly sought access to inward and private dimensions of public lives.[12] Sensibility crept into virtually every discourse over the course of the century, including history; its cultural predominance offered writers models of behavior that were simultaneously transcendent (based on scientific observations of the human body) and particular (recognizable in contemporary representations of virtue and vice).[13] Sensibility lent credibility to fiction by drawing on perceived (but not unproblematic) notions of morality. It also provided a readership, familiar with the conventions of sensibility, who were primed to respond appropriately to their appearance in fiction.

Hagiography is not fiction. Literally meaning "writing about saints," hagiography is rarely understood without reference to historiography. Writing prompted by faith, hagiography cannot pretend to the objective viewpoint or positivism that influenced the development of historiography during the Enlightenment. Like Catholicism, hagiography is not foreign to Britain, "until, that is, the world of discourse in which its relics are lodged [was] determined by humanist, rationalist, and Protestant values."[14] The paradigm shift that displaced the Church of Rome and instituted the Church of England recast the hermeneutics of reading through which readers made sense of and judged the truth value of narratives. The eighteenth-century audience that steadily consumed Hume's, Goldsmith's, and Macaulay's national histories could not access the cultural capital or psychological territory that provided the pre-Reformation reader access to the "legendary feats of prophets, martyrs, and saints."[15] The idea of a "sacred fiction" did not have a place in Protestant Britain; hagiography was at best an embarrassing relic, at worst, heretical. Following on from the positivism of protoscientific methodologies, historians and intellectuals like Edward Gibbon and David Hume "condemned saints' lives to the world of popular polytheism and credulity"; their faith in "objectivity" and the ability to recover an authentic past informed their scathing contempt for hagiography.[16] Dedicated to rational inquiry into the past, Enlightenment thinkers could not countenance the conventionally "fallacious biographical details and fantastic phenomena" of hagiographic narratives.[17] Hume associates hagiography with the savagery of pre-Reformation England, locating it—and by extension, Catholicism—in a primitive past; in Gibbon's *The Rise and Fall of the Roman Empire*, the worship of saints and relics corrupts the "pure and perfect simplicity" of the Christian model that Luther's Reformation returned to the world.[18] The firm connection between Catholicism, superstition, savagery, and ignorance was, as Charles Dodd wrote in his *Church History*, "nurse's language to all Protestant children."[19] Hagiography, pushed firmly into the past by Enlightenment models of historical inquiry, was the product of a previous age whose faults were corrected by positivistic, natural history.

By the mid-eighteenth century, however, hagiography became associated with a particularly pernicious kind of fiction. The energy with which its detractors forced it into the past, insisting on its obsolescence, draws on similarly determined efforts to categorize contemporary forms of writing as distinct from "the fictions of the last age" with their "improbabilities" and "invention."[20] Samuel Johnson's discussion in 1750 clearly outlined the parameters for appropriate fiction: they were meant to delight "the present generation." For Johnson, fictions "can neither employ giants to snatch away a lady from the nuptial rites, nor knights to bring her back from captivity; it can neither bewilder its personages in desarts, nor lodge them in imaginary castles."[21] His distinction rests on an implicit consensus as to what constitutes "accurate observation" and is important precisely because of the emulative potential and didactic nature of any text:

> In the romances formerly written, every transaction and sentiment was so
> remote from all that passes among men, that the reader was in very little dan-
> ger of making any application to himself; the virtues and crimes were equally
> beyond his sphere of activity; and he amused himself with heroes and with
> traitors, deliverers and persecutors, as with beings of another species, whose
> actions were regulated upon motives of their own, and who had neither faults
> nor excellences in common with himself.[22]

Johnson makes the mistake of thinking that readers of romantic texts are Quixotes. He underestimates the power of typology; of mapping a textual experience onto a real, lived one in a manner that is instructive but not enslaved by a notion of fidelity. The romance offers an idealized and extreme model for behavior. The exaggerated plots, characters, settings, style, and language of the romance is precisely the force that allows the reader to recognize similar situations in their own lives; it allows them to read lived experiences in light of the text and to draw instructive comparisons between the two. Reading the romance is the analogical step that precedes the anagogical, the transcendent, and the saintly truth. Hagiography, as a sacred fiction, was not concerned with the "factual account of human achievement" but with the expression of holiness "so that a mundane audience can have access to . . . transcendent experience."[23] Faith in transcendence finds expression in both hagiography and early romances via typology, which Julia Reinhard Lupton argues is due to the "subsumption [of hagiography] into new forms such as the novella, secular drama, and humanist biography . . . [it] functions then as the consummate model . . . a generic paradigm."[24] Johnson's directions for appropriate fiction insist on the particular and the shared, valuing the experience of "general converse" for authors rather than the practice of storing up "some fluency of language . . . retir[ing] to his closet, let[ting] loose his invention, and heat[ing] his mind with incredibilities": "a book was thus produced without fear of criticism, without the toil of study, without knowledge of nature, or acquaintance with life."[25] This description of process recalls Protestant stereotypes of Catholic practices, attributes, and ignorance: easily swayed by convincing language, preferring monastic isolation, content with blind faith in church leaders, and woefully resistant to study and (Protestant) knowledge. Hagiography shares with "romances formerly written" an apparently cavalier attitude to facts and physical possibility only if understood from outside of its epistemological matrix; it is threatening because it survives "beyond the moment of [its] historical supersedure."[26]

History—for both Matilda and Ellinor—is what happens to other people; their narrative, though marked with probability is not possible. Both women spend their energies desperately seeking recognition or acknowledgment of who they are. This gradually fades from the desire for a full-scale royal proclamation, complete with a pardon for their imprisoned mother from Elizabeth I, to a private meeting with their brother, then King James I (VI). Ellinor in particular, rages against her enforced anonymity, driven by her own ambition and her anger at being the unwitting dupe of Elizabeth in signing a "confession" denying her identity and that of Matilda, on a promise of freedom for the Queen of Scots. Although Matilda's long suffering provides the novel with its structure, Ellinor's shorter but considerably more dramatic narrative completes the range of available positions for those excluded from history: Matilda fades away; Ellinor burns out. Neither achieves anything close to their goals of public recognition or, at least, familial reconciliation. Assimilated (married off to various loyal Elizabethan courtiers) or annihilated (Ellinor's madness, Matilda's incarceration), they are persistently denied access to or inclusion in official history if they insist on their personal histories and identities. And yet, as evident in Matilda's opening address, at least one has survived. Matilda's earnest wish at the beginning (which is her ending) is that her "feeble frame be covered with the dust from which it sprung, and no trace of my ever having existed . . . remain" (7). Her narrative already mitigates this, excavated like a relic and thrust back into public view to be recognized by those readers with "hearts . . . enriched with sensibility" (5). But her wish also points to the inevitable return of everything buried and the impossibility of leaving "no trace."

The enigmatic "Advertisement" is thus a parergon, a framing device that is simultaneously inside and external to the narrative,[27] a boundary that marks its status both as fiction and as historical artifact. It is precisely at this moment that we can witness Lee's challenge to the epistemological frameworks that preserve the divide between history and literature—and with that, the dominant Protestant ethos and the beleaguered Catholic minority. The packet of letters prepared and presented by the fictional editor via the Advertisement is written by Matilda and contains Ellinor's own conflicting version of the same events. A note that barely registers in the Advertisement is that *The Recess* is apparently part of a larger manuscript, from which it has been "extracted" (5). Following Matilda's story does not lead the reader to any clarity, and the Advertisement insists that the confusion of the text presented is part of its claim to authenticity, preserved due to an "inviolable respect for truth" (5). This is not exactly the "truth" that Johnson might expect from a text; rather, it is an admixture of verifiable fact (the existence of Elizabeth and her court) with the imagined (every move that Matilda and Ellinor make in the novel). The imagined destabilizes the real, and the real buttresses the imagined. In this indeterminate space, Matilda concludes her story on yet another mystery: the "casket" that the named reader, Adelaide de Montmorenci, receives as her inheritance from Matilda (326).

Caskets are particularly resonant within the history of Mary, Queen of Scots. In 1567–1568, Mary was implicated in the murder of Henry Stuart, Lord Darnley, her second husband, as a conspirator with her alleged lover (and third husband), James Hepburn, Earl of Bothwell. Mary's opponents claimed that discovery of a casket filled with letters belonging to Bothwell, incriminated Mary as a willing partner in Darnley's suspicious death. The documents comprised letters and sonnets, allegedly written to Bothwell by

Mary. Their authenticity has been the subject of debate since and has not been conclusively decided.[28] These letters provided Elizabeth with the rationale for keeping Mary in England and "stained [Mary's] reputation across western Europe."[29] Mary's long life of incarceration ended with another secret correspondence: the Babington Plot. This conviction, like the casket letters and the story of Elizabeth's accidental signing of the warrant for Mary's death, takes historiography into the realm of speculation and belief. Briefly, the Babington Plot was a conspiracy to assassinate Elizabeth and place Mary on the throne. It originated among a group of English Catholics close to the court, including the Spanish ambassador and had the blessing of Philip of Spain. Anthony Babington, a young conspirator, engineered a correspondence with Mary, Queen of Scots, that was, unbeknownst to either party, monitored closely by Walsingham. After discovery, Babington briefly fled London but was imprisoned and executed. Mary remained ignorant of the failure of the plot, and her exact knowledge of the extent of the conspiracy has not been conclusively ascertained. Mary protested her innocence throughout her trial at Fotheringay Castle, especially of the plotters' final aim of assassination, but the correspondence with Anthony Babington was sufficient to condemn her.[30] Hume claims her willingness to die regardless of her innocence as the result of a life "filled with bitterness and sorrow" and in Mary's belief that her devout Catholicism threatened England's reformed religion.[31] Neither George Buchanan (1506–1582) nor John Knox (1514–1572), old enemies who vilified Mary for her gender, her politics, and her religion, lived to comment on the Babington Plot or Mary's execution. Their attacks on Mary's reign before and during her imprisonment in England had already established the characteristics that endured in her reputation after death.[32] Adam Blackwood (1539–1613), a Roman Catholic apologist, eulogized Mary and defended her innocence, though from France, which did little to improve the opinion of Catholicism in England.[33] For Hume, Robertson, and Goldsmith, there is little doubt of her guilt. Hume's portrait of Elizabeth, though admitting her jealousy of the personal attractions of Mary, Queen of Scots, considers Mary endowed with only the "superficial gestures of court" learned during her residence in France, while Elizabeth's "education" led her to the truth of the reformed religion.[34] Goldsmith admits the casket letters are "not free from the suspicion of forgery" but concludes, "the reasons for their authenticity seem to prevail."[35]

The need for authenticity not only indicates the anxiety surrounding interpretation, subjectivity, and speculation in historical writing but also demonstrates the neurotic obsession in eighteenth-century national histories to account for those elements that it cannot explain or subsume. The caskets and secret letters that marked Mary's reign have become fetishized objects for

historiographers. Even when the contents of the casket and the letters are categorized, inventoried, and pawed over by generations of historians, the truth
of Mary's intentions in either affair remains entirely opaque. Beyond the limit
of the casket lies the unexplained and inexplicable. What carries the reader
past this radical indeterminacy is not reason but the acceptance of mystery.

For eighteenth-century historiographers, the persistence of mystery in history is problematic, for example, to admit that Catholicism was not simply
the loser in the Reformation, but another participant in a series of reformations challenges, with the account of that story from the winners' perspective
(Protestantism). But the persistence of Mary, Queen of Scots, as a sympathetic figure into the eighteenth century demonstrates the ways in which
Protestantism struggled to contain Catholicism within prescribed boundaries.
Even Mary's eventual resting place, the magnificent marble tomb in Henry
VII's chapel in Westminster Cathedral, gestures toward this national confusion as to her place in history. A convicted traitor and conspirator, Mary was
nonetheless buried with some ceremony in Peterborough Cathedral; James
I later moved her remains to Westminster Cathedral.[36] In spite of Mary's
stained record, she rests in the spiritual heart of the nation. In the novel, it
is Elizabeth who revives Mary almost immediately after her death. With the
Queen of Scots and Ellinor safely dead and Matilda exiled, Elizabeth ends
her days nonetheless "sunk in the chilling melancholy of despair and hope-
less age" (266). Ellinor's sudden reappearance—a bodily resurrection from
Elizabeth's point of view—precipitates Elizabeth's final madness and death.
Ophelia-like, Ellinor confronts Elizabeth with the deaths of Essex, Matilda,
and the Queen of Scots, anticipating her own end and desiring only that
Elizabeth allow her to be "buried in Fotheringay; and be sure I have *women*
to attend me; *be sure* of that—you know the reason" (267).[37] Ellinor has,
quite literally for the terrified queen, escaped her casket; she is the return of
the repressed, a "being supernatural" who quite undoes Elizabeth's "mighty
mind" (268, 269).

The destruction of the recess and surrounding ruins while Ellinor lives
there as the wife of the Duke of Arlington leads to the discovery of "a small
iron chest strongly fastened" (208). The servant who proposes the demoli-
tion of the ruins to the great distress of Ellinor and pleasure of her husband
and jailer, Lord Arlington, dies after a lingering illness but requests a final
meeting with Ellinor, without which he "could not have departed in peace"
(208). During the improvement of Arlington's property, the servant observes
a "common labourer turn up something which tried his whole strength"
(208). Forcing the laborer to accept him as a partner in the discovery, the
servant takes the uncovered "casket" into hiding on the pretense of meeting
again with this laborer to open and divide evenly the bounty. Taking the

casket "with a purpose God has severely punished," the servant finds, "under a number of papers and trifles of no value," a "large sum in gold, and a few jewels" (208). Replacing these with an "iron crucifix and several rusty keys," he then locks the casket, allows the laborer to wrestle with opening it for no gain. Buying secrecy with twenty nobles, the servant makes plans to escape to London with his "guilty gains." (208) But the treasure is not simply there for anyone: "from [that] moment, peace, appetite, and rest have fled me . . . the idea that my treasure was stolen, has made me often start up . . . I have flown in the dead of night to convince myself it was safe—imaginary whispers have ever been near my bed, and uncertain forms have glided into my chamber—the dawn of day never gave me relief, every eye seemed to dive into my secret, and every hand to be intent on impoverishing me" (208–9). It is, of course, the papers, not the jewels, that tempt Ellinor to promise a vow of silence about the discovery of the casket.

Like so many items in Gothic novels, the casket dug out of the dust that covers the recess has a will of its own. It is more than a simple relic, and only a very specific audience (Ellinor) can properly understand it. The fabulous coincidence of Ellinor's acquisition of the casket is based on the servant's remembering, on the point of death, that she was "said to have been brought up in these ruins" (209). That slight memory leads him to the tenuous conclusion that in passing on the casket to Ellinor, he might "only restore it to the right owner" (209). Possessed of a "strange desire to examine the papers," Ellinor forgets the servant almost immediately and considers the casket a "gift [that] heaven seemed so strangely to have put into my hands" (209). Her "strange desire" is connected by the repetition of the word to the gift's divine provenance. The jewels and gold might offer "assistance and comfort" to her lost sister, Matilda, and provide the rationale for "receiving and secreting" the casket from her husband, whose wealth she refuses to use for that purpose "had I been the unlimited mistress of it" (209). Her "strange desire" is answered in the discovery that the papers "consisted chiefly of the correspondence between Mrs. Marlow and Father Anthony, while yet they were lovers" (209). Reading the letters "recall[s]" Ellinor to "life and sensibility":

> I raised my eyes to heaven in search of their pure translated souls, and wandering from planet to planet, fancied there must be one peculiarly allotted to lovers now no longer unhappy—A thousand trifles whose value must ever be ideal and local, were preserved with these letters:—cyphers, hair, sonnets, dear perpetuators of those bright hours of youth we look back on with pleasure to the last moments of decaying life. I kissed the innocent reliques of such an unhappy attachment with devout regard, and held them not the least part of my legacy. (210)

Ellinor's attentions to the casket's contents verge on worship. The letters communicate far more than the sentiments of the writers; they allow Ellinor to transcend her suffering, to project her own unhappiness into an imagined community of fellow sufferers. Ellinor later stages her own death, going so far as to "plac[e] herself *and treasure* in the homely coffin" (218). Safely away, she reburies the casket: "To the earth that gave, I have restored the remainder; it is buried eastward under the spreading chestnut tree planted by Edward IV" (219).

There are several caskets and packets throughout the novel, containing secret and potentially treasonous writing that connects Matilda and Ellinor to their various origins, including testimonials of their true birth and parentage. Like their illustrious mother, Matilda and Ellinor struggle with questions of authenticity and forgery, their motivations, like Mary's, extracted from letters, testimonials, and other documents. After narrating the story of her life, and the twins' true parentage and birth, Mrs. Marlow delivers a casket "which contained the papers she mentioned and divers attestations, signed by herself, and the late Lady Scrope" (36). Matilda does not specify whether this casket accompanies them when they leave the recess with Lord Leicester, but Elizabeth uncovers the truth when the testimonials are found on Ellinor's person, as well as her correspondence with Essex (170–71). Matilda, on the verge of meeting King James, recalls "several caskets" hidden at Kenilworth Castle by Lord Leicester to which she had added "Mrs. Marlow's papers and the testimonials of my birth" (273). Returning to the now-changed castle, she finds the hiding place secure and the "well-remembered caskets" still in place (275). The casket bequeathed at the end of the novel remains closed, its contents a mystery, but it recalls episodes within each of the fictional sister's story and with the infamous casket letters that initiated the long imprisonment of Mary, Queen of Scots. In *The Recess*, particular objects, carried secretly in caskets or worn close to the body, take on the force of religious relics. The transmission, concealment, and revelation of each casket and packet in the novel, like the documents that incriminated and finally condemned Mary, depend on the intentions of their readers for their meaning and effect. Meaning, in all of these cases, exceeds the moment of production and intended audience. The letters and documents become "caskets" for the meaning that they convey. After their moment, they are buried over time and are excavated alongside other artifacts whose accidental propinquity might be misunderstood as causal. Mary's sonnets (if she is indeed the author) to Bothwell indicate a connection between them, but it is potentially fallacious to presume that connection implicates her in the plot to kill Darnley. Viewed from this perspective, the historical narrative appears as fabulous as any fiction. The "truth" must lie elsewhere. To some characters, the letters that circulate through *The Recess* are inert (the servant who finds the casket in the ruins of the Abbey), but in the right hands, these same missives are extremely volatile (Ellinor's transcendent experience of reconnection with the long-dead Mrs. Marlow). The lesson of Lee's novel is that texts are targeted; not every text is for every reader. Lee's "editor" recommends the novel to readers of a particular sensibility; likewise, the correspondence between Norfolk and Mary, Father Anthony and Mrs. Marlow require a reader with particular sympathies. Lee's ideal reader transcends particularities, admits mystery, and does not mistake realism for the real. In short, the reader trusts the text. This connection to the spirit of the writers, beyond the narrative that the writing contains, verges on the supernatural, or the hagiographic.

Other critics have noted a similar dynamic in the portrayal of Mary, particularly in the descriptions of her from both Matilda and Ellinor. In her study of the afterlife of the Queen of Scots, Jayne Elizabeth Lewis spends some time on the single appearance of Mary in *The Recess* as an example of an encounter with the sublime.[38] In Lewis's reading, Mary "belongs very much within the sentimental tradition: she lives and does not live; and the story of her life is that of her death."[39] The "sentimental tradition," then, comes very close to the faith required by hagiography. Echoing the trademark of hagiographic narratives, Mary suffers, she is weak, and enters the scene supported by "two maids, without whose assistance she could not move" (75). Throughout, even the mere mention of Mary's name produces sensational results: Ellinor's invocation of her murdered mother leads to Elizabeth's madness and death; the news of their mother's execution renders both Matilda and Ellinor insensible; in exile, the twins find that "Mary" is a cultural shibboleth, indicating the motivations of diverse characters. The twins meet their mother in an episode that establishes the particularly charged power that Mary lends objects that contain and define her. Buried in the recess, the young girls invent stories about the "whole-length pictures" that adorn "the best room" (9). The portrait of Norfolk, who Ellinor strongly resembles, returns Matilda's gaze, "full of a tender sweetness," and inspires a "sentiment of veneration, mingled with surprising softness [that] pierced my soul at once" (9), But it is the next picture that elevates this veneration to "a thousand melting sensations," prefiguring their later response in Mary's brief presence:

> If the last picture awakened veneration, this seemed to call forth a thousand melting sensations; the tears rushed involuntarily into our eyes, and, clasping, we wept upon the bosoms of each other. "Ah! Who can these be?" cried we together. "Why do our hearts thus throb before inanimate canvas? surely everything we behold is but part of one great mystery; when will the day come, destined to clear it up?" (10)

The vitality of the portraits makes them far more than simply representations of Mary and Norfolk: they are Mary and Norfolk. The relationship between the twins and these particular portraits grants them access to a "great mystery." Mrs. Marlow's narrative, which follows soon after, "clears up" some part of the mystery, but the greater part of it, the "partialities and prejudices" that led to the mystery, remain hidden (5). Ignorant of the subjects of the painting and unaware of any rational reason for their reactions, Matilda and Ellinor nonetheless "lived in the presence of these pictures as if they understood us, and blushed when we were guilty of the slightest folly" (10).

From echo to encounter: early in the novel, Matilda and Ellinor attempt to visit their imprisoned mother. What they find is "the Saint" (75). Mary, Queen of Scots, is not a historical figure or a sublime object. Lee, via Matilda's narrative voice, sanctifies the renegade queen. Matilda's reaction has all the hallmarks of sensibility:

> Our emotions were too rapid and strong for description; we wept—we incoherently exclaimed—and striking ourselves eagerly against the bars, seemed to hope some supernatural strength would break them. . . . I neither could behold her for my tears, or resolve to lose a look by indulging in them.—She drew near the spot where we stood, when our hands, which we had thrust, in supplication, through the bars, caught her attention.—She raised her fine eyes, with their usual divine composure, to the window—I would have spoke, but my lips denied all utterance. . . . When she withdrew her eyes, she carried my very soul with her; all my strength failed at once, and I sunk in a swoon in my sister's arms. (75–76)

"Supernatural," "divine," "supplication:" this is the language of worship, of rapture, of hagiography. Mary's entire presence in this scene calls up a particularly Catholic set of images. Mary and her two attendants resemble the three Marys at the crucifixion.[40] The "habit of plain purple" connects her with Christ, "dressed in a purple robe" by Pilate's soldiers.[41] The veil, beads, and cross belong to a cloistered nun. Taken as a whole, this portrait of a "weakened" and suffering woman specifically recalls the Marian iconography of the *mater dolorosa*: a touchstone of Catholicism. Lee's portrayal of the Queen of Scots decisively pushes any possible interpretation of the historical woman into hagiography.

To understand *The Recess*, the reader must hold two contradictory precepts in mind: s/he must acknowledge the facticity of the setting *and* populate it with characters and events that, quite simply, never happened. Lee's caskets are metonymic for the processes of the novel as a whole. The ways in which characters interact with caskets, letters, mementos, and portraits indicates that objects participate in systems of representation. They become iconic. They invite spectrality and speculation into a positivistic framework. Just as the caskets in the story are more than mere receptacles, and carry within them a mystery that reveals by its concealment, and just as the novel contains within it a necessary fiction (that is, that Mary's daughters survived) without which the novel ceases to make sense (especially to the Protestant mind), so ultimately, does hagiography function. It conceals a truth in the garments of faith, or better still, locates it in the recesses of national history. This is crypto-Catholicism in a Protestant milieu—truth is a question of belief as much as it is the product of empirical observation. Lee's novel is an epistemological bridge between the literary and the historical, the hagio- and the historio. The Protestant communion—the British nation—at the end of the eighteenth century was an act of faith as much as it was a product of Enlightenment rationality.

Notes

1. Julie Reinhard Lupton, *Afterlives of the Saints: Hagiography, Typology and Renaissance Literature* (Stanford, CA: Stanford University Press, 1996), xxviii.
2. David Punter, *Gothic Pathologies: The Text, the Body, and the Law* (Basingstoke, UK: Macmillan, 1998), 1. Punter specifically locates the Gothic on the "site of vanished cultural territory." The Gothic properties of *The Recess* have been the subject of considerable scholarship, and the novel is now considered part of the Gothic "canon."
3. Hippolyte Delehaye, SJ, *The Legends of the Saints: An Introduction to Hagiography* (1907), trans. V. M. Crawford; introduction by Richard J. Schoeck (Notre Dame, IN: University of Notre Dame Press, reprinted 1961), 2.
4. Delehaye, 63.
5. Delehaye, 70.
6. Delehaye, 3.
7. Lupton, xxviii.
8. Lupton, xxi.
9. Delehaye, 3.
10. Sophia Lee, *The Recess; Or, A Tale of Other Times* (1783–1785), ed. April Alliston (Lexington, KY: The University Press of Kentucky, 2000), 5. All further references are from this edition and will be noted parenthetically in the text.
11. G. J. Barker-Benfield, *The Culture of Sensibility: Sex and Society in Eighteenth-Century Britain* (Chicago and London: University of Chicago Press, 1992).
12. Mark Salber Phillips, "Adam Smith and the History of Private Life: Social and Sentimental Narratives in 18th-Century Historiography," in *The Historical Imagination in Early Modern Britain: History, Rhetoric, and Fiction, 1500–1800*, ed. David Harris Sacks and Donald R. Kelley (Cambridge: Cambridge University Press, 1997), 319 [318–42].
13. See Barker-Benfield, 1–37.

14. Lupton, xxx.
15. Linda L. Coon, *Sacred Fictions: Holy Women and Hagiography in Late Antiquity* (Philadelphia: University of Pennsylvania Press, 1997), 7.
16. Coon, 5.
17. Coon, 5.
18. David Hume, *The Natural History of Religion*, introduction by John Mackinnon Robertson (London: A. & H. Bradlaugh Bonner, 1889), http://files.libertyfund.org/files/340/Hume_0211_EBk_v6.0.pdf; Edward Gibbon, *The History of the Decline and Fall of the Roman Empire*, 6 vols. (London: printed for W. Strahan and T. Cadell, 1776–1789), chapter 25, http://www.fordham.edu/Halsall/source/gibbon-decline28.asp.
19. Charles Dodd, *Dodd's Church History of England, from the Commencement of the Sixteenth Century to the Revolution in 1688; with Notes, Additions, and a Continuation by The Rev. M. A. Tierney, F.S.A*, 8 vols. (London: Charles Dolman, 1839), vol. 2, 106.
20. Samuel Johnson, *The Rambler*, no. 4, Saturday, March 31, 1750, in *The Yale Edition of the Works of Samuel Johnson*, 16 vols., ed. W. J. Bate and Albrecht B. Strauss (London: Yale University Press, 1969), vol. 3, 20 [19–25].
21. Johnson, 20.
22. Johnson, 21.
23. Coon, xxi, 9.
24. Lupton, xxxi.
25. Johnson, 20.
26. Lupton, xxix.
27. See Jacques Derrida, "The Parergon," in *The Truth in Painting*, trans. Geoff Bennington and Ian McLeod (Chicago: University of Chicago Press, 1987), chapter 1, part II.
28. A. E. MacRobert, *Mary Queen of Scots and the Casket Letters* (London: I. B. Tauris, 2002).
29. MacRobert, 1.
30. The Babington Plot is the necessary ending of any biography of the Queen of Scots: see Antonia Fraser, *Mary Queen of Scots* (London: Phoenix, 2009); John Guy, *My Heart Is My Own: The Life of Mary Queen of Scots* (London: Fourth Estate, 2004); Jayne Elizabeth Lewis, *The Trial of Mary Queen of Scots: Sixteenth-Century Crisis of Female Sovereignty* (Basingstoke, UK: Palgrave Macmillan, 1999).
31. David Hume, *The History of England, from the Invasion of Julius Caesar to the Revolution of 1688*, 6 vols. (1754–1762) (London: printed for T. Cadell, 1778), vol. 5, 50.
32. George Buchanan was Mary's tutor but later converted to the Reformed Church and published *Detectio Mariae Regina* (London, 1571), which accused Mary of involvement in Darnley's murder; John Knox was the author of *The First Blast of the Trumpet against the Monstrous Rule of Women* (Geneva, 1558), a text that earned him the ire of Elizabeth I as well as Mary.

33. Adam Blackwood, *Martyre de la Royne d'Escosse, Douairiere de France; contenant le vray discours des traïsons à elle faictes à la suscitation d'Elizabet Angloise, par lequel les mensonges, calomnies, et faulses accusations dressées contre ceste tresvertueuse, tres-catholique et tresillustre princesse son esclarcies et son innocence averse* (Edinburgh [Paris]: Jean Nafield, 1587).

34. David Hume, *The History of England*, vol. 5, 8.

35. Oliver Goldsmith, *The History of England: From the Earliest Times to the Death of George II*, 4 vols. (London: T. Davies and T. Cadell, 1771), vol. 3, 66. William Robertson also believed that the casket letters were genuine and agrees with Hume's portrayal of Mary's devout faith as the real reason for her execution. William Robertson, *The History of Scotland* (London, 1759), 175, 264–65.

36. Beside Mary's tomb is that of Margaret, Countess of Lennox, her mother-in-law; at the foot of Margaret's tomb is the kneeling figure of Lord Darnley, Mary's second husband.

37. As Alliston notes in her edition of *The Recess*, Hume, Robertson, and Goldsmith all report Mary's harsh treatment from Elizabeth's deputies, including their refusal to allow any of her women to accompany her to the block. See *The Recess*, 359, n51.

38. Jayne Elizabeth Lewis, *Mary, Queen of Scots: Romance and Nation* (London: Routledge, 1998), 136–46.

39. Lewis, 145.

40. John 19:25.

41. John 19:2.

CHAPTER 8

Stripped of Their Altars: Film, Faith, and Tudor Royal Women from the Silent Era to the Twenty-First Century, 1895–2014[1]

William B. Robison

Films depict the Tudor era with varying degrees of accuracy and invention but generally do a poor job of portraying the period of reform in England, particularly as it pertained to women. Indeed, from the first Tudor movie in 1895 to the new wave of Tudor films in the twenty-first century, they incorporate religion, if at all, merely as a subplot. They are frequently inaccurate, seldom show much understanding of doctrine and practice, and often bring presentist perspectives to their handling of religion, privileging tales of intolerance and persecution over stories about devotion and charity. Most deal with royalty and emphasize romance, especially Henry VIII and his wives, Elizabeth I and her suitors, and the tragic marriages of Mary, Queen of Scots. Few focus on the less amorous Henry VII, Lady Jane Grey, and Mary I, while Edward VI is a major character only in the many versions of *The Prince and the Pauper*.[2]

Films about the era of Tudor kings (1485–1553) generally relegate royal women to secondary, transitory, and "traditionally female" roles, offering little indication that Margaret Beaufort and Elizabeth of York were major church benefactors or that Katherine of Aragon, Anne Boleyn, and Katherine Parr were intelligent, influential Christian humanists (they give even shorter shrift to lesser figures like Margaret Roper and Anne Askew). Films about regnant Tudor queens (1553–1603) differ in that Lady Jane Grey, Mary I, Elizabeth I, and Mary, Queen of Scots, take center stage and exercise authority usually reserved to male rulers; however, this does not always lead to fuller or more accurate exposition of religion's role in their reigns.

The first Tudor royal women were Margaret Beaufort and Elizabeth of York, Henry VII's mother and queen, respectively. Genuinely devout, Margaret established the Lady Margaret Professorship of Divinity at Cambridge (1502), refounded Christ College (1505), left a bequest to create St. John's College (c.1511–16), patronized religious writers, translated *The Mirror of Gold for the Sinful Soul* and part of *The Imitation of Christ*, earned papal recognition for promoting the Feast of the Name of Jesus, and turned her chapel into a library of devotional works and center for composing spiritual music. But if BBC's *The Shadow of the Tower* (1972) depicts Margaret Beaufort (Marigold Sharman) fairly accurately, it refers to her benefactions only when Henry VII (James Maxwell) advises her to build colleges and leave governing to him (episode 12). Though Elizabeth of York (Norma West) is a major character, the series emphasizes her role in court politics and as wife and mother, failing to indicate that she followed Margaret Beaufort's example as a patron. The ludicrously gothic *Princes in the Tower* (2005) makes Margaret (Sally Edwards) the murderer of Edward V and Richard, Duke of York, and has Elizabeth (Nadia Cameron-Blake) accept Perkin Warbeck as the real incarnation of the latter, who was her brother. Elizabeth, overshadowed by her mother-in-law in real life, gets more screen time, appearing in some filmed versions of William Shakespeare's *Henry VI* and *Richard III*; however, she is essentially a political pawn in the struggle between the houses of Lancaster and York.[3]

The cinematic fate of Henry VII's daughters, Princesses Margaret and Mary, is even more outlandish. In season one of *The Tudors* (2007), Margaret (Gabrielle Anwar) is a weird amalgamation of both sisters and does little that Margaret Tudor did; the fictional Margaret marries and murders the King of Portugal, remarries to Charles Brandon, and opposes the marriage of Henry VIII to Anne Boleyn (Natalie Dormer). Otherwise, the series ignores her faith. In reality, Mary married but did not murder Louis XII of France, remarried to Brandon, and opposed the Boleyn marriage on religious grounds; however, she appears only in the fictionalized romance, *When Knighthood Was in Flower* (1922), based on the 1898 novel by Edwin Caskoden (pseudonym for Charles Major), and the Disney remake, *The Sword and the Rose* (1953), played, respectively, by Marion Davies and Glynis Johns.[4]

Far more popular with filmmakers are Henry VIII's six wives, whose reputations film has done much to shape.[5] Few films focus exclusively on one wife, but equally rarely do they take account of the religious context for the king's serial marriages. Many concentrate on the king-queen-mistress love triangle of Henry, Katherine of Aragon, and Anne Boleyn that sparked the

Henrician Reformation, but they pay little attention to religion or, in Katherine's case, portray it in a negative light. Typically, they feature Katherine in her last decade, when Henry abandoned her, and portray her as pathetic victim and/or stubborn adherent of the old, superstitious faith. In fact, she received an exemplary education, won praise from Erasmus and Jean Luis Vives, was her husband's intellectual match, and was a patron of the Church (especially Observant Franciscans), Oxford and Cambridge, and such scholars as John Leland, Thomas Linacre, Richard Pace, Vives, and Thomas Wyatt. She was neither credulous nor superstitious, supported reform from within the Church, and displayed a profound inner-directed piety. Though she had ascetic tendencies early on that may have influenced her behavior after Henry initiated divorce proceedings in 1527, it took enormous courage and well-grounded faith to resist his might as she did.[6]

Unsurprisingly, Anne Boleyn is in more films, where often her life segues into a second romantic triad with Jane Seymour, but this scenario also tends to undervalue religion. Anne's intellect, learning, and zeal for religious reform—generally acknowledged by modern scholars—receive scant attention. The emphasis on romance instead is unfortunate, for while Henry's love letters to her survive, much of their amorous activity on camera is the fruit of scriptwriters' imagination. The real Anne, though fond of a good time, encountered evangelical thought at the French court in her youth, became an avid student of scripture, assisted importation of English-language Bibles, reportedly gave Henry copies of Simon Fish's *Supplication of the Beggars* and William Tyndale's *Obedience of the Christian Man*, sought to convert monasteries to educational purposes, and was the patron of evangelical clerics, such as Thomas Cranmer, William Barlow, William Bill, Edward Fox, Thomas Goodrich, Hugh Latimer, Matthew Parker, and Nicholas Shaxton, as well as reformist scholars at Cambridge.[7] Jane, the least well studied of Henry's wives, probably was religiously conservative (supposedly she tried to dissuade Henry from dissolving the monasteries), but she is somewhat enigmatic.[8]

The latter three wives get less attention on film. When they do appear, Anne of Cleves frequently overlaps with Katherine Howard and Katherine Parr, but most filmmakers ignore the religious background to the Cleves and Howard marriages and downplay Parr's Protestantism. The best-known religious aspect of Anne's story is that Thomas Cromwell encouraged the marriage to secure an alliance with the Lutheran Schmalkaldic League, of which her brother, Duke Wilhelm, was a member. Though contemporaries like Thomas Becon and Thomas Elyot regarded her as devout, in most cases filmmakers use her for comedic purposes.[9] No one applies the adjective "devout" to the adulterous Katherine Howard, but her ultimately tragic marriage to Henry was a temporary victory for the conservative religious faction led by her uncle, Thomas Howard, third Duke of Norfolk, and Bishop Stephen Gardiner.[10] Finally, Katherine Parr, far from the dowdy widow who often appears on film, was well versed in Christian humanism, a patron of religious scholars, and an author and translator who published under her own name *Prayers or Meditations* (1545) and *Lamentations of a Sinner* (1547), the latter of which shows Calvinist and Lutheran influences. According to traditional accounts, her evangelical tendencies made her the target of a 1546 plot in which the religious conservatives Gardiner, William Paget, Richard Rich, and Thomas Wriothesley nearly succeeded in having her prosecuted for heresy.[11]

Henry VIII and his wives—like the Tudors in general—were popular in the silent era. Katherine of Aragon and Anne Boleyn were well-known to theatre audiences from Shakespeare and John Fletcher's *The Famous History of the Life of King Henry the Eight*, which focuses upon the fall from power of the Duke of Buckingham, Cardinal Wolsey, and Katherine but downplays religion. Based on that play are *Henry VIII* (1911), now lost, with Violet Vanbrugh as Katherine and Laura Cowie as Anne, and *Cardinal Wolsey* (1912), with Julia Swayne Gordon as Katherine and Clara Kimball Young as Anne, a role she also played in *Anne Boleyn* (1912), which is lost, too. The treatment of religion in *Cardinal Wolsey* is absurdly ahistorical. In one scene Katherine drives Henry from a room by holding up a cross as though he were a vampire, while Wolsey sides with her against Anne, excommunicates Henry, and asks the pope to prevent the divorce. Meanwhile, *Anne Boleyn* (1911) is a far-fetched tale in which Jane dupes Henry into believing Anne (Madeleine Roch?) is committing adultery. Though she sets the trap by placing a letter in Anne's prayer book, the focus is intrigue, not religion.[12]

The wildly inaccurate *Anne de Boleyn* (1913) is largely a tale of romance with Laura Cowie in the title role. The unknown actress who portrays Katherine has only a bit part, though an intertitle slide tells viewers, "Queen Katherine takes little part in the gaities [*sic*] of Henry's court—finding her happiness in good deeds." If this unfairly suggests that the queen was not much fun, it at least acknowledges her goodness. Jane appears only long enough for Anne to discover Henry kissing her hand. The most important silent film about Henry's reign is Ernst Lubitsch's *Anna Boleyn* (1920), which does explore the religious dimensions of the king's marital dilemma—at one point Henry tells Anne she has a "holy duty" to give England a male heir—but it gives no attention to the individual faith of Anne (Henny Porten), Katherine (Hedwig Paul Winterstein), or Jane (Aud Egede Nissen). The last silent film Katherine (Theresa Maxwell Conover) appears in, *When Knighthood Was in Flower* (1922), is mainly about Henry's sister Mary and Charles Brandon and sheds little light on the queen's faith. Similarly, *Hampton Court Palace* (1936) deals with circumstances surrounding the execution of

Katherine Howard (Gabrielle Morton), while *A Princess of Destiny* (1929) features the final pre-sound Anne (Doris Lloyd) and Jane (Dorothy Gould), though little else is known about it.[13]

Foreshadowing Katherine's subsequent filmic fate, the first major English-language feature film with sound, *The Private Life of Henry VIII* (1933), dismisses her with a title slide: "Henry VIII had six wives. Katherine of Aragon was the first but her story is of no particular interest—she was a respectable woman. So Henry divorced her. He then married Anne Boleyn. This marriage also was a failure—but not for the same reason." Unusually, the film concentrates on the last four wives, dealing summarily with Anne Boleyn (Merle Oberon), who is in the Tower awaiting execution when it begins. Jane (Wendy Barrie) also is gone quickly, and the film devotes considerable time to Elsa Lanchester's comic turn as Anne of Cleves and the romance between Katherine Howard (Binnie Barnes) and Thomas Culpeper (Robert Donat), with Katherine Parr (Everley Gregg) turning up briefly as a comedic nagging wife. Although Charles Laughton's portrayal of Henry has been tremendously influential, and the many subtleties of this broadly comic film repay repeated viewing, it says nothing about religion. Though the later 1930s brought a spate of films about regnant Tudor queens, it was over a decade before the next film to concentrate on Henry's reign, *The Rose without a Thorn* (1947), based on Clifford Bax's highly romanticized 1932 play about Katherine Howard (Victoria Hopper) and Culpeper (John Bryning). Both films drew heavily on Francis Hackett's popular but non-scholarly biography, *Henry the Eighth* (1929) and Martin Hume's *The Wives of Henry VIII* (1905).[14]

A new wave of Tudor films and television began in the 1950s, inspired to a considerable degree—as Tom Freeman notes—by two plays, Maxwell Anderson's *Anne of the Thousand Days* (1948) and Robert Bolt's *A Man for All Seasons* (1954), which in turn owed much to Hackett, Hume, and R. W. Chambers' *Thomas More* (1935). All emphasize Henry's brutality and pay little attention to religion. Anderson's Anne Boleyn is a strong woman, who among other things controls her own sexual destiny, but her faith and learning are insignificant. The play took two decades to make it from stage to big screen because of its frank talk about adultery, bastards, and incest. However, for the debut of Alastair Cooke's *Omnibus* on CBS, Anderson scripted an adaptation, *The Trial of Anne Boleyn* (1952), in which Anne (Lilli Palmer) bravely dies rather than agree to an annulment making her daughter Elizabeth illegitimate, though without reference to her faith. Bolt makes Thomas More a secular champion of liberty of conscience, discounting his devotion and the fanaticism that led him to persecute reformers, and ignoring Katherine of Aragon and Anne Boleyn, the women at the heart of the crisis that brought him to the scaffold. His only woman of wit is More's daughter

Margaret, whose dialogue is confined to humanism minus the Christianity that routinely accompanied it. Bolt adapted his radio play (1954) into a BBC television production (1957), and a longer version appeared on Australian television (1964) before the award-winning Fred Zinneman film (1966) and Charlton Heston's teleplay (1988), but Katherine appears in none and Anne (Vanessa Redgrave) only in a nonspeaking role (1966).[15]

Despite publication of Garrett Mattingly's seminal and sympathetic biography, *Catherine of Aragon*, in 1941, the first two talking films to include Katherine as a character fail to show any positive manifestations of her religiosity. *The Sword and the Rose* (1953), a remake of *When Knighthood Was in Flower*, depicts Katherine (Rosalie Crutchley) as a prude and a shrew. *The White Falcon* (*BBC Sunday Night Theatre*, 1956) is an excellent drama, but it portrays Katherine (Margaretta Scott) as cold, humorless, stern, stiff, and stubborn; Anne (Jeanette Sterke) as opportunistic and smug; and Jane (Jennifer Browne) as conniving and coy. Religion does feature in the film, but either in the form of ritual (the pageant of the White Falcon to insure St. Anne's blessing for Anne Boleyn's pregnancy) or references to superstition for humorous effect (Henry's acquisition of vials containing a tear of Christ and drops of sweat from St. Michael).[16]

Katherine Parr also appears in several films from this time, including *A Queen's Way* (*Hallmark Hall of Fame*, 1953), in which Sarah Churchill (Winston's daughter) portrays Katherine but about which little else is known. *Young Bess* (1953) is based on Margaret Irwin's 1945 novel, which drew inspiration from J. E. Neale's *Queen Elizabeth* (1934), and emphasizes another romantic triangle involving Katherine Parr (Deborah Kerr), Elizabeth (Jean Simmons), and Thomas Seymour (Stewart Granger). One sequence addresses religion, though more as a matter of the king's authority than of doctrine. Prince Edward (Rex Thompson) tells Elizabeth that Katherine Parr will not last because she is arguing with Henry VIII (Charles Laughton) about religion, and soon—aboard *The Great Harry*—the king berates Archbishop Cranmer (Lumsden Hare) and threatens Katherine with the penalties of heresy for authorizing the printing of an English Bible while acting as regent during his absence in France. The scene is invented, but she did put herself in jeopardy by debating theology with Henry. Katherine Parr (Gwen Cherrell) is in the same three-way romance in *The Young Elizabeth* (1964, Valerie Gearon), directed by Charles Jarrot, who soon did likewise with Anderson's play.[17]

Jarrot's *Anne of the Thousand Days* (1969) is very much a product of its time. Anne (Genevieve Bujold) is a liberated woman who speaks her mind but shows her strength mainly in her refusal to become mistress to Henry (Richard Burton) and her sophistication largely in sexual terms. Her faith and learning are not evident, and she prays only as death approaches. The film exhibits Henry's certainty that he is doing God's will, fear of excommunication for breaking with Rome, and cynical attitude to Wolsey (Anthony Quayle), but it ignores the Reformation. Moreover, at times Anne seems to mock Henry's conviction. Katherine of Aragon fares somewhat better. Though she is a secondary character and has only limited on-screen time, Irene Papas gives her considerable depth. Despite her austere black clothing—in sharp contrast to Anne's brightly colored dresses—she is not dour; in fact, at one point she admonishes one of her ladies, who is performing a sad tune on the lute, to play something cheerful. She experiences considerable woe as the story progresses but clearly draws strength from her faith, wears a large crucifix, and has a private altar in her chamber. When Henry asserts that they are living in sin, she replies that her conscience is clear and affirms that she never consummated her previous marriage to the king's brother, Arthur. Regarding Princess Mary (Nicola Pagett), she defiantly declares to Henry: "Neither you nor the pope can make my child a bastard," which implicitly recognizes that she was no unthinking minion of the papacy. Later, she refuses to recognize the authority of the legatine court—Cardinals Campeggio (Marne Maitland) and Wolsey—to examine the validity of her marriage, proclaiming, "To God I commit my cause."[18]

The Six Wives of Henry VIII (1970) is one of the more accurate depictions of Henry (Keith Michell) despite some invention and time compression. Episode 1 for the first time shows a young, beautiful, and intelligent Katherine of Aragon (Annette Crosbie), though it skips over the period between the death of her infant son (Henry, Duke of Cornwall) in 1511 and Henry's decision to seek a divorce in 1527. Still, there is little overt reference to her faith, though the king praises her learning, her ladies describe her as "devout," and she once appears silently praying. A flirtatious Anne Boleyn (Dorothy Tutin) appears in the first episode, but episode 2 is concerned with the breakdown of her romance with Henry amid increasing desperation over her inability to bear a male child. Terrified when the king warns her to pray for a son, she seeks counsel from Cranmer (Bernard Hepton), and after he hears her confession in the Tower prior to her execution, he says, "You shame us all." But the educated, evangelical Anne is missing as usual. Episode 3 is a series of flashbacks while Jane Seymour (Anne Stallybrass) receives the last rites in a chapel. This is the innocent, modest Jane, concerned about monks and nuns evicted from the monasteries and rebels punished after the Pilgrimage of Grace and acting as a prick to Henry's conscience. In episode 4 Anne of Cleves (Elvi Hale) is again comic, though clever enough to outsmart Henry; however, there is real religious drama for Anne and Cranmer with the end of the Schmalkaldic alliance, the fall of Cromwell (Wolfe Morris), and the martyrdom of the evangelical Robert Barnes (Robert James), all of which places them in jeopardy. In episode 5 Katherine Howard (Angela Pleasence), as usual, represents Henry's attempt to regain his youth and the conservative Howards' evanescent triumph. Episode 6 emphasizes the personal faith of Katherine Parr (Rosalie Crutchley) and the struggle at court between conservatives and evangelicals.[19]

Keith Michell reprised his role with a different cast in the feature film, *Henry VIII and His Six Wives* (1972). It portrays Katherine of Aragon (Frances Cuka) as long-suffering, inclined to mortify her flesh with hair shirts, and stubborn. At various points the king is angry at Anne Boleyn (Charlotte Rampling) for presenting a play ridiculing the fallen Wolsey (John Bryans), blames her for the death of More (Michael Goodliffe), resents her attitude to Princess Mary (Sarah Long), and accuses her of having a witch's mark (a mole)—all offenses with religious overtones, though none that present her in a positive light. Jane Seymour (Jane Asher), again mild-mannered, begs mercy for the northern rebels to no avail; Anne of Cleves (Jenny Bos) gets little time on-screen but is once more played for laughs; and Katherine Howard (Lynne Frederick) is the usual sad story. However, Henry quizzes Katherine Parr (Barbara Leigh-Hunt) about her "new faith," and she admits to favoring freedom of conscience and opposing the burning of a fifteen-year-old boy who has spoken against the sacraments. A new film of Shakespeare and Fletcher's *Henry VIII* (1979) treats Katherine of Aragon (Claire Bloom) sympathetically but avoids the subject of her religion. In *God's Outlaw* (1986), a dramatized biography of William Tyndale (Roger Rees), Anne Boleyn (Oona Kirsch) favors his translation of the Bible into English and shares his *Obedience of the Christian Man* with Henry (Keith Barron).[20]

The twenty-first century has brought new on-screen interpretations of Henry and his wives without adding much about the Reformation. Granada Television's *Henry VIII* (2003), with Ray Winstone consciously channeling Tony Soprano, is notorious for its inaccuracies. It emphasizes his quest for a son, focuses on Anne Boleyn (Helena Bonham Carter), and pays little attention to Christian humanism (More is not a character) or religion in general. Still, if it ignores Katherine of Aragon's learning, it does take account of her devotion. She (Assumpta Serna) prays to St. Casilda of Toledo for a son, plans a pilgrimage to the shrine of Our Lady of Walsingham, and wears a hair shirt. Anne's story, on the other hand, is all bold manipulation and tragic romance. Jane Seymour (Emilia Fox) is a sympathetic character who again urges mercy for Robert Aske and the Pilgrims. Anne of Cleves (Pia Girard) has no lines, the scenes with Katherine Howard (Emily Blunt) seem almost like child pornography, and there is no reference to Katherine Parr (Clare Holman) having evangelical sympathies, her writings, or the plot against her. The two film versions of *The Other Boleyn Girl* are rife with howlers. Katherine of Aragon (Yolanda Vazquez 2003, Ana Torrent 2008) is a minor character, and Anne Boleyn (Jodhi May 2003, Natalie Portman 2008) is anachronistically feminist, obnoxiously brash, sexually assertive, and cruelly manipulative, but neither learned nor devout, showing concern for her soul only on the eve of her execution. In *The Twisted Tale of Bloody Mary* (2008) Katherine (Victoria Peiró) has an almost negligible role, and Anne Boleyn (Lisa Marie Kennedy) is a monstrous caricature.[21]

Despite its faults, *The Tudors* (2007–10) occasionally slips religion in with the political power games, sex, and violence. It is hard to disentangle politics and religion with Katherine of Aragon (Maria Doyle Kennedy)—the intrigues of Eustace Chapuys (Anthony Brophy), hostility of Wolsey (Sam Neill), and support of More (Jeremy Northam)—but some moments emphasize her faith. Appropriately for this sex-drenched drama, in Episode 1.01 she invites Henry to her chamber, but when he arrives, she is praying in her chapel, so he romps with her maid instead. In 1.04 the royal couple attend mass together; in 1.05 she observes the ritual of creeping to the cross at Lambeth, distributes alms to the poor, and is praying when Henry announces that their marriage is invalid; in 1.07, during an outbreak of sweating sickness (1528), she, Henry, and Princess Mary pray together; and 1.08 has Campeggio failing to convince her to enter a nunnery and hearing her confession, as well as a fairly accurate portrayal of her refusal to cooperate with the legatine court trying the divorce. Faith underlies her stoic response to Anne's increasing prominence at court and her own banishment, her separation from Mary, her refusal to renounce the title of Queen or take the Oath of Supremacy, and her final illness (she dies in 2.07).[22]

Susan Bordo reports that Natalie Dormer persuaded series creator Michael Hirst to give Anne Boleyn more intellectual heft. While sexuality overpowers other aspects of her character—especially after the signature "seduce me" scene (1.04)—her faith comes up repeatedly. In 1.08 Cromwell delivers from Simon Fish a copy of Tyndale's *Obedience of a Christian Man* (1528), warns her to be careful, and notes that they are both of the true religion (actually Fish probably sent Anne his own *Supplication of the Beggars* and not via Cromwell). In 1.09 Anne tells Henry, "Some on good authority care not for popes," and says she has a book (presumably Tyndale) that argues the king is both emperor and pope, an idea actually attributable to Cromwell. In 1.10 she claims that Wolsey has kept similar books from him. Subsequently, Henry tells Chapuys that prelates should live according to the gospel and the Church Fathers, that Luther was right to attack clerical vice even if he went too far with the sacraments, and that he will advance reform in England. More burns Fish on *The Tudors*, though in reality it was Archbishop Warham who condemned the *Supplication*, and Fish died of plague in 1531. In 2.03 Anne encourages her servants to read Tyndale's Bible in her chambers, saying there is no more papal idolatry, and in 2.04 she admonishes Madge Shelton to read scripture. Miraculously, in 2.06 she watches John Bale's *King John*, which ridicules the Catholic church but was written in 1538, two years after her death. There are the usual references to her being a witch, and she worries about a prophecy that a queen of England will be burned. In 2.08 she dispenses alms and washes parishioners' feet. At the Tower in 2.09 she asks for the sacrament so that she may pray, and in 2.10 she receives absolution from Cranmer and prays while her ladies sleep. Much of this reflects Anne's real convictions, though it comes amid a welter of factual errors and inventions.[23]

Without Katherine and Anne, *The Tudors* loses much of its dramatic tension in Seasons Three and Four, and the quality of the episodes—even as historical fiction—deteriorates. The script conflates the Lincolnshire Rising and the Pilgrimage of Grace while making a hash of the details, though it is broadly correct in having Jane Seymour plead unsuccessfully for the king to show mercy to the rebels and in making her religious allegiance a matter of uncertainty.[24] After Jane dies, Cromwell arranges a marital alliance with Protestant Cleves, whereupon viewers are expected to suspend belief to the point of regarding Joss Stone's Anne of Cleves as ugly. As the king's disillusionment with his fourth wife mounts, Sir Francis Bryan procures a "distraction" from the Dowager Duchess of Norfolk's house, which looks distinctly like a brothel, and indeed Katherine Howard comes across as an extraordinarily silly and immature harlot. As Henry's new love, Tamzin Merchant is so youthful looking that her trysts with the unconvincingly aging king and her paramour Culpeper seem like more quasi-child-porn. Though there is politico-religious intrigue in the background, Anne and Katherine's religiosity is inconsequential, and the emphasis is upon illicit sex—the king even sleeps with his ex-wife (which has no basis in fact).[25]

Midway through Season Four, Katherine Howard is executed for adultery, and Henry begins courting Katherine Parr (Joely Richardson) and launches a campaign to capture Boulogne. Religion returns to the forefront, as Henry leaves Katherine as regent during his absence in France, and she makes Hugh Latimer her chaplain (this never happened) and announces her intention to advance the cause of reformation (which she did). Bishop Gardiner meanwhile campaigns against heresy, Katherine refuses to cooperate, and, upon the king's return to England, the prelate sets his sights on her. Again, the broad outline of the plot against her is correct—she presents Henry with a copy of *Lamentations of a Sinner*, discusses her translations, and argues theology, which annoys him; Gardiner seeks to exploit this after torture fails to compel Anne Askew to implicate the queen as a heretic; and Katherine narrowly escapes after submitting to her husband's "wisdom." However, many of the details are wrong, and the final episode has Henry talking to the ghosts of his other wives while Hans Holbein belatedly paints his famous portrait of the king. It is not a stellar finale.[26]

Prior to his death, Henry restored Mary and Elizabeth to the royal succession, but by the rule of primogeniture the throne went first to their younger brother, Edward VI (1547–53), who was only nine years old. Intelligent and devout, he was also vigorous and healthy, and but for his unexpected illness, there might have been no regnant Tudor queens. Political power lay with the reformers—initially his uncle Edward Seymour, Duke of Somerset, and later John Dudley, Duke of Northumberland—while Cranmer dominated the church, conservatives Gardiner and Norfolk were imprisoned in the Tower of London, and the realm became genuinely Protestant. This led to considerable strife between Edward and the Catholic Mary, notably at Christmas in 1550. When Edward realized he was dying in 1553, he tried to preserve Protestantism by passing the throne to his cousin Lady Jane Grey, a devout reformer married to Northumberland's son, Guilford Dudley.[27]

Edward's reign has received little attention from filmmakers except for adaptations of Mark Twain's novel *The Prince and the Pauper*, which tone down its sharp critique of religious intolerance and only tacitly acknowledge government promotion of Protestant reform. Therefore, it is hardly surprising that they pay little attention to faith in depicting Mary, Elizabeth, and Jane, who are minor characters, compared to Edward and the fictional Tom Canty and Miles Hendon, and are heavily fictionalized themselves. If religion comes up at all, it is to emphasize Mary's heartlessness, as in Disney's 1962 version, where she criticizes "Edward" (Tom) for pardoning a witch, or the 1996 miniseries, where she regards his life-threatening illness as God's work.[28]

Lady Jane's reign lasted only nine days before Mary took the crown and imprisoned her in the Tower, where she remained until her execution after Wyatt's Rebellion in 1554. Jane has been the main character in three films, all essentially fictionalized love stories about her marriage, though they differ in their treatment of religion. In the silent film, *Lady Jane Grey: The Court of Intrigue* (1923), Jane (Nina Vanna) calls upon her followers to defend the Reformed Church, and Mary "yearns to restore Catholicism and punish all who helped Henry VIII divorce her mother." In contrast, *The Tudor Rose* (aka *Nine Days a Queen*, 1936) never mentions that Jane (Nova Pilbeam) was a Protestant and only obliquely hints that Mary is Catholic by having her appear near a large crucifix. While *Lady Jane* (1986) rightly emphasizes that Jane (Helena Bonham Carter) had a humanist education and supported reform, it ignores her family and teachers' Protestantism and modernizes her into "a proto-socialist feminist."[29]

The devout and well-educated Mary I (1553–58) freed Gardiner and Norfolk, imprisoned Cranmer, and contracted marriage with the Catholic Philip of Spain, whose father—and her first cousin—Emperor Charles V involved England in his war with France. Her proposed marriage sparked Wyatt's failed uprising, after which Mary imprisoned Elizabeth and executed Lady Jane Grey. She restored England's allegiance to Rome and in 1556 appointed her cousin Cardinal Reginald Pole as Archbishop of Canterbury. Meanwhile, she experienced a false pregnancy in 1554; began burning heretics in 1555 (including Cranmer in 1556); suffered abandonment by her husband, who became King of Spain the same year; and lost Calais, England's last Continental outpost, in 1558. All the while she kept a close and suspicious eye on Elizabeth. Mary was long the villain in Protestant accounts of the English Reformation, and there is no denying the brutality of the religious persecutions that earned her the nickname "Bloody Mary." However, in recent decades historians have provided a more multi-dimensional account of her life and reign, emphasizing the emotional torment she endured as princess and genuine achievements of her government.[30]

The film industry has yet to catch up with these changes in historiography. Moreover, although Mary figures as a child in movies about Henry, a popish princess in those about Edward and Jane, and the bad old queen in those about Elizabeth, she is largely limited to small parts. She is only a minor character in *Anne of the Thousand Days* (1969, Nicola Pagett), *The Six Wives of Henry VIII* (1970, Verina Greenlaw and Alison Frazer), *Die Liebe und die Königin* (1977, Inge Keller), *Henry VIII* (2003, Lara Belmont), *The Other Boleyn Girl* (2008, Constance Stride), and *Tudor Rose* (2008, Rebecca Bigler). Among films in which Mary has a larger role, Daphne Slater offers the best and most accurate portrayal opposite Glenda Jackson in *Elizabeth R* (1971), a miniseries whose first episode fairly depicts both her anger and anguish over heresy, rebellion, her sister's uncertain loyalty, her loveless marriage, and her failure to produce an heir. On the other hand, while Kathy Burke does a good job of acting in *Elizabeth* (1998) with Cate Blanchett, and though the burning of heretics (apparently Hugh Latimer, Nicholas Ridley, and a fictitious female victim) is realistic, on the whole Michael Hirst's vehemently anti-Catholic film script is hard to swallow and Shekhar Kapur's staging of Mary's scenes seems more appropriate for a heavy-metal music video than a film about Tudor queens.[31]

Hirst does somewhat better with the younger Mary in *The Tudors* (2007–10), which gives more attention to Mary than any other filmic event, and Sarah Bolger offers a nuanced portrayal of the princess as a sweet but sorrowful girl who gradually develops the bitter edge that led her to burn nearly 300 heretics later on. Mary and Katherine of Aragon (Maria Doyle Kennedy) are among the few female characters the Showtime series does not exploit primarily as sex objects. However, Mary never has been the primary subject of a serious movie unless one counts the largely forgotten film versions of Victor Hugo's play *Marie Tudor*, which is pure fiction and sheds no meaningful light on her faith, or the amateurish independent film, *The Twisted Tale of Bloody Mary* (2008). The latter is extremely problematic, despite favorable quotes on its website from critic Ian Levine and author Alison Weir. Director Chris Barnard claims, "History has called her 'Bloody Mary,' but how fair is this? This film paints another picture, of a woman true to her beliefs pushed towards a terrible psychological disintegration." In fact, it demonizes Protestants in much the same way that Kapur's films do with Catholics, implies that Edward VI's death was divinely inspired, and largely excuses her burning of heretics.[32]

The majority of films about regnant Tudor queens focus on Elizabeth I, whose troubled youth and forty-five-year reign (1558–1603) offer a fascinating cast of characters and a host of real problems—all with religious overtones—that lend themselves to dramatization, including repeated attempts to exclude her from the succession; her incarceration and banishment from court under Mary; her refusal to marry or defer to male councilors and members of Parliament; her own uncertain beliefs and alleged unwillingness to make windows into other men's souls; her domestic conflicts with Catholic recusants (though there were also Catholic loyalists) and Puritan reformers intent upon purging the church of lingering popish elements; her reluctant involvement in the French Wars of Religion (1562–98), the Dutch Revolt (1567–1609), and the Anglo-Spanish War (1585–1604); her constant risk of assassination; her employment of adventurers who often operated outside the law; and—running through it all—her religiously charged rivalry with her sister Mary, her cousin Mary, Queen of Scots, and her brother-in-law Philip II.[33]

Like her sister, Elizabeth appears as a child or young adult in films about Henry VIII and Edward VI, though not Lady Jane Grey. However, she was seventeen years younger than Mary I and only thirteen when her father died, so films about Henry give less attention to her faith than to Mary's. This is true even of *The Six Wives of Henry VIII* and *The Tudors*, though these at least indicate something of her precocious intelligence and humanist education. Aside from various versions of *The Prince and the Pauper*, the only film set during Edward's reign in which she is a major character is *Young Bess*. Except for *The Twisted Tale of Bloody Mary*, Elizabeth is cast as the hero and victim of Marian religious persecution in films in which the sisters appear as adults, e.g., *Elizabeth R*, *Elizabeth*, and *Elizabeth I: the Virgin Queen* (2005), all discussed below. Films that deal with the first and last decades of her reign often focus on fictionalized romances with, respectively, Robert Dudley, Earl of Leicester and Robert Devereux, Earl of Essex, though they make take some account of religion. However, the greatest emphasis on religious conflict comes in films that include her struggles with Mary, Queen of Scots, and Philip II.[34]

Elizabeth's fate was closely intertwined with that of Mary Stuart, who became queen of Scotland as an infant upon the death of her father, James V (1514–42). In a conflict known as the "rough wooing," Henry VIII tried to force the Scots to accept Mary Stuart's marriage to Prince Edward; however, her mother, Marie of Guise, sent her to France, where she grew up at the court of Henri II and Catherine de Medici, eventually marrying their son, Francis II (1559–60). Upon Mary Tudor's death, she claimed to be the rightful queen of England on the grounds that Elizabeth was both a bastard and a heretic. When Francis died, she returned to Scotland, where her marriage in 1565 to her cousin Henry Stuart, Lord Darnley made her an even greater threat to Elizabeth, for both bride and groom were the grandchildren of Henry VII's daughter Margaret. Mary famously quarreled with Scottish Protestants, especially firebrand preacher John Knox. She was possibly involved in Darnley's 1567 murder with the Earl of Bothwell, whom she subsequently married. Facing revolt by the Scottish nobility, in 1568 she fled to England, where for nineteen years she was Elizabeth's prisoner and the center of a series of plots to oust the Protestant queen and restore Catholicism. Reluctantly, Elizabeth ordered her execution in 1587, which provided both a putative motive for Philip II to attempt an invasion in 1588 and the opportunity to do so without the risk of replacing Elizabeth with Mary, whose Guise relatives were his enemies.[35]

This rivalry between royal cousins has appealed to filmmakers and audiences throughout the history of film and television. As it has played out on the large and small screens, Elizabeth has emerged triumphant again. Although many films feature only one queen or the other, Elizabeth appears much more frequently. Even films with both queens typically give precedence to one or the other, and those in which Elizabeth is the "headliner" tend to depict Mary in a negative light, while those in which the Scots queen is the star cast aspersions on her English cousin. Again, though, the advantage lies with Elizabeth, and not just in terms of screen time. While aesthetic quality and historical accuracy vary widely, overall the films concentrating on Elizabeth are better written, directed, and produced, and the actresses portraying the English queen generally give stronger performances. This is not to say there has been a conscious, continuous effort to privilege Elizabeth, but there certainly is a contrast in their depiction.

Elizabeth's cinematic predominance is likely due to a combination of factors, including Anglocentrism in British and American cinema, her much longer reign and greater success, the brilliance of the Elizabethan court and culture, the legendary adventures of Elizabethan explorers and privateers, the drama of her relationship with Parliament, the cinematic appeal of her alleged romances, and movie audiences' fondness for a winner. However, most pertinent in the present context are the crucial religious milestone represented by the Elizabethan Settlement, her defeat of the series of plots intended to enthrone Mary Stuart, the iconic status of the Armada campaign, her near deification as the Virgin Queen and Gloriana, and her mythic role in "the rise of the English nation," in which there is a strong and persistent strain of Protestant providentialism. In a very real sense, Elizabeth's "victory" over Mary in terms of screen time and quality is also a "triumph" of Anglo-Protestantism over Catholicism.[36]

The same is true of Elizabeth's on-screen "defeat" of Philip II, though the Spanish king has an even heavier load to bear than the Queen of Scots. In films made during the 1930s and early 1940s, he is often an analogue for Hitler, an intolerant Continental tyrant whose threat to liberty and true religion inspires the growth of English sea power. More recently, Philip is the primary example of what some observers see as Shekhar Kapur's use of Spanish Catholicism as a means to comment on Islamist terrorism in *Elizabeth* (1998) and *Elizabeth: The Golden Age* (2007). In the latter film, the Spanish king is a most unsympathetic character, who—Islamist overtones or not—evokes comparison to Darth Vader, Sauron, and Voldemort. The only filmic representation that treats Philip with subtlety and even a degree of sympathy is *Elizabeth R*, which appeared in a period more inclined to limn characters in shades of gray than stark black and white.[37]

One of the earliest surviving films is Thomas Edison's *The Execution of Mary Stuart* (Robert Thomae as Mary), an 1895 short that illustrates the culmination of the Scots queen's contest with her cousin for control of Britain, though—with a running time of eleven seconds—it does not provide much backstory, an appearance by Elizabeth, or any comment about religion. Since 1895, there have been only a few films in which Mary appears without Elizabeth. Among silent films both *Marie Stuart et Rizzio* (1911) and *Mary Queen of Scots* (1911) are lost, while *Maria Stuart* (1927)—which *Variety* panned as a "resounding flop"—focuses on the period between Mary's return to Scotland and her flight to England. Twentieth-century sound films that exclude Elizabeth usually give Mary only minor supporting roles that say little about her faith. More recently, the little known 2013 film, *Mary, Queen of Scots*, omits Elizabeth as a human character, though she does appear as a puppet, and Mary (Camille Rutherford) delivers as monologues the contents of letters she writes but does not send to the English queen. It botches the depiction of religion, making Darnley the chief Catholic fanatic and implying that Knox performed the marriage ceremony for Mary and Bothwell. At least thus far, the new CBS series *Reign* has no Elizabeth either, given that it deals with the young Mary (Adelaide Kane) in France prior to her marriage. Its ludicrous plot—replete with Nostradamus' prophecies, pagan sacrifices, poisoning, fictional ladies-in-waiting, and a love triangle involving Mary, Francis, and the latter's imaginary half-brother Bash—owes little to history where religion or anything else is concerned.[38]

Meanwhile, the first film to feature Elizabeth was 1912's *Queen Elizabeth* (*Les Amours de la reine Élisabeth*), released by the aptly named Histrionic Films, offering a weirdly distorted account of her relationship with Essex (Lou Tellegen), and characterized by overacting from Sarah Bernhardt that is remarkable even by silent film standards. Because it occurs after Mary Stuart's death, she does not appear, nor does it mention religion. Elizabeth appeared without Mary in several silent films: *Drake's Love Story* (1913) deals obliquely with religion via the Armada campaign, *The Life of Shakespeare* (1914) concerns the bard, *Old Bill through the Ages* (1924) is comic fantasy, and *The Virgin Queen* (1928) is about Elizabeth and Walter Raleigh.[39] In the sound era Elizabeth has minor roles minus Mary in numerous films about Shakespeare and some major ones that are discussed below. Like her father, she is so well-known that she also appears in cartoons, comic spoofs, and time-traveling tales, all obviously ahistorical in nature.[40]

The earliest film to feature both queens is a 1913 silent short, *Mary Stuart*, the first of many film versions of Friedrich Schiller's play *Maria Stuart*, which is friendly to Mary though largely fictional. Later versions appeared in 1957 (twice), 1959, 1960, 1963, 1969, 1980, 1982, 1986, 1991, and 2008; Gaetano Donizetti's opera *Maria Stuarda*, which uses Schiller as the basis for the libretto, has also been filmed on numerous occasions. In 1923 Elizabeth and Mary appeared in a pair of silent movies, both now lost: in *The Virgin Queen*, Robert Dudley (Carlyle Blackwell) saves Elizabeth (Diana Manners) from an assassination attempt by the Countess of Lennox (Norma Whalley), presumably acting on behalf of her daughter-in-law Mary (Maisie Fisher), while *The Loves of Mary, Queen of Scots* apparently deals primarily with the Scots queen (Fay Compton) before her imprisonment in England by Elizabeth (Ellen Compton). In 1924 the two queens had supporting parts in *Dorothy Vernon of Haddon Hall*, which stars Mary Pickford in the title role. Director Marshal Neilan was usually drunk during filming, and it shows in the convoluted, confusing plot. There is also a great deal of typical silent film overacting, especially from Clare Eames as the haughty Elizabeth, and a bogus love affair between Mary (Estelle Taylor) and a fictional male character but (again) not much about religion.[41]

Elizabeth had major roles in several talking movies without Mary Stuart in the 1930s and early 1940s, all concentrating on love and religious war.

Drake of England (aka *Drake the Pirate*, 1935) focuses on Drake (Matheson Lang) with a fictionalized account of his crusade against Catholic Spain, from Nombre Dios in 1567 to the Armada Campaign in 1588, and his marriage to Elizabeth Sydenham (Jane Baxter). It does not address the issues troubling the Elizabethan church or the personal faith of Elizabeth I (Athene Seyler), but she and Drake are emblematic of English Protestant patriotism. English Catholics plot for the Duke of Alba to invade the realm and restore the "rightful queen," presumably Mary (not a character), and Drake declares after defeating the Armada, "Henceforth we shall fear only God." *Fire over England* (1937), which parallels events in 1588 with the Nazi threat in the 1930s, recounts the adventures of the fictional Michael Ingolby (Laurence Olivier) and his romance with Cynthia (Vivien Leigh), an attendant of Elizabeth I (Flora Robson). The Catholics clearly are bad guys. Early on the Inquisition burns Ingolby's father for heresy, and the film uses fire throughout as a symbol for Spanish tyranny, existence of which it takes for granted. Philip II (Raymond Massey) asserts, "Only by fear can the people be made to do their duty," and a courtier warns against "treating your enemies like human beings." Naturally, the climax comes with the defeat of the Armada.[42]

The Private Lives of Elizabeth and Essex (1939) deals with the period after the Armada campaign and is primarily a love story between Elizabeth (Bette Davis) and Essex (Errol Flynn). It opens with Essex returning from his 1596 expedition against Cadiz and includes a lengthy exposition of his 1599 Irish campaign but does nothing to explain the religious context of either.

The Sea Hawk (1940) is the entertaining tale of another fictional adventurer, Geoffrey Thorpe (Flynn again), who is clearly based on Drake. Even more obviously than *Fire over England*, it calls attention to the German Nazi threat, particularly when Elizabeth (Robson again) delivers a long speech after the defeat of the Armada. But the religious dimensions of the Anglo-Spanish war, though perhaps well known to 1940 audiences, receive little attention. Following a lengthy hiatus and the release of *Young Bess* (1953), the next major film to feature Elizabeth sans Mary was *The Virgin Queen* (1955), which goes back to 1581 for a fictional love triangle involving Elizabeth (Davis again), Raleigh (Richard Todd), and Beth Throgmorton (Joan Collins). Irish rebels clearly are a problem in this film, but it fails to explain the religious reasons why.[43]

Early in the sound era brought attempts to treat Mary sympathetically when she shared the screen with Elizabeth. The first talking movie to feature both queens is John Ford's *Mary of Scotland* (1936), based on the Maxwell Anderson play, with Katherine Hepburn in the title role and Florence Eldridge as Elizabeth. By all rights, this should have been a huge success, but it was a critical and a box office failure. Both play and screenplay present

Mary as an admirable person who makes unwise choices, while Elizabeth is calculating, envious, and harsh. Neither actress quite carries off her role, and both are foiled by inappropriate accents. Thus, it is hard to take either "good" Mary or "bad" Elizabeth seriously. Ford, like Anderson, cannot resist revising history to have the two queens meet, and he turns Mary's execution into melodrama. But he does give considerable attention to the religious conflict between Mary and Knox (Moroni Olsen). *The Pearls of the Crown* (*Les perles de la couronne*, 1937) is a tongue-in-cheek film that follows the history of seven pearls from the sixteenth century to the twentieth. The pearls travel from Pope Clement VII to Mary (Jacqueline Delubac) and, after her execution, to Elizabeth (Yvette Pienne), but this is hardly a penetrating study of personal faith or religious conflict.[44]

The Heart of a Queen (*Das Herz de Königin*, 1940), like many German films made in the Nazi era, is well-crafted propaganda. Using the theme of the two queens' hearts, it contrasts an unfeeling Machiavellian Elizabeth (Maria Koppenhöfer) with a Mary (Zarah Leander) who only wants to find love. Though the film follows the general trajectory of Mary's career, it deviates from history at various points, not least in its sharply anti-English depiction of Elizabeth. To be fair, Schiller's and Anderson's plays and Ford's film earlier did the same. However, a positive portrayal in a Nazi film was not necessarily the best thing for Mary's image, and its political agenda leaves no room for religion. ABC's *Pulitzer Prize Playhouse* produced Anderson's *Mary of Scotland* in 1951, with Mildred Natwick as Elizabeth and Helen Hayes as Mary. Natwick later portrayed Mary in Walter Cronkite's *You Are There: The Execution of Mary Queen of Scots February 8, 1587* (1954), with Carmen Mathews as Elizabeth.

A turn toward more positive portrayals of Elizabeth and less laudatory depictions of Mary came with *Seven Seas to Calais* (*Il dominatore dei sette mari*, 1962). Though primarily about the adventures of Drake (Rod Taylor), it gives prominent billing to Irene Worth as his queen, while Esmerelda Ruspoli has a much smaller role as Mary during the heroic privateer's fictional efforts to root out Catholic treachery at the English court. The fictionalized British television series, *Sir Francis Drake* (Terence Morgan, 1961–62) portrays Elizabeth (Joan Kent) in a positive light, though at times she exhibits the foibles and weaknesses of a 1950s' stock female character. For obvious reasons, the Spanish frequently are villains, but the emphasis is on swashbuckling, not rival forms of piety. "Queen of Scots," the one episode that involves Mary (Noelle Middleton) is peculiar. After Sir Francis Walsingham and fictional courtier Munro fail to persuade Elizabeth to execute Mary, they trick the Scots queen into replying to a letter about a planned invasion of England forged by Thomas Phillips. That much is based in reality, but from here on fiction takes over. Elizabeth shows Mary's letter to Drake, who is skeptical; she sends him in disguise to discover the truth. Walsingham warns Sir Amyas Paulet, Mary's jailer, who captures Drake, threatens to have him shot, and throws him into a cell. Naturally, however, Drake tricks a sentry, escapes, evades other guards, and finds Mary, who admits writing about the planned invasion but denies plotting to murder Elizabeth. Drake forces Phillips to give him the original letter and to admit that he works for Walsingham, which hardly would have been a surprise to Elizabeth. Hotly pursued by Paulet, Drake escapes with Mary's assistance and delivers the original letter to Elizabeth. She shows it to Walsingham, forgives him his well-intentioned subterfuge, and burns it, predicting that it will not be the last and that the next may not be so easy to forgive.

The Queen's Traitor (1967), a BBC children's series about Elizabeth (Susan Engel) and Mary (Stephanie Beacham), is lost, but the title suggests that it was unfavorable to Mary. Elizabeth also appeared in the Hallmark Hall of Fame production of Maxwell Anderson's *Elizabeth the Queen* (1968), the play upon which *The Privates Lives of Elizabeth and Essex* is based. It features both the Irish Rebellion and an interesting bit of Elizabethan ambivalence when, after Essex's arrest, the queen asks Penelope to bring her the prayer book, changes her mind—saying, "There is no god but death"—and then asks for it again. The young Elizabeth also appears in the religiously charged fourth episode of *The Six Wives of Henry VIII* (1970).[45]

The BBC's *Elizabeth R* (1971) is the longest (six ninety-minute episodes) and arguably the best dramatization of Elizabeth's life ever to appear on film or television. Because the episodes are thematic in nature, there is some loss of chronological continuity, and this approach tends to understate the threats from Mary, Queen of Scots, and Philip II until "their" episodes. Naturally, it involves considerable dramatization (e.g., of conversations) and some time compression, but rarely does the narrative contradict the known facts. Not only does it provide a more nuanced account of religious conflict, it also includes many impressive smaller details. Episode 1, "The Lion's Cub," focuses on Elizabeth's trials during her two siblings reigns but also shows Cranmer presenting the new *Book of Common Prayer* to Edward VI, depicts the dying king altering the succession in favor of Lady Jane Grey, presents a plausible argument between Elizabeth and Mary I about theology and liberty of conscience, and gives an accurate sense of why Philip cultivated his putatively Protestant sister-in-law in order to maintain the delicate balance with France, where Mary, Queen of Scots, was betrothed to the heir.[46]

Episode 2 focuses on romance but also takes full account of the religious implications of "The Marriage Game." The Spanish Bishop de Quadra and Count de Feria seek to maneuver Elizabeth into wedding their Catholic sovereign Philip II, who has qualms about her "heresy" but urges her to seek a papal dispensation allowing her to marry her dead sister Mary's widower. Elizabeth and Cecil weigh the pros and cons of matrimony with the Protestant Earl of Arran of Scotland and Eric XIV of Sweden and the Catholic Archdukes Ferdinand and Charles. The newly crowned Francis II of France and his bride, Mary, Queen of Scots, advance her claim to the English throne on the grounds that Elizabeth is a heretic. Elizabeth and Robert Dudley tease an unhappy Quadra about marrying them. The Privy Council agonizes over the danger to the Protestant succession when the queen nearly dies of smallpox, and Parliament subsequently beseeches her to marry. After Francis II's death and Mary's return to Scotland, Elizabeth attempts via Lord Melville to arrange a Protestant marriage for her cousin to Dudley, now Earl of Leicester. The only purely invented event is Elizabeth and Leicester's near meeting at St Swithin's Church, apparently to marry, near the end of the episode.

Episode 3, "Shadow in the Sun," begins with Elizabeth giving the French ambassador, Fenelon (Bertrand de Salignac), a withering dressing-down in the wake of the St Bartholomew's Day Massacre of 1572. It then proceeds to a fierce debate between the Privy Council, who advocate harsh measures against Mary, Queen of Scots, and English Catholics, and the queen, who prefers watchful toleration. The main storyline concerns the Duke of Alençon's courtship of Elizabeth, English Protestants' objections to a French marriage, and her eventual decision not to wed her "Frog." The episode accurately depicts England's need to conciliate Catholic France, the Council's worries about possible war with Catholic Spain, and Alençon's role in the Netherlands in the midst of the Calvinist Dutch Revolt.

Mary appears only in episode 4, "Horrible Conspiracies," which deals at length with the Babington Plot, Francis Walsingham's entrapment of the Scots queen, Elizabeth's anguish over what to do about her troublesome cousin, and Mary's trial and execution. It includes a chilling scene with notorious priest-hunter Richard Topcliffe and accurate portrayals of the roles that Spanish ambassador Bernardino de Mendoza played in the plot and of turncoat Gilbert Gifford's role in thwarting it. Because the series is largely factually accurate and emphasizes the English queen's reluctance to have her Scots cousin executed, and because Glenda Jackson is extraordinarily compelling as Elizabeth and Vivian Pickles much less so as Mary, viewers are almost certain to have a more favorable opinion of Elizabeth. She resists her council—at one point denouncing Walsingham as "a piss-pot of self-righteousness"—and grieves Mary's death.

Episode 5, "The Enterprise of England," of course deals with the Armada. It gives much more attention to the Spanish side than usual, treating Philip with some sympathy and referencing the strategic debate between the Duke of Parma and the Marquis de Santa Cruz, the involvement of the English Cardinal William Allen and the reluctant Duke of Medina Sidonia. There is even an appearance by magus John Dee and his sidekick Edward Kelley. In the end, the episode presents the English victory as well deserved. It ends with Leicester's death, which mars the triumph for Elizabeth. The only real flaw is the absence of battle scenes. Finally, episode 6, "Sweet England's Pride," deals with Elizabeth's relationship with Essex (much more accurately than other films) before concluding with her death. Though religion is a factor in the conflict with Ireland and in the succession of James VI of Scotland, its role is understated.

Director Charles Jarrot attempted to recapture the magic of *Elizabeth R* with the cinematic release the following year of *Mary, Queen of Scots* (1971), in which Glenda Jackson reprises her role as Elizabeth. Vanessa Redgrave is a better Mary than Pickles and thus represents the only real improvement over *Elizabeth R*, but—like Hepburn in *Mary of Scotland*—she is not at her best here. Though the film shows her resistance to the papal mandate to reinstate Catholicism, her initial toleration for Protestants, and her struggles with Scottish lords and Knox, it makes the already complex and shifting politico-religious alliances in Scotland even more confusing, and it inaccurately turns David Riccio into a papal agent and brings the Catholic priest John Ballard to Scotland. In addition, the movie emphasizes Mary's poor judgment while on the throne, sharply compresses the two decades of her imprisonment (when she demonstrated greater strength of character), and invents an insult-laden meeting between the two queens. The net effect is that her faith seems simplistic, and she appears childish in comparison with Elizabeth.[47]

La dernière nuit (1981), a French film, is a predictably more sympathetic account of the Scots queen's execution, with Catherine Rethi as Elizabeth and Annie Giradot as Mary. *Border Warfare* (1990) is a filmed stage performance portraying battles between the English and the Scots from prehistory to the 1980s, so it gives fairly short shrift to the Tudor period. Worse, it shows John Knox (Derek Anders) sending the "harlot" Mary (Maria Miller) to England, promising that her son James will one day rule there, and it has Elizabeth (Juliet Cadzow) signing a document promising him the throne.

Shekhar Kapur's *Elizabeth* (1998) and *Elizabeth: The Golden Age* (2007) are visually beautiful but anti-Catholic to the point of nastiness, and it would take an essay longer than this one to catalog all of their historical inaccuracies, so a few examples must suffice. The first film distorts the Elizabethan Settlement, having Walsingham (Geoffrey Rush) lock Gardiner (Terence Rigby)—who died in 1555—and other hostile bishops in a cellar while Elizabeth (Blanchett) employs her womanly wiles to win over the rest of the dour prelates and members of Parliament to the Act of Uniformity of 1559. Its treatment of her courtships is a chronological muddle and utterly lacks the sophistication and subtlety of *Elizabeth R.* Ballard (Daniel Craig) attempts to assassinate Elizabeth at least two decades early, Dudley (Joseph Fiennes) is disgraced after plotting with Norfolk (Christopher Eccleston) and Spanish agents, and there is a bloodbath of Catholics more reminiscent of *The Godfather* than of England in the 1560s. Oddly, the main thing it does well is completely fictional, for although Elizabeth never consciously chose to emulate the Virgin Mary or to "become the Virgin Queen" as she puts it, the film is not off target in suggesting that she replaced the Holy Mother in the affections of many Englishmen.[48]

Elizabeth: The Golden Age (2007), deals with the period during which Mary Stuart was imprisoned in England and the subsequent attack by the Armada. Blanchett gives her usual strong performance, which no doubt enhances Elizabeth's stature with casual viewers despite the plot consisting largely of ahistorical nonsense. Samantha Morton plays a fairly malevolent Mary with an over-the-top Scots accent hardly to be expected from a woman who grew up in France. More disturbing is that Kapur and screenwriter Hirst use her, just as they did Mary Tudor in *Elizabeth*, to promote a virulently anti-Catholic message, driven home by a darkly venomous Philip II, Walsingham's imaginary papist brother, William, a Jesuit who tries to assassinate Elizabeth, and so on. At the same time, the film presents Elizabeth as the defender of very modern sounding concepts of liberty and toleration. Equally bad, though, is that all this is subordinated to another invented love story, this time with Sir Walter Raleigh (Clive Owen), who appears to defeat the Spanish Armada single-handedly.[49]

Meanwhile, *Gunpowder, Treason and Plot* (2004), a BBC miniseries filmed in Romania, is in part an attempt to rehabilitate Mary that is completely undermined by its own absurd plot elements. There is relatively little continuity between the two episodes, the first covering Mary's reign from 1561 to 1568, and the second concentrating on the Gunpowder Plot against James VI almost four decades later. A common element is gunpowder, used in attempts to kill Mary's husband, Lord Darnley, in 1567, and their son in 1605. Another is the emphasis on the union of England and Scotland. The first episode, which focuses on Mary's effort to produce an heir who will inherit both kingdoms, seems primarily intended to set up the second, in which James fulfills her wish. As Mary, Clémence Poésy (famous as Fleur Delacour in the Harry Potter movies) has the right accent (French instead of Scots) and the wrong hair color (blond instead of red). As Elizabeth, Catherine McCormack has a hyper-curled hairdo reminiscent of Charlie Brown's little redheaded girl in *Peanuts* as well as the bearing of a children's TV-movie heroine, which hardly enhances the program's attempt to portray her as a cunning and devious manipulator. The story wrongly has "Lord James"—the Earl of Moray—oppose Mary's participation in private Catholic services, makes Bothwell her protector when a Protestant mob disrupts her first mass, transforms Knox into a royal councilor, skips over Mary's flight to England and imprisonment (completely omitting the period 1568–87), and has James (Robert Carlyle) visit Cecil (Tim McInnerny)—an amalgamation of William and Robert—to approve his mother's execution.

The Channel Four/HBO collaboration, *Elizabeth I* (2005), filmed in Lithuania and starring Helen Mirren and a talented cast, is outstanding as a work of art but problematic as an account of history. One problem is that its two episodes are built around twin love stories that are largely fabricated, the first with an aging Earl of Leicester (Jeremy Irons) between 1579 and 1588 and the second with the young Earl of Essex (Hugh Dancy) thereafter. Inevitably, this distorts history by downplaying other characters and events or presenting them only as they relate to the queen's two love interests. Episode 1 begins with the erroneous statement that the "Catholic powers" were a monolithic force united in their determination to dethrone Elizabeth, and episode 2 opens with this bit of post-hoc Protestant providentialism: "By 1589 Elizabeth I was the heroine and saviour of her country. The defeat of the Spanish Armada had secured the English nation and the English Protestant Church." In reality, the Anglo-Spanish War lasted until 1604. Though the miniseries features a realistic debate among Privy Councilors about how her proposed marriage to Alençon might affect the Dutch Revolt, it wrongly has Leicester oppose the match for romantic rather than religious reasons. Elsewhere, it resorts to outright invention, most egregiously by having Elizabeth meet both Mary (Barbara Flynn) and her son James VI (Ewen Bremner), neither of which happened. Muddled chronology further mars the narrative, and for some reason a completely imaginary plot involving Gilbert Gifford takes the place of the real Throckmorton Plot of 1583. On the other hand, viewers may find the torture and execution scenes all too realistic—for example, it shows the executioner chopping off John Stubbs' hand and Mary's head, as well as disemboweling several traitors. In the end, the miniseries works well enough as art, and Mirren is so good that it enhances Elizabeth's stature while portraying Mary as an inept but evil-intentioned plotter.[50]

The BBC miniseries *Elizabeth I: The Virgin Queen* (2005) does not work well as art or as history. It apparently is an attempt to appeal to a young audience by casting young actors and keeping them perpetually youthful; however, Anne-Marie Duff and Tom Hardy are utterly unconvincing as Elizabeth and Leicester. Overall the miniseries emphasizes Elizabeth's romances with Dudley, Anjou, and Essex at the expense of politics, religion, and warfare. Like the Mirren miniseries, it suggests the existence of a monolithic Catholic alliance internationally. It oversimplifies her relationship with English Catho-lics and largely ignores the existence of Puritans other than the unfortunate Stubbs. The story skips over the years 1565–70 and severely compresses the events of the decade 1578–88, which attenuates its treatment of Mary (Char-lotte Winner)—there is no mention of James VI's birth, Darnley's murder, or the Bothwell marriage. The Throckmorton Plot disappears again, though the broad outlines of the Babington Plot are correct. There is no meeting between the queens, but almost as bad is that Mary "speaks" to Elizabeth in the form of voice-overs. Ultimately, though, this miniseries does nothing positive for the image of either queen or for the history of religion.[51]

Finally, among the most noteworthy Tudor films to feature Elizabeth as a character in the last decade-and-a-half are *Shakespeare in Love* (1998) and *Anonymous* (2011), both of which are largely fictional. The former is immensely entertaining, consistently engages in obvious self-mockery, and lets the audience in on the joke, while the latter is an overly serious, self-important attempt to revive the discredited notion that the seventeenth Earl of Oxford wrote the bard's works. Both feature memorable Elizabeths (Judi Dench in the first, Joely Richardson and Vanessa Redgrave in the latter) but neither has anything to say about the queen's faith. A new film, titled *Mary, Queen of Scots*, is in preproduction for 2014, with Saoirse Ronan as Mary and Elizabeth as yet uncast. The screenwriter is Michael Hirst, who also wrote *The Tudors* (2007–10) and Shekhar Kapur's *Elizabeth* films; consequently, historians can be forgiven for tempering their enthusiasm about this project. Reportedly, Kapur plans a third Elizabeth movie with Cate Blanchett, though no doubt this will concern her life after the Armada campaign and thus will not involve Mary.[52]

Clearly, films seldom do justice to Tudor royal women in terms of religion. There may even be reason to ask whether they do more harm by ignoring religion completely or by offering an error-ridden account within a warped perspective. In the end, of course, the filmmaker's goal is not didactic but to entertain audiences and generate profits, and as that is unlikely to change, historians must decide whether and how to respond. Some scholars suggest that historians should simply ignore "historical films." However, such films profoundly influence popular belief, and historians have a responsibility to engage them unless history is to concede the field to fiction. This is especially important at a time when some postmodernists contend that any account of history is just as good as another, an argument that—if true—would make the historical enterprise pointless. Moreover, films in general are prone to stereotyping women, and historical films provide a particularly useful oppor-tunity to counter simplistic or negative images with hard evidence from his-tory. On the other hand, historical films can serve a practical purpose, for discussing them in the classroom and the public forum—as well as scholarly publications—can encourage interest in real history, stimulate critical thinking, and reinforce memory. With proper guidance, students and others can be remarkably adept at comparing films with works of history and ferreting out errors. The extraordinary popularity of Tudor films makes them particularly useful in this regard. Therefore, rather than merely bemoaning their manifold flaws, it behooves Tudor historians to expose their errors while exploiting their appeal.[53]

Notes

1. This essay draws on research for Sue Parrill and William B. Robison, *The Tudors on Film and Television* (Jefferson, NC: McFarland, 2013) but focuses on the filmic representation of Tudor royal women and religion in a way not possible in that volume due to considerations of length and structure. There are links at www.tudorsonfilm.com to Blu-ray, DVD, or VHS editions of films discussed here if available or to the Internet Movie Database (IMDB) or British Film Institute Film and Television Database (BFI) for those that are lost or inaccessible. One caveat for using IMDB is that this film database is not vetted by scholars but user-written and user-edited. Citations are included in the notes only for rare films and video held by the British Film Institute or the Library of Congress. Entries appear in the book for all films discussed here except a few released in 2012 and after, for which entries appear on the website; therefore, the notes do not include separate citations to the book. As used here, the term "film" refers to all filmic representation, including television; however, although the book and website include documentaries, some of which incorporate dramatizations, this essay addresses only fictional or fictionalized films about the Tudor period. I would be remiss not to acknowledge Sue Parrill, my longtime friend and colleague at Southeastern Louisiana University (where she was a member of the Department of English), who has been a wonderful collaborator and has contributed immeasurably to my knowledge of film history. We benefited greatly from the extensive literature concerning the Tudors on film; Susan Doran and Thomas S. Freeman, eds., *Tudors and Stuarts on Film: Historical Perspectives* (New York: Palgrave Macmillan, 2008) is a particularly outstanding collection but does not include television; other important works dealing with films about the Tudor period include Thomas Betteridge and Thomas Freeman, *Henry VIII and History* (Surrey, UK: Ashgate, 2012); Susan Bordo, *The Creation of Anne Boleyn: A New Look at England's Most Notorious Queen* (New York: Houghton Mifflin, 2013); Mark Thornton Burnett and Adrian Street, eds., *Filming and Performing Renaissance History* (New York: Palgrave Macmillan, 2011); Annaliese Connolly and Lisa Hopkins, eds., *Goddesses and Queens: The Iconography of Elizabeth I* (Manchester: Manchester University Press, 2008); Michael Dobson and Nicola J. Watson, *England's Elizabeth: An Afterlife in Fame and Fantasy* (Oxford: Oxford University Press, 2002); Susan Doran and Thomas Freeman, *The Myth*

of Elizabeth (New York: Palgrave Macmillan, 2003); Elizabeth A. Ford, *Royal Portraits in Hollywood: Filming the Lives of Queens* (Lexington, KY: University Press of Kentucky, 2009); Denis Gifford, *The British Film Catalogue 1895–1985* (New York: Facts on File, 1986); Sue Harper, *Picturing the Past: The Rise and Fall of the British Costume Film* (London: British Film Institute, 1994); Andrew Higson, *English Heritage, English Cinema: Costume Drama Since 1980* (Oxford: Oxford University Press, 2003); Michael Klossner, *The Europe of 1500 to 1815 on Film and Television: A Worldwide Filmography of Over 2550 Works, 1895 Through 2000* (Jefferson, NC: McFarland, 2002); Bethany Latham, *Elizabeth I in Film and Television: A Study of the Major Portrayals* (Jefferson, NC: McFarland, 2011); Mark Rankin, Christopher Highly, and John N. King, eds., *Henry VIII and His Afterlives: Literature, Politics, and Art* (Cambridge: Cambridge University Press, 2009); Greg Colón Semenza, ed., *The English Renaissance in Popular Culture: An Age for All Time* (New York: Palgrave Macmillan, 2010); Tatiana String and Marcus Bull, *Tudorism: Historical Imagination and the Appropriation of the Sixteenth Century* (Oxford: Oxford University Press, 2011); Gore Vidal, *Screening History* (Cambridge, MA: Harvard University Press, 1992); and Greg Walker, *The Private Life of Henry VIII: British Film Guide* (London: I. B. Tauris, 2003). Work related to Tudor films will continue with *History, Fiction, and The Tudors: Sex, Politics, Power, and Artistic License in the Showtime Television Series* (forthcoming 2015), a collection of essays that I am editing for Palgrave Macmillan's *Queenship and Power* series. I have had the opportunity to discuss Tudor films with many of the aforementioned experts and a host of others at a Center for Shakespeare Studies Workshop at the Folger Shakespeare Library, "Reassessing Henry VIII: Directions for Future Research" (2010), and when presenting various bits of related material at the British Scholar Conference, the Gulf Medieval and Renaissance Conference (formerly the Louisiana Consortium of Medieval and Renaissance Scholars), the Louisiana Historical Association, the Sixteenth Century Studies Conference, the Southern Conference on British Studies, the Symposium on Medieval and Renaissance Studies, and in various public lectures, library programs, and university seminars. I am especially grateful to Stephen Alford, Keith Altazin, Caroline Armbruster, Tom Betteridge, Susan Bordo, Sara Butler, Marie-Therese Champagne, Susan Doran, Lauren Doughty, Charles Elliott, Tom Freeman, Ron Fritze, Elizabeth Lane Furdell, Steve Gunn, Jeff Hankins, Maria Hayward, Rob Hermann, Megan Hickerson, Chris Highley, Krista Kesselring, Harry Laver, Carole Levin, Catherine Loomis, Scott Lucas, Margaret McGlynn, Bill Parrill, Samantha Perez, Beth Quitslund, Glenn Richardson, Jim Rogers, Karl Roider, Jerry Sanson, Robert Scully, Victor Stater, Tania String, Bill Tighe, Scott Walker, Kristen Walton, and Retha Warnicke for the information and insights they have shared, the encouragement they have offered, and their consistently delightful company. I similarly appreciate Julie Chappell and Kaley Kramer's vision in conceiving the present volume and their generosity in accepting my contribution to the project. Considerations of space make it impossible to cite at length the extensive literature on film history and "history films" or the vast historiography on the Tudor church and state, the Tudor kings, the English

Reformation, or early modern women, though for the historical characters in Tudor films the endnotes reference biographical entries in the *Oxford Dictionary of National Biography* (Oxford: Oxford University Press, 2004–2014), online edition [ODNB hereinafter] where extensive citations to relevant scholarship may be found.

2. The first Tudor film, *The Execution of Mary, Queen of Scots* (1895), silent and a mere eleven seconds long, offers little opportunity for religious commentary; of all the Tudor films produced in the last 120 years, only one concentrates on a religious figure—*God's Outlaw* (1986), a mediocre account of William Tyndale's life; productions of *A Man for All Seasons* downplay Thomas More's faith as a motive for martyrdom.

3. S. J. Gunn, "Henry VII (1457–1509)," ODNB (2004–14), doi.org/10.1093/ref:odnb/12954; Michael K. Jones and Malcolm G. Underwood, "Beaufort, Margaret, Countess of Richmond and Derby (1443–1509)," ODNB, doi.org/10.1093/ref:odnb/1863; Rosemary Horrox, "Elizabeth (1466–1503)," ODNB, doi.org/10.1093/ref:odnb/8635; *The Shadow of the Tower* is an underrated BBC series about Henry VII's reign that was the prequel to *The Six Wives of Henry VIII* (1970), but it was unavailable and largely unknown after its initial showing until it was released on DVD in 2011; *Princes in the Tower* is convoluted and ridiculous; English-language Shakespearean "Elizabeths" include Carlotta De Felice as princess and Carey Lee as queen in *The Life and Death of King Richard III* (1912), Mary Kerridge in Laurence Olivier's *Richard III* (1955), Jane Wenham in *An Age of Kings* (1960), Katherine Barker as princess and Susan Engel as queen in *The Wars of the Roses* (1965), Rowena Cooper in *Richard III* (1983), Ann Penfold in the English Shakespeare Company's *The Wars of the Roses* (1989), Sorcha Cusack in the animated *Richard III* (1994), Kate Stevenson-Payne as princess and Annette Bening as queen in *Richard III* (1995), Angelina Szostak as princess and Caroline Burns Cooke as queen in *Richard III* (2005), Daniela Melgoza as princess and Maria Conchita Alonso as queen in *Richard III* (2008).

4. Richard Glen Eaves, "Margaret [Margaret Tudor] (1489–1541)," ODNB, doi.org/10.1093/ref:odnb/18052; David Loades, "Mary [Mary Tudor] (1496–1533)," ODNB, doi.org/10.1093/ref:odnb/18251; S. J. Gunn, "Brandon, Charles, First Duke of Suffolk (c.1484–1545)," ODNB, doi.org/10.1093/ref:odnb/3261. Mary is also a character in *La reine galante* (*Au théâtre ce soir*, 1974); Margaret (Wendy Spinks) appears briefly as a child in *The Shadow of the Tower*.

5. E. W. Ives, "Henry VIII (1491–1547)," ODNB, doi.org/10.1093/ref:odnb/12955; despite the proliferation of works on the king and his reign, J. J. Scarisbrick, *Henry VIII* (New Haven, CT. and London: Yale University Press, 1997) remains essential. Of the many books that deal with the six wives collectively, the most useful are Antonia Fraser, *The Wives of Henry VIII* (New York: Alfred A. Knopf, 1992); David Loades, *The Six Wives of Henry VIII*, second edn. (Stroud, Gloucs.: Amberley Publishing, 2010); and David Starkey, *Six Wives: The Queens of Henry VIII* (New York: Vintage, 2004). For an excellent survey of Henry's reign on film, see Thomas S. Freeman, "A Tyrant for All Seasons: Henry

VIII on Film," in Doran and Freeman, *Tudors and Stuarts on Film*, 30–45; see also Tom Betteridge, "Henry VIII and Popular Culture," Rankin, Highley, and King, *Henry VIII and His Afterlives*, 208–22; Tatiana String, "Myth and Memory in Representations of Henry VIII," 201–22; and Greg Walker, "A Great Guy with His Chopper: The Sex Life of Henry VIII on Screen and in the Flesh," in String and Bull, *Tudorism*, 223–42.

6. Katherine's parents, Ferdinand of Aragon and Isabella of Castille, had her educated by the Dominican reformer Pascual de Ampudia and the Italian humanists Alessandro and Antonio Gerladini. In 1523 Katherine brought Vives to England and commissioned his *De institutione foeminae Christianae*. C. S. L. Davies and John Edwards, "Katherine [Katherine of Aragon] (1485–1536)," ODNB, doi.org/10.1093/ref:odnb/4891; Garrett Mattingly, *Catherine of Aragon* (New York: Little, Brown and Company, 1941) is the classic biography; important new works are Julia Fox, *Sister Queens: The Noble, Tragic Lives of Katherine of Aragon and Juana, Queen of Castile* (New York: Ballantine, 2012); Giles Tremlett, *Catherine of Aragon: The Spanish Queen of Henry VIII* (New York: Walker & Company, 2010); and Patrick Williams, *Catherine of Aragon* (Stroud, Gloucs.: Amberley Publishing, 2012).

7. E. W. Ives, "Anne [Anne Boleyn] (c.1500–1536)," ODNB, doi.org/10.1093/ref:odnb/557, and *The Life and Death of Anne Boleyn*, second edn. (Oxford: Blackwell, 2004); Retha Warnicke, *The Rise and Fall of Anne Boleyn* (Cambridge: Cambridge University Press, 1989); Starkey, *Six Wives*; G. W. Bernard, *Anne Boleyn: Fatal Attractions* (New Haven, CT: Yale University Press, 2010), in which the resolutely contrarian Bernard questions her Protestantism and influence on the Henrician Reformation as well as much else that is usually taken as given about her life but is less than convincing on this point; Glenn Richardson, *Anne of the Thousand Days* in Doran and Freeman, *Tudors and Stuarts on Film*, 60–75.

8. Her brothers, Edward (later Duke of Somerset and Lord Protector) and Thomas, became active proponents of Protestantism during her son Edward VI's reign but had not yet done so in the 1530s. Barrett L. Beer, "Jane [Jane Seymour] (1508/9–1537)," ODNB, doi.org/10.1093/ref:odnb/14647.

9. Retha M. Warnicke, "Anne [Anne of Cleves] (1515–1557)," ODNB, doi.org/10.1093/ref:odnb/558, and *The Marrying of Anne of Cleves: Royal Protocol in Early Modern England* (Cambridge: Cambridge University Press, 2000); Mary Saaler, *Anne of Cleves: Fourth Wife of Henry VIII* (Ontario, Canada: Rubicon Press, 1995).

10. Retha M. Warnicke, "Katherine [Katherine Howard] (1518x24–1542)," ODNB, doi.org/10.1093/ref:odnb/4892, and *Wicked Women of Tudor England: Queens, Aristocrats, Commoners* (New York: Palgrave Macmillan, 2012), chapter 3; Lacey Baldwin Smith, *Catherine Howard* (Stroud, Gloucs.: Amberley Publishing, 2010).

11. According to the traditional account, their arrest and brutal torture of the openly heretical Anne Askew failed to compel her to implicate the queen, but Gardiner obtained a warrant for Katherine Parr's arrest on the basis of her possession of

heretical books, and she escaped only by humbly submitting herself to the king and adopting a lower profile for the remainder of his reign; Susan E. James, "Katherine [Katherine Parr] (1512–1548)," ODNB, doi.org/10.1093/ref:odnb/4893, and *Catherine Parr: Henry VIII's Last Love* (Stroud, Gloucs.: The History Press, 2009); Linda Porter, *Katherine the Queen: The Remarkable Life of Katherine Parr, the Last Wife of Henry VIII* (New York: St. Martin's Press, 2010); however, Thomas S. Freeman, "One Survived: The Account of Katherine Parr in Foxe's 'Book of Martyrs,' *Henry VIII and the Court*, ed. Tom Betteridge and Suzannah Lipscomb (Aldershot: Ashgate, 2013), 235–54 questions the traditional account of Gardiner's plot.

12. Anne Boleyn debuted in Georges Melies' *La Tour de Londres et les derniers moments d'Anne de Boleyn* (1905), now lost, as is *Henry VIII and Catherine Howard* (1910, misdated in IMDB); *Anne Boleyn* (1911), likely the same film as *Une Intrigue à la cour d'Henry VIII d'Angleterre*, released in America as *Jane Seymour and Henry VIII of England*, with Madeleine Roch as Anne; Richard Abel, *The Ciné Goes to Town: French Cinema 1896–1914* (Berkeley: University of California Press, 1998), 311; *Henry VIII* (1911); Robert Hamilton Ball, "The Shakespeare Film as Record: Sir Herbert Beerbohm Tree," *Shakespeare Quarterly* 3.3 (July 1952): 227–36; *Cardinal Wolsey* (1912, incomplete, British Film Institute Archives, title/28744); *Anne Boleyn* (1912, http://www.silentera.com/PSFL/data/A/AnneBoleyn1912.html); William Shakespeare, *Henry VIII*, Folger Shakespeare Library, ed. Barbara A. Mowat and Paul Werstine (New York: Simon & Schuster, 2007).

13. *Anne de Boleyn* (1913, incomplete, Library of Congress, FRA 3515); Katherine, Anne, and Jane likely were characters in *The Threefold Tragedy* (1922), now lost; *When Knighthood Was in Flower* (1953); *Hampton Court Palace* (*Haunted Houses and Castles of Great Britain*, 1926); *A Princess of Destiny* (*Great Events*, 1929); see also Scott Eyman, *Ernst Lubitsch: Laughter in Paradise: A Biography* (New York: Simon & Schuster, 1993).

14. Anne's inclusion in *Private Life* was primarily a vehicle for launching the career of actress Merle Oberon. Freeman, "A Tyrant for All Seasons," 33–39; Francis Hackett, *Personal History of Henry the Eighth* (London: Jonathan Cape, 1929); Martin Hume, *The Wives of Henry the Eighth and the Parts They Played in History* (London: E. Nash, 1905); Walker, *The Private Life of Henry VIII*; on films in the 1930s and 1940s, Harper, *Picturing the Past: The Rise and Fall of the British Costume Film*.

15. Palmer's real-life husband, Rex Harrison, reprised his onstage role as Henry VIII in *Anne of the Thousand Days* for *The Trial of Anne Boleyn* (*Omnibus* 1.01, November 9, 1952, Library of Congress VBE 5417–18); Anne (Beatrice Straight) also shared screen time with Walter Cronkite in *The Crisis of Anne Boleyn* (*You Are There*, June 20, 1954); *A Man for All Seasons* (1957; 1964; 1966, directed by Robert Zinnemann with Paul Scofield as More and Robert Shaw as Henry; 1978, directed by Charlton Heston, who also played More); see also Maxwell Anderson, *Anne of the Thousand Days* (New York: William Sloane, 1948); Robert Bolt, *A Man for All Seasons* (New York: Samuel French, 1960); Bordo, *The Creation of*

Anne Boleyn (I am grateful to Dr. Bordo for sharing her chapter on Anne on film prior to its publication); Colin Chambers, "Bolt, Robert Oxton (1924–1995)," ODNB, doi.org/10.1093/ref:odnb/59804; R. W. Chambers, *Thomas More* (London: Jonathan Cape, 1935); Freeman, "A Tyrant for All Seasons," and Peter Marshall, "Saints and Cinemas: *A Man for All Seasons*," in Doran and Freeman, *Tudors and Stuarts on Film*, 40–42, 46–59; Glenn Richardson, "The 'sexual everyman'? Maxwell Anderson's Henry VIII," 195–206, and Ruth Ahnert, "Drama king: The Portrayal of Henry VIII in Robert Bolt's *A Man for All Seasons*," 207–22 in Betteridge and Freeman, *Henry VIII and History.*

16. *BFI: The White Falcon* (www.screenonline.org.uk/tv); for the pageant of the White Falcon, see Alice Hunt, *The Drama of Coronation: Medieval Ceremony in Early Modern England* (Cambridge: Cambridge University Press, 2008).

17. Margaret Irwin, *Young Bess* (New York: Harcourt Brace, 1945); J. E. Neale, *Queen Elizabeth* (New York: Harcourt Brace, 1934).

18. No doubt as a result of the previous success of *A Man for All Seasons*, Thomas More appears more often in the movie than in Anderson's original play, but his main function is to warn others, notably Thomas Cromwell, against letting Henry know the full extent of his power; however, little is made of his faith; Richardson, "Anne of the Thousand Days," Doran and Freeman, *Tudors and Stuarts on Film*, 60–74.

19. Although Henry speaks learnedly about religion, it does not figure in his discussion with Katherine of Aragon on their wedding night of his plans for a "golden age." When years later he presents her with his argument from Leviticus that their marriage is invalid, she weeps hysterically but does not argue with his interpretation. Subsequently, she defends the sanctity of her marriage to Cardinal Campeggio but only on the grounds that her first marriage to Arthur was never consummated. When Campeggio urges her to enter a nunnery, she declares that she has no calling to the "religious" life, but this is an accurate reflection of her refusal to give up marriage for monasticism. Though she angrily and courageously defends herself against Henry and Wolsey, she does not do so on scriptural or theological grounds. The closest she comes to a statement of faith is at her brief appearance before the legatine court, when she tells Henry that if he will not hear her, she will appeal to God, and later when she worries that the king is "endangering his immortal soul." The episode's final verdict is that Katherine followed "conscience and love." However, much like *A Man for All Seasons* does with Thomas More, it gives Katherine's "conscience" a rather generic meaning rather than one clearly rooted in faith. Later, Anne Boleyn actually hopes after her own arrest that Henry will send her to a nunnery rather than the scaffold. Rosalie Crutchley returns as Katherine Parr in *Elizabeth R* (1971), though only in a flashback after Elizabeth (Glenda Jackson) and Thomas Seymour (John Ronane) are arrested in 1549. A young, unmarried Katherine of Aragon (Adrienne Byrne) appears briefly in the last episode of *The Shadow of the Tower* but only as a pawn in diplomatic negotiations between Henry VII and her parents, Ferdinand and Isabella.

20. Camille Saint-Saens' opera, *Henry VIII* (1991), with Michèle Command as Katherine, is likewise favorable, being based on the Shakespeare–Fletcher drama and another play, *La cisma de Ingalaterra*, by Pedro Calderon de la Barca, a seventeenth-century Spanish Catholic priest, poet, and dramatist. Gaetano Donizetti's *Anna Bolena*, of which there are several filmed versions (1984, 2007, 2011) is distinctly ahistorical; what happens in the obscure film, *Great Harry and Jane* (1994) is unknown.

21. Director Pete Travis calls *Henry VIII* (2003) "*The Godfather* in tights"; both versions of *The Other Boleyn Girl* are based on the novel by Philippa Gregory, *The Other Boleyn Girl* (New York: Scribner, 2001).

22. See also Jerome de Groote, "Slashing History: The Tudors," in String and Bull, *Tudorism*, 243–60; Ramona Wray, "Henry's Desperate Housewives: The Tudors, the Politics of Historiography, and the Beautiful Body of Jonathan Rhys Meyers," in Semenza, *The English Renaissance in Popular Culture*, 25–42, and "The Network King: Re-creating Henry VIII for a Global Television Audience," in Burnett and Streete, *Filming and Performing Renaissance History*, 16–32.

23. More claimed after Fish's death that he had returned to the Catholic Church. As Chancellor, More was responsible for burning several heretics, but not Fish.

24. There are two Janes—Anita Briem at the end of season two and Annabelle Wallis in season three. Although the second Jane is pregnant with Prince Edward, Henry has an affair with the imaginary Ursula Misseldon (Charlotte Salt), who later assists Jane in her labor, and whom Jane incongruously asks to be a "comfort" to the king if something should go wrong.

25. Season three offers a great deal of nonsense about religion (e.g., making Henry the author of the Six Articles of 1539 and having him rewrite the Lord's Prayer). Also, with Archbishop Cranmer having departed the show at the end of season two, Bishop Gardiner is now ubiquitous, though in reality he was in France between 1536 and 1538.

26. Season four, like its predecessor, proceeds without Cranmer, a key adversary of Gardiner. It also invents a conflict between Gardiner and Ann Stanhope. On the positive side, it correctly emphasizes Katherine Parr's possession of heretical books.

27. Dale Hoak, "Edward VI (1537–1553)," ODNB, doi.org/10.1093/ref:odnb/8522.

28. Mark Twain, *The Prince and the Pauper* (Boston: James R. Osgood and Co., 1881); *The Prince and the Pauper* (1909, 1915, 1920, 1937, 1943, 1957, 1960, 1962, 1969, 1972, 1976, 1977, 1996, 2000, 2005); see also Vidal, *Screening History*, 1–30.

29. Alison Plowden, "Grey, Lady Jane (1537–1554)," ODNB, doi.org/10.1093/ref:odnb/8154; Eric Ives, *Lady Jane Grey: A Tudor Mystery* (New York: Wiley-Blackwell, 2011); Carole Levin, "Lady Jane Grey on Film," in Doran and Freeman, *Tudors and Stuarts on Film*, 76–87 (the quote is from 82).

30. Ann Weikel, "Mary I (1516–1558)," ODNB, doi.org/10.1093/ref:odnb/18245; see also Eamon Duffy, *Fires of Faith: Catholic England under Mary Tudor* (New Haven, CT: Yale University Press, 2009); Linda Porter, *Mary Tudor: The First*

Queen (New York: Little, Brown, 2007); Anna Whitelock, *Mary Tudor: England's First Queen* (London: Bloomsbury, 2009).

31. *Elizabeth* (1998); *Tudor Rose* (2008); see also Christopher Haigh, "Kapur's Elizabeth," in Doran and Freeman, *Tudors and Stuarts on Film*, 122–35; Latham, *Elizabeth I in Film and Television*, 148–65.

32. *Maria Tudor* (1911); *Marie Tudor* (1912, misdated to 1917 at IMDB); *Maria Tudor* (aka *Judgment*, 1920); *Mary Tudor* (1923), possibly the American release of the 1920 film; *Marie Tudor* (1966).

33. Patrick Collinson, "Elizabeth I (1533–1603)," ODNB, doi.org/10.1093/ref:odnb/8636; see also Stephen Alford, *The Watchers: A Secret History of the Reign of Elizabeth I* (London: Bloomsbury Press, 2012); John Cooper, *The Queen's Agent: Sir Francis Walsingham and the Rise of Espionage in Elizabethan England* (Glendale Heights, IL: Pegasus, 2013).

34. See also Thomas Betteridge, "A Queen for All Seasons: Elizabeth I on Film," *The Myth of Elizabeth*, ed. Susan Doran and Thomas Freeman (Basingstoke, UK: Palgrave Macmillan, 2003), 242–59; Susan Doran, "From Hatfield to Hollywood: Elizabeth I on Film"; Judith Richards, "Lady in Waiting: The Young Elizabeth on Film," in Doran and Freeman, *Tudors and Stuarts on Film*, 88–121; Adrienne L. Eastwood, "The Secret Life of Elizabeth I," in Semenza, *The English Renaissance in Popular Culture*, 43–54; Elizabeth A. Ford and Deborah C. Mitchell, *Royal Portraits in Hollywood: Filming the Lives of Queens* (Lexington, KY: University Press of Kentucky, 2009), 126–56, 226–94; Latham, *Elizabeth I on Film and Television*, passim.

35. Julian Goodare, "Mary (1542–1587)," ODNB, doi.org/10.1093/ref:odnb/18248; see also Rosalind Marshall, *Mary, Queen of Scots* (Edinburgh: National Museums of Scotland, 2013).

36. See Will Coster, "The Armada, War and Propaganda in the Cinema," in Doran and Freeman, *Tudors and Stuarts on Film*, 150–63.

37. Glyn Redworth, "Philip (1527–1598)," ODNB, doi.org/10.1093/ref:odnb/22097; see also Vivienne Westbrook, "*Elizabeth: The Golden Age*: A Sign of the Times?" in Doran and Freeman, *Tudors and Stuarts on Film*, 164–77; Latham, *Elizabeth I in Film and Television*, 165–78.

38. Sound films featuring Mary but not Elizabeth include *Campbell of Kilmhor* (1939, Elliott Mason); *Princess of Cleves* (1961, Renée-Marie Potet); *Father Came Too!* (1964, Hugh Lloyd); *Mistress of Hardwick* (1972, Gilly McIver); *A Traveller in Time* (1978, Heather Chassen); *Les grandes conjurations: Le tumulte d'Amboise* (1978, Véronique Delbourg); *A korona aranyból van* (1979, Georgiana Tarjan); *Highlander: The Raven: Thick as Thieves* (1999, Peggy Frankston); new entries are forthcoming at www.tudorsonfilm.com on Mary's very minor appearances in *Campbell of Kilmor, Father Came Too!, Highlander: The Raven: Prince of Thieves*, and *Princess of Cleves*, as well as her more lengthy, if still historically insubstantial, appearances in *Mary, Queen of Scots* (2013) and *Reign* (2013).

39. See also Latham, *Elizabeth I in Film and Television*, 16–39.

40. See, for example, *The Prince and the Pauper* (1962, 1976). On Shakespeare: *Will Shakespeare* (1938, Nancy Price); *The Dark Lady of the Sonnets* (1946, Dorothy Black); *Will Shakespeare* (1953, Mary Clare); *You Are There: The First Command*

Performance of Romeo and Juliet 1597 (1954, Mildred Dunnock); *BBC Sunday Night Theatre: The Dark Lady of the Sonnets* (1955, Beatrix Lehmann); *Life of Shakespeare* (1978, Patience Collier); *The Merry Wives of Windsor* (1980, Diane Cameron). Cartoons: *Magic Grandad: Famous People—Elizabeth I* (1994, Robin Weaver); *Tudor Rose* (2008, Mimi Forrester). Comedy: *Decisions, Decisions* (1975, John Cleese); *Carry on Laughing! Orgy and Bess* (1975, Hattie Jacques); *Black-adder II, Blackadder's Christmas Carol, Blackadder Back & Forth* (1986, 1988, 1999, Miranda Richardson); *The Girls Next Door: Surely, You Joust!* (2007). Time travel: *Time Flies* (1944, Olga Lindo); *Doctor Who: The Executioners* (1965, Vivienne Bennett, 1965); *Doctor Who: The Shakespeare Code* (2007, Angela Pleasence); *Doctor Who: The Day of the Doctor* (2013, Joanna Page). Other: *I Married an Angel* (1942, Edwina Coolidge); *Kenilworth* (1957, Maxine Audley); *The Story of Mankind* (1957, Agnes Moorehead); *Queen's Champion: Betrayal* (1958, Peggy Thorpe-Bates); *ITV Play of the Week: In the Shadow of the Axe* (1958, Catherine Lacey); *Elizabeth Is Dead* (1960, Mecha Ortiz); *Thursday Theatre: The Young Elizabeth* (1964, Valerie Gearon); *Kenilworth* (1967, Gemma Jones); *The Ghosts of Motley Hall: Ghost Writer* (1978, Christine Rose); *Jubilee* (1978, Jenny Runacre); *Drake's Venture* (1980, Charlotte Cornwell), *Titans: Elizabeth I* (1981, Frances Hyland); *Gloriana* (1984, Sarah Walker); *Mapp & Lucia: Battle Stations* (1985, Geraldine McEwan); *T-Bag and the Ring of Olympus: Torture* (1991, Sarah Berger); *Orlando* (1991, Quentin Crisp); *In Suspicious Circumstances: An Evil Business* (1996, Helen Baxendale); *Gloriana* (2000, Josephine Barstow); *Mentors: Her Grace under Pressure* (2001, Margot Kidder); *Renaissance Girl: The Short Film* (2005, Gay Linn Kirkpatrick); *Sword of Hearts* (2005, Mary Kababik); *Mandragora* (2006, Lindsay Kemp); *Secret Mysteries of America's Beginnings* (2006–07, Gay Linn Kirkpatrick).

41. Schiller: *Mary Stuart* (1913, Miriam Nesbitt as Elizabeth, Mary Fuller as Mary); (1957, Paul Wessely as Elizabeth, Kathe Dorsch as Mary); *Maria Stuart (Omnibus Ford Theatre,* 1957, Eva Le Gallienne as Elizabeth, Irene Worth as Mary); *Marie Stuart* (1959, Elénore Hirt as Elizabeth, Maria Mauban as Mary); *Mary Stuart (Play of the Week,* 1960, Eva Le Gallienne as Elizabeth, Signe Hasso as Mary); *Maria Stuart* (1963, Elfriede Kuzmany as Elizabeth, Agnes Fink as Mary); *Mary Queen of Scots (BBC Play of the Month,* 1969, Pamela Brown as Elizabeth, Virginia McKenna as Mary); *Maria Stuart* (1980, Gisela Leipert as Elizabeth, Gertraud Dreissig as Mary); *Maria Stuart* (1982, cast unknown); *Maria Stuart* (1986, Daniela Ziegler as Elizabeth, Anja Kruse as Mary); *Maria Estuard* (1991, Maife Gil as Elizabeth, Anna Lizaran as Mary); *Maria Stuart* (2008, Paul Dombrowski as Elizabeth, Susanne Wolff as Mary); *The Virgin Queen* (1923); *The Loves of Mary, Queen of Scots* (aka *Marie, Queen of Scots,* 1923); *Dorothy Vernon of Haddon Hall* (1924, Library of Congress FCA 8553–55).

42. *Drake the Pirate* (1935, Library of Congress VAG 4856); see also Latham, *Elizabeth I in Film and Television,* 65–76; Vidal, *Screening History,* 31–64.

43. See also Doran, "From Hatfield to Hollywood," and Paul E. J. Hammer, "The Private Lives of Elizabeth and Essex and the Romanticization of Elizabethan Politics," in Doran and Freeman, *Tudors and Stuarts on Film,* 97–98, 190–203; Latham, *Elizabeth I on Film and Television,* 40–49.

44. See also Latham, *Elizabeth I in Film and Television*, 41–65.
45. *Elizabeth the Queen* (1968, Library of English VHS E.T.I. Video).
46. See also Latham, *Elizabeth I in Film and Television*, 191–216.
47. See also John Guy, "Mary Queen of Scots (1971), in Doran and Freeman, *Tudors and Stuarts on Film*, 136–49; Latham, *Elizabeth I in Film and Television*, 130–48.
48. See also Christopher Haigh, "Kapur's Elizabeth," in Doran and Freeman, *Tudors and Stuarts on Film*, 122–35; Latham, *Elizabeth I in Film and Television*, 148–65.
49. See also Latham, *Elizabeth I in Film and Television*, 165–78; Courtney Lehmann, "Where the Maps End: *Elizabeth: The Golden Age* of Simulacra," in Semenza, *The English Renaissance in Popular Culture*, 55–74; Westbrook, "*Elizabeth: The Golden Age:* A Sign of the Times?" in Doran and Freeman, *Tudors and Stuarts on Film*, 164–77.
50. See also Latham, *Elizabeth I in Film and Television*, 239–68.
51. See also Latham, *Elizabeth I in Film and Television*, 220–39.
52. For information on the new film projects about Mary, Queen of Scots see http://www.imdb.com/title/tt2328900/ and especially http://www.bbc.co.uk/news/uk-scotland-highlands-islands-22652469; see also the last line of an article about Shekhar Kapur which indicates a "third instalment of *Elizabeth*" at http://www.hollywoodreporter.com/news/shekhar-kapur-london-fields-martin-amis-266616.
53. For the argument that historians should ignore historical films, see David Herlihy, "Am I a Camera? Other Reflections on Film and History," *American Historical Review* 93 (1988): 1186–92; on the responsibility of historians to engage them, Thomas S. Freeman, "Introduction: It's Only a Movie," in Doran and Freeman, *Tudors and Stuarts on Film*, 1–28; and on their usefulness in the classroom, Eric Josef Carlson, "Teaching Elizabeth Tudor with Movies," *Sixteenth Century Journal* 38 (2007): 419–40. My own classes on history and film have confirmed that students can learn a great deal by combining lecture, discussion, reading, and viewing of historical films. Tudor scholars have a larger body of films to employ than perhaps anyone except historians of the American Civil War and World War II. For some further thoughts on "doing history" in the postmodern era, see my reviews of Keith Jenkins, *On "What Is History?": From Carr and Elton to Rorty and White*, and Frank Ankersmit and Hans Kellner, *A New Philosophy of History*, in *Clio: A Journal of Literature, History and the Philosophy of History*, 28.3 (1999): 354–64, and 28.4 (1999): 464–73, respectively.

List of Contributors

Sharon L. Arnoult is Associate Professor of History at Midwestern State University. She has contributed articles to numerous collections, including "Prayer Book, Polemic and Performance," in *Negotiating the Jacobean Printed Book*, ed. Pete Langman (Ashgate, 2011); "'Some Improvement to Their Spiritual and Eternal State': Women's Prayers in the Seventeenth-Century Church of England," in *Early Modern Women and Transnational Communities of Letters*, ed. Julie D. Campbell and Anne R. Larsen (Ashgate, 2009); "'Spiritual and Sacred Publique Actions': The *Book of Common Prayer* and the Understanding of Worship in the Elizabethan and Jacobean Church of England," in *Religion and the English People, 1500–1640: New Voices, New Perspectives*, ed. Eric J. Carlson (Sixteenth Century Essays and Studies, Volume 45, Truman State University Press, 1998); and "The Sovereignties of Body and Soul: Women's Political and Religious Actions in the English Civil War," in *Women and Sovereignty*, ed. Louise O. Fradenburg (Edinburgh University Press, 1992).

Amanda L. Capern teaches at the University of Hull in the United Kingdom. She is author of *The Historical Study of Women: England 1500–1700* (Palgrave, 2008, 2010) and is currently working on a second monograph, *Women, Land and Family in Early Modern England*. She is editor (with Louella McCarthy) of the book series *Gender and History* (Palgrave) and was coeditor (with Judith Spicksley) of *Women, Wealth and Power*, a special issue of *Women's History Review* (2007). She has published in numerous academic journals. Forthcoming chapters in books include: "Rumour and Reputation in the Early Modern English Family" in *Fama and her Sisters: Gossip and Rumour in Early Modern Europe*, ed. Claire Walker and Heather Kerr (Brepols, 2014) and "Visions of Monarchy and Magistracy in Women's Political Writing, 1649–1670" in *From Republic to Restoration*, ed. Janet Clare (Manchester University Press, 2014). She was one of the subeditors on *Female Biography*, vols. 1–6, ed. Gina Luria Walker (Pickering & Chatto, 2013, 2014) and is editor of and contributor to *The Routledge History of Women in Early Modern Europe* (forthcoming, 2016).

Julie A. Chappell is Professor of English at Tarleton State University. She is editor and translator of *The Prose Alexander of Robert Thornton: The Middle English Text with a Modern English Translation* (Peter Lang, 1992) and author of *Perilous Passages:* The Book of Margery Kempe *1534–1934* (Palgrave Macmillan, 2013). She is coeditor with Kamille Stone Stanton of *Transatlantic Literature of the Long Eighteenth Century* (Cambridge Scholars, 2011) and *Spectacle, Sex, and Property in Eighteenth-Century Literature and Culture* (AMS, 2014). A collection of her poetry, *Faultlines: One Woman's Shifting Boundaries*, was released by Village Books Press in October 2013, and she is coeditor with Marilyn Robitaille of a collection of creative works by Texas writers, *Writing Texas* (Lamar University Press, 2014).

Rebecca A. Giselbrecht is Teaching and Research Associate at the University of Zurich Theological Faculty, Institute for Swiss Reformation Studies and the Department of Practical Theology. Her dissertation, completed in September 2014, is entitled: "A Hermeneutic of Female Testimony in the Zurich Reformation: Heinrich Bullinger and Women (1525–1575)." Her publications "Reforming a Model: Zwingli, Bullinger and the Virgin Mary in Sixteenth-century Zurich," in *Following Zwingli: Applying the Past in Reformation Zurich*, ed. Luca Baschera, Bruce Gordon, and Christian Moser (Ashgate, 2014); "Beza over polygamie," in *Théodore de Bèze: Zijm Leven*, ed. W. Balke, J. C. Klok, and W. van't Spijker (Uitgeverij Kok, 2012); "Zwingli und Bullinger: Väter des reformierten 'Wybsbilds'" in *Kirche, Theologie und Politik im reformierten Protestantismus*, ed. Matthias Freudenberg and Georg Plasger (Neukircher Verlag, 2011); and "Myths and Reality about Heinrich Bullinger's Wife Anna" in *Zwingliana*, ed. Christian Moser and Peter Opitz (Theologischer Verlag Zurich, 2011).

Kaley A. Kramer is a Lecturer in eighteenth-century literature at York St John University (York, UK). She studied at Queen's University and the University of Windsor (Canada) before undertaking doctoral work at the University of Leeds (UK). She specializes in eighteenth-century women's writing, history, and authorship. She has previously published work on Mary Wollstonecraft, Charlotte Smith, Elizabeth Griffith, and Frances Sheridan. Her current research interests include eighteenth-century English Catholicism and the representation of Canada in eighteenth-century British literature.

Janice Liedl is Associate Professor of History at Laurentian University in Sudbury, Ontario. She is the coeditor of *The Hobbit and History* (Wiley, 2014), *Star Wars and History* (Wiley, 2012), and *Love and Death in the Renaissance* (Dovehouse, 1991). Her articles have appeared in *Rethinking History, The Sixteenth Century Journal, The Greenwood Encyclopedia of Love, Courtship* *and Sexuality through History, The Dictionary of Literary Biography,* and in *London Lives.* Her current research examines mothering and stepmothers in early modern England.

Lisa McClain is Professor of History and Gender Studies at Boise State University. She is the author of the book *Lest We Be Damned: Practical Innovation and Lived Experience among Catholics in Protestant England 1559–1642* (Routledge, 2004), as well as articles in journals such as the *Sixteenth Century Journal, Church History, Tulsa Studies in Women's Literature,* and the *Journal of Religious History.*

William B. (Bill) Robison is Professor of History and Head, Department of History and Political Science at Southeastern Louisiana University, where he teaches undergraduate and graduate courses on British and Early Modern European History. He earned the PhD in History at LSU (1983). He is coeditor (with Ronald H. Fritze) of the *Historical Dictionary of Stuart England* (1996) and *Historical Dictionary of Late Medieval England* (2002); coauthor (with Sue Parrill) of *The Tudors on Film and Television* (McFarland, 2012), for which he maintains the interactive website www.tudorsonfilm.com; author of numerous articles on the history of early modern England, film history, and popular culture; editor of and contributor to a forthcoming volume of essays featuring twenty other scholars that is tentatively titled *"The Tudors," Sex, Politics, and Power: History, Fiction, and Artistic License in Showtime's Television Series;* director of the film, *Louisiana During World War II;* a musician; and a published poet.

Valerie Schutte earned her PhD at the University of Akron. Her dissertation is entitled "'To the Mooste Excellent and Vertuous Queene Marye': Book Dedications as Negotiations with Mary I," in which she examines book dedications as an arena in which Mary Tudor and her dedicators negotiated patronage, politics, religion, and gender roles. She has published two articles on Anne Boleyn in *In, Out and Beyond: Studies on Border Confrontation Resolution and Encounters,* ed. Antonio Medina-Rivera (Cambridge Scholars, 2011) and *Retrospect* Graduate History Journal (vol. II, spring 2011). She has also published an article on *The Merchant of Venice* in *ANQ* (vol. 26, 2013) and has forthcoming articles in the *Journal of the Early Book Society* and *Early Modern Women,* both dealing with royal Tudor women and print.

Index

Abbot, George
  as Archbishop of Canterbury, 93, 99
Act for Printers and Binders of Books
    (1534), 22
Act for Succession (1534), 22–23
Act of the Submission of the Clergy
    (1533), 22–3
Acts of Union, 132, 166
Amsterdam, 100, 102, 113 n57, n58
Anabaptist, 47, 53
Anderson, Maxwell
  Anne of a Thousand Days (1948), 149,
    173 n15
  Elizabeth the Queen (1930), 163
  Mary of Scotland (1933), 161, 162
Anger, Jane, 74, 86 n22
Anglesey, Earl of, 117
Anglo-Catholic, 38, 84 n3
Anglo-Spanish War, 157, 161, 167
Anna Boleyn (1920), 148
Anne Boleyn (1911), 148
Anne Boleyn (1912), 148
Anne de Boleyn (1913), 148
Anne of Cleves
  in film, 147, 149, 151, 152, 154
  see also Becon, Thomas; Cromwell,
    Thomas; Elyot, Thomas; Lutheran
    Schmalkaldic League; Wilhelm,
    Duke
Anne of the Thousand Days (1948),
    149
  see also Anderson, Maxwell
Anne of the Thousand Days (1969),
    150, 156
Anonymous (2011), 168

anti-Catholicism, 3, 58, 93, 154, 156,
    165, 166
Antichrist, 94–6, 102
Antwerp, 18, 53, 54, 56
Archbishop of Canterbury
  see under individual names
Armada, 159, 160, 161, 164, 166, 167,
    168
Armagh, Archbishop of
  see Ussher, James
Arminianism, 93, 94, 100, 111 n29
Arthur, Prince of Wales, 23, 32, 151,
    174 n19
Askew, Anne
  arrest and torture of, 172 n11
  interrogation of, 11 n14, 38
  in film, 145, 154
  marriage of, 6
  martyrdom of, 3
Ayer, Richard, 34
  see also Pole, Margaret, Countess of
    Salisbury

Babington, Anthony
  Babington Plot and, 136
Babington Plot
  in film, 164, 168
  Mary, Queen of Scots and, 136, 143
    n30
Bales, John, 11 n14
  King John (1538), 154
Ballard, George, 93, 111 n13
Ballard, John
  in film, 165–6
Barca, Pedro Calderon de la, 175 n20

Elizabethan settlement, 159, 165
in film, 145–9, 157–8, 161–4, 167–8
Henry VIII and, 157
Mary, Queen of Scots and, 3, 157, 158
Parkhurst, John and, 58
Philip II of Spain and, 157, 158
in *The Recess*, 129–44
Elizabeth (2000), 157
Elizabeth I (2005), 167
Elizabeth I: The Virgin Queen (2005), 157, 167
Elizabeth, Lady Tanfield, 75
Elizabeth of York, 145, 146
in film, 146
Elizabeth R (1971), 156, 163–5, 166
Elizabethan church, 161
Elyot, Thomas, 147
Emperor Charles V
see under Charles V, Holy Roman Emperor and King of Spain
equivocation, 79
Erasmus of Rotterdam
Beaufort, Lady Margaret and, 20
book dedications by, 17, 18–25
Bullinger and, 63
Colloquia, 19
correspondence of, 27 n14
Froben, Johannes and, 18
humanism of, 3, 19, 20
Institution of Christian Matrimony (aka *Christiani matrimonii institutio*), 18–25
Katherine of Aragon and, 17, 18–25, 147
on marriage, 18, 19, 20, 21–2, 23
Mary I, 24
Matrimonii encomium, 19
Mountjoy, Lord William and, 20–1
Paraphrases of, 25
The Execution of Mary Stuart (1895)
see under Edison, Thomas
Exeter conspiracy, 7, 29–30, 34–5, 38
exile, 3, 8, 102, 137, 140
see also Marian Exile

Falkland, Viscount
see Cary, Henry, (Viscount) Lord Falkland; Cary, Lucius, (Viscount) Lord Falkland
The Famous History of the Life of King Henry the Eight (1623)
see under Fletcher, John; Shakespeare, William
feme sole, 17, 32
Fenwick, Ann
as preacher, 100
The Saints Legacies (1629), 100
Ferdinand of Aragon, 24, 172 n6, 174 n19
film, 9, 145–78
see also under individual titles
Fire Over England (1937), 161
The First Tome or Volume of the Paraphrases of Erasmus upon the Newe Testament (1548)
see under Udall, Nicholas
Fish, Simon
death of, 154, 175 n23
in film, 153
Supplication of the Beggars (1529), 147
Fisher, John, Bishop of Rochester, 20
Fitzwilliam, William, Earl of Southampton, 37, 38, 40
Fletcher, John
The Famous History of the Life of King Henry the Eight (1623), 148
Shakespeare, William and, 148, 152
Flodden Field, 24
Ford, John
Mary of Scotland (1936), 161
The Foundation of Christian Religion (1591)
see under Perkins, William
Fox, Edward, 147
Foxe, John
Actes and Monuments (1563, 1570, 1576, 1583), 11 n14, 100
Francis II, King of France, 158
Frankleyn, Oliver, 39

Parr, Katherine and, 11 n17, 150
Pole, Margaret and, 31–2, 33, 40
Pole, Reginald and, 33
Reformation of, 1, 2, 4, 7, 9, 35
Stuart, Mary and, 158
successors of, 4
Tyndale, William and, 10 n12
wives of, 17, 20, 146, 148, 149: *see also* Anne of Cleves; Boleyn, Anne; Howard, Katherine; Katherine of Aragon; Parr, Katherine; Seymour, Jane
Henry VIII (1613)
see under Fletcher, John; Shakespeare, William
Henry VIII (1911), 148
Henry VIII (1979), 152
Henry VIII (2003), 152, 156
Henry VIII and His Six Wives (1972), 152
Henry the Eighth (1929)
see under Hackett, Francis
Hilles, Anna
birth of, 48
Bullinger and, 46, 48–9, 50, 52, 54, 60, 62 n8, 64 n27
children: Hilles, Barnabas; Hilles, Daniel, Hilles, Gerson; 48
death of , 48
Hilles, Richard and, 46, 48, 49, 53
independence of, 49
as Marian Exile, 48
parents of, 48
piety of, 49
Protestantism and, 49, 60
Hilles, Richard, 46–9, 53, 63 n22
Bullinger and, 47, 48
Hilles, Anna and, 46, 48, 49, 53
as Marian Exile, 48
historiography, 92, 108, 129–32, 136, 156, 169–70 n1
history, 8, 15, 25, 51, 58, 61, 62 n7, 71, 91, 93, 129–35, 137, 142
in film, 157, 158, 160, 162, 165, 167, 168–9

women's writing and, 51, 69, 70, 95, 96, 99, 101, 107, 129
Holy Maid of Kent
see under Barton, Elizabeth
Hooper, Anne (aka Anne Tserclaes)
Borgonge, Jacques de, 53
Bullinger and, 46, 54–6, 57, 60, 62 n8
children: Hooper, Daniel, 56, 57; Hooper, Rachel, 54, 55, 56, 57
death of, 57
escape to Antwerp of, 53, 56
Hooper, John and, 46, 53–5, 56, 57
as Marian Exile, 54, 56–7
Hooper, John
as Bishop, 56
Bullinger and, 46, 54–5
education, 54
execution of, 57
Hooper, Anne and, 46, 53–5, 56, 57
imprisonment of, 55, 56
as Marian Exile, 58
Howard, Katherine
in film, 25, 147, 149, 152, 154
Henry VIII and, 2, 147
Howard, Thomas, Third Duke of Norfolk, 33, 148
in *The Recess*, 131, 140–1
Hugo, Victor, 157
Hume, David, 129, 133
Hume, Martin
The Wives of Henry VIII (1905), 149
Hyrde, Richard
as translator of *The Instruction of a Christen Woman* (1529), 18, 19

iconoclasm (–tic), 4, 6, 103, 130
Index of Forbidden Books (1559), 19
An Invective ayenste the great and detestable vice, treason, wherein the secrete practices, and traitorous workings of theym, that suffid of late are disclosed
see under Morison, Richard